VALUING YOUR BUSINESS

Also by Frederick D. Lipman

The Complete Going Public Handbook
The Complete Guide to Employee Stock Options
Financing Your Business with Venture Capital
Audit Committees

VALUING YOUR BUSINESS

Strategies to Maximize the Sale Price

Frederick D. Lipman

WILEY

John Wiley & Sons, Inc.

Published by John Wiley & Sons, Inc., Hoboken, New Jersey
Published simultaneously in Canada

For general information about our other products and services, please contact our Customer Care Department within the United States at 800-762-2974, outside the United States at 317-572-3993 or fax 317-572-4002.

Wiley also publishes its books in a variety of electronic formats. Some content that appears in print may not be available in electronic books. For more information about Wiley products, visit our web site at www.wiley.com.

Library of Congress Cataloging-in-Publication Data:

Lipman, Frederick D.
    Valuing your business : strategies to maximize the sale price / Frederick D. Lipman.
        p.   cm.
    Includes index.
    ISBN-13 978-0-471-71454-5
    ISBN-10 0-471-71454-2 (cloth)
    1. Business enterprises—Valuation.   2. Sale of business enterprises
    I. Title.
    HG4028.V3L56   2005
    658.15—dc22   2005002640

Printed in the United States of America
10 9 8 7 6 5 4 3 2 1

To my grandson,
Tyler Keith Lipman

Contents

Contents

PART V
ALTERNATIVES TO SELLING YOUR BUSINESS

PART VI
APPENDIXES

Acknowledgments

I want to acknowledge the helpful comments and editorial efforts of my partners at the Philadelphia office of the law firm of Blank Rome LLP: Chapters 1 and 2: Fred Blume, Esq.; Chapters 3, 4, and Appendix 4: Alan L. Zeiger, Esq.; Chapter 5: Lawrence S. Chane, Esq. and Henry M. Kuller, Esq.; Chapter 10: Robert M. Broder, Esq.; Chapters 11 and 14: Joseph T. Gulant, Esq.; Chapter 14: Arthur Bachman, Esq.; Chapters 15 and 16: Steven Dubow, Esq.; Chapter 18: Francis E. Dehel, Esq., Edward J. Hoffman, Esq., and Jennifer Hale Eagland, Esq.; Chapter 19: Harvey I. Forman, Esq. and Lawrence F. Flick, II, Esq.

I absolve the editors from any responsibility for any errors in this book.

Helpful suggestions for this book were made by Seth Lehr of LLR Equity Partners L.P. and my partner Fred Blume.

Jim Twerdahl, chairman and chief executive officer of Mayco Colors, Inc. was kind enough to permit me to use portions of his comprehensive buyer's due diligence checklist in Chapter 7.

Ken Patton and Matt Crow of Mercer Capital Management Inc. (Memphis, Tennessee, Web site www.mercercapital.com) share their wisdom on valuing Internet businesses in Chapter 21.

Last but not least, I owe a special debt to my secretary, Barbara Helverson, who typed the updated manuscript.

Introduction

This book is intended for entrepreneurs who want to fully understand how to maximize the valuation and ultimate sale price of their business. This process requires careful advanced planning, which should begin as early as five years before your target sale date. Even if your exit date is less than five years from now, this book will enable you in the time remaining to accelerate the maximization of your valuation and help you avoid traps that can reduce the sale proceeds you receive.

Inexperienced business owners may think that it is simple to sell their businesses. They think they can just let it be known that the business is for sale, receive offers, sign legal documents, cash the buyer's check, and then golf for the rest of their lives.

Only one in ten business sales occurs this smoothly. The remaining nine out of ten may be plagued with at least one of the following problems, which can reduce, if not destroy, the value of your business:

- Key employees leave when you announce your decision to sell, taking important customers with them.

- Overvaluing your business can mean that it takes so long to find a buyer that new, well-financed competitors have time to establish themselves before your sale, thereby lowering the value of your business.

- Customers find out about your pending sale and seek out your competitors.

- Competitors find out about your pending sale and use this information to win away existing and potential customers.

- Suppliers who are important to your business start selling to your competitors when they realize that your business will be sold.

- In the course of their due diligence investigation, potential buyers discover your proprietary information and use it to start a competitive business.

- You and your top executives spend so much time involved with the sale process that the business itself begins to go downhill.

- Income taxes can consume more than 50 percent of the proceeds from the sale of your business.

- You are the trustee of family trusts that own shares in your company, and your children, who are the beneficiaries, hire their own lawyers in an effort to maximize their share of the sale price.

- Your spouse, anticipating the sale proceeds, decides to divorce you and hires the most aggressive lawyer in town to maximize his or her share.

Selling your business is an exit strategy and a method of diversifying your assets. Because most businesspeople have the overwhelming percentage of their net worth tied up in their businesses, a sale permits them to diversify their asset portfolios and avoid the risk of business failure.

Most business owners have little experience in the actual sale of a business, however. The skills that permit entrepreneurs to grow a business are not necessarily the skills that would permit them to sell the business successfully. There are also many costly traps for the novice seller.

The six stages of selling your business are described in Table I.1.

The key to maximizing the sale price of your business is careful advance planning, which starts many years before your target sale date. The advance planning steps taken over a five-year period are discussed in detail in Chapters 1 through 6. These steps start with stage 1 and end with stage 3. The purpose of these steps is to enhance the value of your business and its appeal to potential buyers.

Chapter 1 focuses on your motives for selling, which must guide the entire sale process, including your negotiation strategy. Unless you are experienced in selling businesses, you must also assemble a professional team of advisers in advance of the sale. Chapter 1 tells you how.

You must understand how your business will be valued so that you

TABLE 1.1 SIX STAGES IN THE SALE PROCESS

STAGE 1	STAGE 2	STAGE 3	STAGE 4	STAGE 5	STAGE 6
ADVANCE PLANNING (up to 5 years from target date)	ORGANIZATION (up to 1 year from target date)	PREPARATION FOR MARKETING	MARKETING	NEGOTIATIONS	FINALIZATION
• Assess objectives • Maximize valuations • Assemble advisory team • Draft marketing brochure • Eliminate deal killers and impediments • Protect the business • Minimize taxes	• Finalize decision to sell • Ensure commitment from top • Finalize advisory teams	• Finalize marketing brochure • Develop list of potential buyers	• Auction versus negotiated process • Contact potential buyers • Buyer's due diligence	• Selection of serious bidders • Negotiation	• Documentation • Closing

can maximize your sale price through steps taken prior to the sale. Those subjects are covered in Chapter 2.

During the presale years, you must identify and eliminate deal killers and other impediments to the sale. The elimination of deal killers may take many years to accomplish, and consequently, you cannot begin too soon. Chapter 3 discusses these issues.

You also must give careful advance thought to how you will protect your business during the sale. This includes maintaining confidentiality of both your decision to sell and your proprietary information. It is important that your key employees, customers, and suppliers do not become privy to this information earlier than necessary and that you do not inadvertently give potential buyers valuable proprietary information about your business. Chapter 4 tells you what you must do years before your target sale date to protect your business and proprietary information during the sale process.

Finally, you must take steps prior to the sale to minimize the taxes on the sale proceeds, including estate and death taxes, as well as federal and state income taxes. This is discussed in Chapter 5.

Businesses do not sell themselves. You must market your business and understand the motivations of buyers. You would not launch a new product line without careful study of the marketplace and a detailed knowledge of your customers' needs. This study might take several years. The same careful study must be done prior to the marketing of your business. Chapter 6 tells you how to plan for the marketing of your business and discusses the pros and cons of using an investment banker or business broker. Chapters 5 and 6 describe stage 3 and prepare you for stage 4, the actual marketing of the business and the negotiations with the buyer, which are covered in Chapters 7 through 9.

Chapter 7 explains how to survive the buyer's due diligence process.

Chapter 8 provides a negotiation strategy for sellers, including the use of auctions to maximize the sale price.

Chapter 9 covers letters of intent, which may be more binding than you think.

Chapters 10 and 11 cover the structuring and tax issues to which you must be sensitive and teach you to think in "after-tax" terms.

If you are selling to a public-company buyer, Chapter 12 is essential.

Chapter 13 explains the special problems of selling a public company. The sale of a control block of stock in either a public or a private company is also discussed.

Some entrepreneurs would prefer to sell their business to their key employees. Chapter 14 tells you how and explains the surprising tax benefits of selling to an ESOP (employee stock ownership plan).

Chapters 15 and 16 deal with notes and earnouts and the traps inherent to accepting these deferred payouts of the sale price.

Chapter 17 advises you on how to negotiate your employment or consulting agreement with the buyer.

The traps in the agreement of sale and closing (stage 6) are covered in Chapter 18.

Chapters 19 and 20 discuss two possible alternatives to selling your business: leveraged recapitalization and going public. Although neither alternative is possible for all businesses, it is important to understand these alternative exit strategies and their pros and cons.

Chapter 21 discusses the specific valuation problems in valuing Internet businesses after the meltdown of this industry in the year 2000. This chapter was written by Ken Patton and Matt Crow of Mercer Capital Management Inc., located in Memphis, Tennessee, (www.mercercapital.com).

The keys to a successful sale of your business are careful advance planning and a clear understanding of your motivations for the sale. Your motivations will dictate the manner in which you conduct the sale, your strategies for negotiation, and which alternatives you will consider. For example, if you believe that your business is going downhill, you may wish to promote a fast sale and price your business accordingly. You also might instruct your attorney to take somewhat higher legal risks in order to avoid delaying or interfering with a prompt sale.

A clear understanding of your motivations also will prevent you from suffering from seller's remorse or will at least alleviate the symptoms—and a substantial bank account always helps.

This book is intended to guide you through the sale process and around the traps inherent in that process. Every effort has been made to ensure that all information contained in this book is current as of January 2005. However, there is no substitute for an experienced professional team of advisers, including a tax attorney, who should always be consulted to ensure that current statutes of the law and accounting principles are met in each specific circumstance. This book will help you pick such advisers.

VALUING YOUR BUSINESS

PART I

ADVANCE PLANNING

CHAPTER ONE

PRELIMINARY CONSIDERATIONS

Selling a business is a complicated, time-consuming, and at times, emotional experience. You should give consideration to all of the following factors before seriously embarking upon the sale process.

UNDERSTANDING YOUR MOTIVES

It is important that you understand your motivation for selling your business. Your motivation will dictate the nature of your buyer and the structure of your transaction.

For example, if you are no longer interested in operating your business, you do not want to sell to a financial buyer or to have an earnout. An earnout is a provision in the agreement of sale that would measure the purchase price in whole or in part by the future profits of the business.

A financial buyer will typically not have the management in place to run your business and will expect you to remain to operate the business under a long-term employment or consulting agreement. You would not want to agree to an earnout unless you are in control of the business because otherwise, your final purchase price could be significantly reduced by poor performance of the managers installed by the buyer.

Understanding your motives to sell your business also helps you avoid what is called "seller's remorse." In general, seller's remorse results from the significant change in lifestyle that the sale of your business can bring, together with the emotional attachments that you have toward the business. Truly understanding your motivation will help you get through a very natural period of doubt and uncertainty concerning the wisdom of selling your business.

The following are some typical reasons for selling, which are usually a mix of personal and business:

- You are tired of working so hard and are ready to retire.
- You have no children who are interested in taking over the business.
- You have children who want to take over the business, but they are not competent to operate it.
- New competitors are moving into your business area, and you do not have the capital with which to fight them.
- You would like to have enough money in the bank so that you can support your lifestyle for the rest of your life.
- You need more capital resources than you can acquire to grow the business.
- Your business is going downhill, and you would prefer to sell it before it reaches the bottom.
- You were just divorced, and you retained the second-best lawyer in town. Unfortunately, your ex-spouse retained the best lawyer in town, and you owe your ex-spouse a huge amount of money.
- Your partner just died, and you do not have enough life insurance to buy out your partner's family as required by your shareholder agreement.
- You just died, and you did not maintain enough life insurance to pay death and inheritance taxes.

The preceding are only the major motivations; many other reasons may exist. At the beginning of the decision to sell your business, you may have one set of motivations and by the time the process is through, you may have dropped those motivations or added new ones.

What is important, however, is that you fully understand your motivations to sell your business and that you allow those motivations to continually guide the logic of your sale.

ASSEMBLING YOUR PROFESSIONAL TEAM

Your first step should be to assemble an outstanding professional team to advise you.

Most businesspersons select their professional team on the eve of their sale. This is far too late in the sale process. By selecting your professional team several years before the target date for your sale, you can obtain their guidance in the presale years as to methods of minimizing the obstacles. Your professional team will help implement the advance planning recommendations contained in Chapters 2 through 6.

M&A Attorney

The first person on your team should be an attorney specializing in mergers and acquisitions, an M&A attorney. This person might not be your regular attorney, who may be inexperienced in this area. You must carefully interview your attorney to learn about his or her expertise. Ask your attorney how many mergers and acquisitions he or she has handled in the last three years and what size businesses they were.

If a public company is a potential buyer, does your attorney have securities law experience? Has your attorney ever handled the sale to a public company where stock was part of the purchase price consideration?

If you do not get favorable answers from your personal attorney, look elsewhere. Most large corporate law firms maintain groups of attorneys who specialize in M&A. Select someone who not only is well experienced in M&A but also has good business sense and is someone with whom you have a good rapport.

The requirement that your attorney have good business sense cannot be overemphasized. You will need to make delicate trade-offs during negotiations, which require business and legal judgment from your lawyer. You need a lawyer who thinks like a businessperson but also has the necessary legal skills to protect you. It is a mistake to hire a lawyer who is a good scrivener but cannot properly translate legal risks into business risks and assist you in evaluating their importance.

During the sale negotiation, it is not unusual to instruct your attorney to play "bad cop" while you play "good cop." The good cop–bad cop negotiation strategy helps insulate you from the angry emotions of the buyer. This is particularly helpful if you expect to work for the buyer, but is also useful if you want to maintain a distance from the give-and-take of the bargaining. Be certain that your M&A attorney can play the bad cop role but also knows when to stop playing it.

Be wary of attorneys recommended to you by an investment banker or business broker involved in your sale. These attorneys may be experienced in M&A, but they also may feel beholden to the person who recommended them. Carefully interview such attorneys to determine if they are sufficiently independent that they could recommend that you (1) terminate the investment banker or business broker or (2) not proceed with an agreement of sale that is against your interests but would result in a fee to the recommending investment banker or business broker.

Tax Attorney

In addition to an M&A attorney, you will need a tax attorney. This is true even if you have a good tax accountant. Unless the tax consequences of your sale are simple (which you cannot know in advance of its structuring), you will want to double-check any tax advice you receive with a second tax professional. Tax attorneys and tax accountants sometimes approach tax issues differently, and you should solicit the views of both.

If your business is a C corporation for federal income tax purposes, one of the first questions to ask your tax consultant is what the tax consequences would be of changing to an S corporation. There are serious tax disadvantages to selling a C corporation, which are discussed in Chapter 11.

It is worthwhile to weigh the costs of changing to an S corporation five years prior to your sale target date versus staying a C corporation for the same five years and suffering the adverse tax consequences when you sell. This, of course, does not necessarily apply if you have a C corporation that is qualified under Section 1202 of the Internal Revenue Code, which is discussed more fully in Chapter 11 under the heading Fifty Percent Exclusion.

Accountant

It is generally not necessary to select a new accountant in order to sell your business. Most accountants can perform this task.

Some business owners use their accountant to negotiate the business terms of the sale. Caution should be exercised in doing this. Inquire how many sales transactions your accountant has previously negotiated, as well as their size and complexity. Discreetly inquire from other clients of your accountant as to whether they were satisfied. You must be discreet, because you do not want to announce to the world your decision to sell your business.

Your accountant and your personal attorney may be losing a significant portion of their revenues if your business is sold. Be sensitive as to how important your fees are to them.

> **WARNING** Be careful in using any accountants or lawyers with an economic interest in killing your sale. Have a heart-to-heart talk with them before engaging them, and, in case of doubt, look elsewhere.

Investment Banker or Business Broker

As early as five years before your sale target date, you should consider obtaining advice from an investment banker or business broker. The advice should primarily cover the following areas:

- an estimated value of your business as it currently exists and the factors that affect that value (see Chapter 2)
- the likely buyers for a business such as yours

You should seek this advice even if you intend to sell the business yourself and do not expect to retain an investment banker or business broker.

The purpose of this advice is to help guide you in the growth and development of the business during the years prior to the sale target date. If negative factors about your business are identified by the investment banker or business broker, you should take steps to eliminate them to the extent possible.

For example, if you are advised that you have a weak management team, you should consider strengthening your management
structure during the years prior to sale. Likewise, if you are advised
that your overdependence on a single customer will materially reduce your ultimate sale price, you can make efforts to diversify your
customer base in the years prior to sale.

The investment banker or business broker you select as an advi-
sor need not necessarily be the same one you choose to sell your business (see Chapter 6). You should select your investment banker or
business broker based upon their familiarity with your industry and
the quality of their advice.

CHAPTER TWO

MAXIMIZING THE SALE PRICE

I t is important to understand how your business will be valued in order to avoid setting either too low or too high a sale price. The following are methods of valuing your business, along with techniques to maximize that value.

UNDERSTANDING THE METHOD OF VALUING YOUR BUSINESS

You can increase the value of your business if you understand how buyers are likely to value it. Likewise, by understanding the valuation method, you may be able to remove assets from your business prior to sale that do not affect the valuation, thereby effectively increasing the total sale consideration you ultimately receive.

An appraisal of your business, which specifies the primary valuation methods and factors, should be sought from a qualified appraiser well in advance of the expected sale date. Such an appraisal could cost as little as $5,000 to $10,000. Select the appraiser by reputation and personal recommendation.

In general, an appraiser from an investment banker or business broker with *actual* experience in selling businesses in your industry is the most valuable. What is important is not so much an appraisal of what your business is currently worth but rather an understanding of the primary methods of valuation and valuation factors. Someone who actually sells businesses in your industry is best qualified to provide this information.

If you cannot find anyone with such experience, look for appraisers who are members of recognized appraisal groups that require an examination. The prestigious American Society of Appraisers and the somewhat newer Institute of Business Appraisers (typically, certified public accountants) are examples of such groups. The Institute of Business Appraisers does not require any specific valuation experience, in contrast to the more rigorous requirements for the American Society of Appraisers, which requires five years of experience for the designation accredited senior appraiser and two years for the accredited member designation.

These different professional requirements usually are reflected in the cost of the appraisal, with members of the American Society of Appraisers generally charging significantly higher fees.

Appraisal

Appraisal is an art, not a science. Take all appraisals with a large grain of salt. The larger your business, the less likely that the appraisal will be accurate in assessing your business' total valuation. Businesses that are worth more than $5 million to $10 million tend to attract financial as well as strategic buyers. The presence of financial buyers tends to drive up the price.

No one can accurately predict what you are worth to a particular strategic buyer. The strategic buyer may find that the value of your business to them far exceeds the result of any standard valuation formula. Your customer list, sales force, and market identification may blend so well with the market direction of the strategic buyer that a high sale price can result.

The balance of this section presents some of the more common methods used to evaluate a business.

Businesses worth less than $1 million tend to be valued using the rule-of-thumb formulas and the asset accumulation methodology, which are discussed in the sections that follow.

Buyers of businesses worth $5 million or more tend to use the Earnings Before Interest, Taxes, Depreciation, and Amortization (EBITDA) method combined with a comparable transaction analysis. If no significant earnings exist, a discounted cash flow methodology will be used. It is not unusual for the investment banker to also use a discounted cash flow analysis to double-check the valuations obtained using the EBITDA or comparable transaction method.

Caution should be exercised in using any formula to value your business. Every business is unique and thus, using only formulas can give you a very misleading picture of your value because they are not tailored to your particular business. There is no substitute for an appraisal performed by a competent investment banker or business broker.

However, even the best appraisal cannot take into account the value of your business to a specific buyer. For example, a strategic buyer who can lay off all of your back-office employees might be willing to pay an absurdly high price for your business because of the cost savings of the layoffs. Without knowing the pro forma effect of combining your business with the business of a specific buyer, any appraisal becomes little more than an educated guess.

Rule-of-Thumb Formulas

Potential buyers have a variety of rule-of-thumb methods for valuing businesses, depending on the nature of the business. For example, vending machine businesses are typically valued based on the number of locations. Cable TV businesses are typically valued based on the number of subscribers. The accounting income shown by these businesses is only of secondary importance to the buyer, because the buyer will change the business to conform to the buyer's model, thereby making your financial results irrelevant.

Rule-of-thumb valuation methods are more typically used for smaller businesses (usually valued at less than $5 million), particularly where there is a perception that the financial information is not completely reliable. However, rule-of-thumb formulas are occasionally used for larger businesses as well.

If you are in a business that uses these rules of thumb (e.g., vending machine locations or cable TV subscribers), consider increasing your locations or subscribers prior to sale. Thus, by understanding the valuation method for your business, you can increase the likely sale price.

Some valuation experts have criticized this method of increasing valuation because it ignores profitability. They argue that a cable TV system, which is valued at $3,000 per subscriber, can easily add new subscribers by cutting prices or giving away free services. Adding new subscribers at a loss per subscriber should not, they argue, increase the value of the cable TV system.

Some common sense must be used to increase the value of businesses that are valued on a rule-of-thumb basis. If our hypothetical cable TV system, by cutting prices, can cause new subscribers to sign up and still have the lowered "teaser prices" cover the additional costs of these new subscribers, then adding new subscribers is a good strategy. However, if the cable TV company cannot charge prices to new subscribers that will cover the incremental costs of these new subscribers (except for a very short period of time), it is not a good idea to add subscribers by reducing overall profitability.

Many rule-of-thumb formulas exist for valuing specific industries. The following are examples:

Insurance agencies	1 to 2 times annual gross commissions
Real estate agencies	.2 to .3 times annual gross commissions
Restaurants	.3 to .5 times annual gross sales
Travel agencies	.05 to .1 times annual gross sales

Buyers do not apply these rules of thumb universally, as the rules ignore the profitability of the specific business.

First find out the formula for valuing your business. Then attempt to maximize the elements of the formula for the year in which your business will be valued and, if possible, prior years. Typically, this is the year prior to sale.

EBITDA Method

A number of businesses are valued by buyers based upon accounting earnings or income. Indeed, one of the most common methods of valuation is the so-called EBITDA method. This involves the determination of your accounting earnings before interest, taxes, depreciation, and amortization (EBITDA), and multiplication of the EBITDA by the relevant multiplier to obtain a business valuation.

Table 2.1 is an example of the EBITDA method.

Your EBITDA is then adjusted to remove expenses and revenue that will no longer be carried forward into the new business. These adjustments can be quite substantial for a closely held family business.

Most closely held businesses are operated to minimize income taxes. As a result, excessive compensation and perquisites may be

TABLE 2.1 EBITDA CALCULATION

EXAMPLE	
Revenues	$10,000,000
Cost of sales	(8,000,000)
Gross profit	2,000,000
General and administrative costs	(500,000)
Depreciation	(100,000)
Amortization	(50,000)
Interest expense	(250,000)
Total expenses	(900,000)
Net income before taxes	(1,100,000)
Income taxes (40%)	(440,000)
Net income after taxes	($ 660,000)

CALCULATION OF EBITDA	
Net income after taxes	$ 660,000
Interest	250,000
Income taxes	440,000
Depreciation	100,000
Amortization	50,000
EBITDA	$ 1,500,000

provided to the owner and his or her family in order to reduce taxes. The excessive compensation and perquisites are really forms of disguised dividends.

The true cost of replacing the owner and his or her family with a high-level executive usually results in a substantial addition to the EBITDA.

Some buyers will subtract from the adjusted EBITDA any required yearly capital expenditures.

Multipliers

The adjusted EBITDA is then multiplied by a multiplier to obtain an overall valuation for the business (also called "enterprise value"). The multiplier typically ranges from 4 to 6 times adjusted EBITDA, particularly for financial buyers. However, the multiplier has gone below 4 and substantially above 6, depending upon whether it is a buyer's market or a seller's market for the sale of businesses. A multiplier above 6 is more typical for strategic rather than financial buyers.

Multipliers of 20 or more are not unheard of for strategic buyers of companies with strong market niches.

The multipliers are derived from comparable company valuations, including the multipliers applicable to public companies in the same industry. For example, if a public company in your industry has a total market valuation (based on its stock price) of 10 times its EBITDA, this multiplier could be the starting point in determining the appropriate multiplier.

This multiplier would then be discounted by the fact that your company was smaller and had less market dominance.

Many business owners incorrectly assume that the multipliers applicable to larger companies in the industry apply to their smaller company. The multipliers for less dominant companies in an industry are significantly smaller than for dominant companies.

A further discount to the multiplier may be applied to reflect the lack of liquidity of your stock in the hands of the buyer (that is, if no public market exists for your stock).

General

If your business has long-term debt, the overall valuation of your business will be reduced by the market value of this debt (including the current portion of long-term debt). The market value can be greater or less than the principal amount of the debt. For example, long-term debt that bears an interest rate below current interest rates for comparable maturities will have a market value less than its principal amount.

The overall valuation of your business obtained by multiplying the adjusted EBITDA by the applicable multiplier is called the "enterprise value." If your business has no long-term debt, then this figure is the valuation of your business.

Your business will be expected to have a normal amount of working capital at the closing date of any sale. Your working capital is the excess of your current assets (e.g., cash, accounts receivable, inventory, and prepaid assets) over current liabilities (e.g., accounts payable, loans due within one year, accrued payroll, etc.). If your working capital is below normal, this will reduce your ultimate sale price. If your working capital is above normal, you can usually negotiate on a dividend of the excess working capital before closing, which in effect increases your ultimate sale price.

If you have nonoperating assets in the business, the buyer may permit you to remove assets from the business before the sale closing.

Businesses that are likely to be valued on the EBITDA basis should consider methods of increasing their accounting income during the one or two years prior to sale. This requires advance planning.

WARNING Many businesses have inventory cushions. This is an illegal method of minimizing taxes by underreporting the ending inventory. The result of underreporting ending inventory is to increase the cost of sales, which in turn reduces taxable income. Many businesses that have an inventory cushion find that whatever savings they had in taxes over the years by underreporting their taxable income are partially or completely offset by the fact that they never get paid by the buyer for their inventory cushion. The seller merely gets paid for the inventory that was reported. It is not usually possible to eliminate an inventory cushion in one year. Several years are required for this purpose.

For each $1 that you increase your EBITDA during the valuation year, you should arguably receive an additional $4 to $6 in sale price.

Discounted Cash Flow Method

Under this method of valuation, you look at future cash flows projected from the operations and discount them in accordance with time and risk factors. The higher the risk, the higher the discount factor.

The discounted cash flow method begins with a projection of revenues and operating profit. These projected financial results are then adjusted for nonrecurring and nonoperating items of income and expense and are reduced by taxes. The projected operating profit estimates after taxes are then further adjusted by adding back depreciation and amortization and deducting net investments in working capital and capital expenditures.

At the end of a given period, typically five or ten years, a "terminal" or "residual" value is calculated for the business. This terminal or residual value is then combined with the discount cash flows to produce an overall valuation for the business (the enterprise value).

The two most common methods of calculating residual value are the perpetuity method and the multiplier approach. The perpetuity method capitalizes the final year's projected cash flow by a discount rate as if it were an annuity. The multiplier approach applies a multiplier to the final year's cash flow. Because the residual value is typically a large figure, the underlying assumptions in the calculation must be carefully examined.

The net equity value of the business, including the residual value, is then determined by deducting the market value of interest-bearing debt and adding the market value of nonoperating assets that remain in the business. An example of this calculation is contained in Table 2.2.

Obviously, a cash flow ten years from today is not worth the same amount to the investor as a current cash flow. Thus, the formula tends to give little current value to cash flows that are too far in the future.

The sale price of your business using the discounted cash flow valuation assumes that a normal amount of working capital remains in your business at sale closing. As explained, using the EBITDA method, the sale price is typically adjusted for excessive or inadequate working capital at sale closing. Similar adjustments are required under each of the valuation methods discussed in this book.

Discount Factor

The discount factor applicable to the cash flows is arrived at by using various formulas, one of which is the capital asset pricing model (CAPM). The CAPM sets the discount rate at the weighted average cost of equity and debt capital.

The capital asset pricing model estimates the future cost of the corporation's equity through a multifactor equation and then determines the after-tax expected future costs of the corporation's debt.

TABLE 2.2 **FLOW VALUATION**

DISCOUNTED CASH FLOW VALUATION (IN MULTIPLES OF 1,000)

	YEAR 1	YEAR 2	YEAR 3	YEAR 4	YEAR 5	TERMINAL VALUE
Revenues	$30,000	$45,000	$50,000	$55,000	$62,000	
EBIT	3,264	3,825	4,322	4,884	5,519	
Income taxes (cash basis)	1,110	1,301	1,469	1,661	1,876	
Net operating income	2,154	2,524	2,853	3,223	3,643	30,358
Cash flow adjustments						
Plus:						
Depreciation	1,392	1,800	2,034	2,298	2,597	
Less: Net change in working capital	(405)	(731)	(168)	(204)	(244)	
Capital expenditures	(1,966)	(3,675)	(4,161)	(4,398)	(4,697)	
Free cash flows	1,175	(82)	558	919	1,299	
Net present value at 12.0%	1,049	(65)	397	584	737	17,226
Total corporate value						$19,928
Less: Market value of debt						(12,528)
Shareholder value						$ 7,400

The final step is to compute the weighted average cost of capital, which is the weighted average cost of both equity and debt.

The weighted average cost of equity is computed by using the following equation: $re = rf\,B(rm - rf)$, which can be defined as follows:

re = expected future cost of equity

rf = risk-free rate of return

B = the beta factor, which is a measurement of market risk, with the value 1 equaling a normative risk. (One court has defined the beta factor as "the nondiversified risk associated with the economy as a whole as it affects this firm.")

rm = the market risk premium for this particular business

The rm factor, together with the beta factor in the equation, has the effect of discounting the future cash flows by the risk of their nonoccurrence. The greater the risk of the projected cash flow not occurring, the higher the expected future cost of equity.

Your historical financial results are only relevant to this discounted cash flow method to the extent that they give credence to the projections of future cash flow. However, if your business is likely to be valued by this method, assets that do not contribute to your cash flow can be safely removed from the business without affecting its valuation.

Comparable Company Method of Valuation

The comparable company method of valuation typically involves comparing your company to the market capitalization and multiples of certain financial criteria (such as net income; projected net income; earnings before interest, taxes, depreciation, and amortization, revenues; and book value) of comparable public companies. Market capitalization refers to the public trading price of the stock multiplied by the number of outstanding shares. Thus, if a comparable public company had a public trading price of $20 per share and there were two million shares outstanding, the overall market capitalization of that comparable public company would be $40 million.

The market capitalization method of valuation contains a number of limitations. The trading price of shares of a public company does not normally reflect any control premium unless the company is expected to be sold shortly. Consequently, the public trading price

may significantly understate the overall value of the comparable public company in a sale situation where a control premium is paid for
the shares.

In addition, it is difficult to compare a publicly held company
with a privately held company. Shares of public companies typically
trade at a price that reflects the liquidity available to shareholders,
which is not available to shareholders of a privately held company. As
a result, privately held companies tend to sell at a discount compared
to comparable publicly held companies.

Comparable Transaction Method of Valuation

Where information is available on the sale of comparable companies
(whether public or private), this information is very valuable in assessing the value of your company. However, great care must be taken
in using this information. Because every company is unique, significant differences may exist between your company and the so-called
comparable company.

One of the major problems with this method is the lack of sufficient information to be able to judge how "comparable" another
company is to yours. For example, your company may have one customer that accounts for 15 percent of your sales—a negative factor.
You may not be able to determine whether the so-called comparable
company has this same negative factor. Therefore, information on
the sale price of the comparable company may be difficult to assess.
Consider all such information with a certain measure of skepticism.

Asset Accumulation Method

This method involves accumulating the going concern value of each
of the specific assets of your business. This includes off-balance-sheet
assets, such as customer lists, product market identification, value of
your trained workforce, goodwill and other intangible assets, in addition to your balance-sheet assets. In computing going concern value,
three standard appraisal methods are utilized:

- cost approach
- income approach
- market approach

The replacement cost is usually the most favorable method to the seller of valuing both balance sheet and off-balance-sheet assets.

The values of your balance-sheet and off-balance-sheet assets are then combined to calculate the total value of your entire business. The major advantage of this valuation method is that if you eliminate specific assets from the sale (for example, accounts receivable), you can easily adjust the total sale price. This valuation method is more typically used in valuing smaller businesses than midsized and larger businesses.

Asset liquidation value serves as a minimum valuation figure, regardless of whatever other valuation method may be used. Thus, if the rule-of-thumb formula for your business is 1 times annual sales, and your liquidation value is higher, you should receive the liquidation value.

Valuing Goodwill and Other Intangible Assets

As noted, the asset accumulation method of valuation permits you to separately value such goodwill and intangible items as your customer relationship, your market reputation, and your trained workforce. If you have other intangible assets, such as patents, trademarks, and copyrights, they can also be considered as separate assets to be individually valued.

Several classifications of intangible assets are as follows:

- *Technology-related* (e.g., engineering drawings and technical documentation)
- *Customer-related* (e.g., customer lists and customer relationships)
- *Contract-related* (e.g., favorable supplier or other product/service contracts)
- *Data processing-related* (e.g., computer software, automated databases)
- *Human capital-related* (e.g., employment agreements, noncompete agreements, a trained and assembled workforce)
- *Marketing-related* (e.g., trademarks and trade names)
- *Location-related* (e.g., leasehold interests, certificates of need)
- *Goodwill-related* (e.g., going-concern value)
- *Engineering-related* (e.g., patents, trade secrets)

- *Literary-related* (e.g., literary copyrights, musical composition copyrights)

As previously noted, three common methods of valuing both tangible and intangible assets are the cost approach, the income approach, and the market approach.

In valuing intangible assets, the seller usually obtains the highest valuation using the replacement cost method. However, few buyers will pay full replacement costs. Buyers will argue that if they are requested to pay 100 percent of the replacement costs, they might as well actually replace these intangible assets. The seller's counter to that is "time is money," and replacement of these intangible assets could take years. Despite this counter by the seller, only very motivated buyers will pay 100 percent of replacement costs.

As a result, goodwill and other intangible assets typically sell for some significant discount from actual replacement cost. Many buyers refuse to pay anything for goodwill, particularly if the business does not have superior earning power or is incurring a loss.

Intangibles, such as patents that actually produce royalty income to the seller, can typically be separately valued on an income approach using a discounted cash flow method of valuation.

Some sellers believe that they should be separately paid for their goodwill and other intangibles even if a macro financial method of business valuation is used, such as the EBIDTA, discounted cash flow, comparable company, or comparable transaction valuation methods. Unfortunately, each of these methods values your business as a whole and therefore, any goodwill items are included as part of the valuation. Thus, goodwill is not added to the enterprise value computed under these methods.

Goodwill and other intangibles are valued separately under the assets accumulation method and certain formulas discussed further on, including orderly liquidation.

The assets accumulation method or other valuation methods discussed in the following section, which permit separate valuation of goodwill, are usually used because the EBITDA and other macro valuation methods do not produce as favorable a price to the seller.

Other Valuation Formulas

A myriad of other valuation formulas are used today.

If your business is asset intensive, some have suggested that your business value is equal to your hard assets plus goodwill. Hard assets refer to the total fair market value (which can be replacement cost) of your fixed assets and equipment, leasehold improvements, accounts receivable, and inventory. Your goodwill is your discretionary cash for one year—that is, the amount of cash you received as salary and dividends.

Another formula used for smaller businesses focuses on the seller's discretionary cash per year and multiplies this figure by 2.2727 to arrive at a sale price.

None of these formulas or the many others currently in use are universally applied. What is important is that you understand the particular valuation formula most likely to be applied to your business.

MINIMUM VALUE FORMULAS

The minimum value of your business is the higher of (1) its value-to-service acquisition debt or (2) its liquidation value.

Acquisition Debt Value (Leveraged Buyout Analysis)

If your business produces positive cash flow earnings before interest, taxes, and depreciation amortization (EBITDA), that cash flow can service (that is, pay interest and principal) a certain amount of acquisition debt for the buyer. The amount of acquisition debt that can be so serviced is the minimum value for your business, particularly to a financial buyer.

For example, assume that the excess cash flow of your business (EBITDA) is $500,000 per year, and that, based upon current interest rates, that $500,000 is sufficient to pay the interest and principal due on $3 million of bank debt, which matures over a five-year loan term (exclusive of the balloon principal payment in the fifth year, which can be refinanced). The minimum value of your business would be $3 million, particularly to a financial buyer.

There is a limit to the amount of debt senior lenders will provide for a given business without an equity component. Therefore, once that debt limit is reached, your cash flow must be high enough to be able to attract equity investors.

In this sense, you can determine the minimum value of your business using a leveraged buyout analysis (see Chapters 14 and 19).

Liquidation Value

Some businesses are worth only the liquidation value of their assets. Liquidation value refers to the price that would be received in an orderly liquidation, not in a fire sale. These businesses are typically not producing positive cash flow and have no prospects for doing so.

SPECIFIC FACTORS THAT AFFECT VALUATION

Let us assume that your business has an identical EBITDA to one of your competitors, and in your industry, businesses generally sell for 5 times EBITDA. Should both businesses sell for the same price? Not necessarily.

EBITDA is merely the beginning of the valuation process. Certain specific favorable and unfavorable factors to your business increase or decrease the multiplier of 5. Table 2.3 gives some examples.

These specific valuation factors will affect all of the valuation formulas, not just the EBITDA method.

You must analyze the strengths and weaknesses of your business and be prepared to point out the strengths and acknowledge the weaknesses, which the buyer will probably discover in its due diligence process.

The valuation of your business will also vary with the nature of the buyer. Financial buyers (e.g., leveraged buyout funds) will typically pay less than strategic buyers, as more fully discussed in Chapter 8. Strategic buyers who, by definition, are already engaged in your business, have the ability to reduce your work force, particularly your back office, and can consolidate operations with their own. These post-sale cost-saving activities can increase your value to a strategic buyer.

Your valuation can also vary based upon the needs of the buyer. A financial buyer who needs to demonstrate progress in the use of the investment funds to their fund investors may overpay for your business. Likewise, a strategic buyer who wants access to a particularly important customer of yours may be willing to pay more for your business to obtain such access.

TABLE 2.3   FACTORS THAT INFLUENCE VALUATION

FACTORS INCREASING VALUATION	FACTORS DECREASING VALUATION
1. Strong customer relationships at all levels	1. Weak customer relationships and frequent turnover
2. Proprietary products or services	2. Lack of proprietary products or services
3. No single customer accounts for more than 5% of revenues or profits	3. A single customer accounts for over 15% of revenues or profits
4. Strong management team (important mainly to financial buyers)	4. A weak management team (so-called "one-man-show syndrome")
5. Excellent employee turnover and relations	5. Poor employee turnover and relations
6. Consistent revenue and earnings trends	6. Inconsistent revenue and earnings trends
7. Plant and equipment in good repair	7. Plant or equipment has been neglected and requires significant repairs
8. Intellectual property assets, which are legally protected	8. Lack of legally protected intellectual property assets

RECENT SALES OF BUSINESSES

Appendix 1 contains examples of sales of businesses of all types and sizes with a sale price of between $10 million and $1 billion.

Appendix 2 contains examples of sales of businesses with sale prices ranging from $500,000 to $10 million. Appendix 3 contains examples of sales of businesses with sale prices ranging from $100,000 to $500,000. Appendices 2 and 3 use the abbreviation SDCF to refer to the seller's discretionary cash flow, which is the equivalent of EBITDA plus the owner's salary and nonbusiness-related expense.

The information in Appendixes 2 and 3 has been supplied by BIZCOMPS, which collects information from business brokers throughout the United States. BIZCOMPS also supplies similar information on businesses sold for less than $500,000. The contact information for BIZCOMPS is: Jack R. Sanders, P.O. Box 711777, San Diego, CA 92171; 858-457-0366.

Other computerized databases include the following:

* *Mergerstat Review*, an annual and monthly publication of merger and acquisition transactions (www.mergerstat.com)
* Thomson Financial Securities Data (www.tfibcm.com)

The special considerations involved in valuing Internet businesses are discussed in Chapter 21.

INCREASE YOUR NET BOOK VALUE

Regardless of what valuation is placed on your business, some buyers will not, at closing of the sale, pay more cash for your business than its net book value. Any excess of the sale price over the net book value is deferred by such buyers. Net book value refers to your total assets less your total liabilities as reflected on your financial statements. This is the same figure as your shareholder equity as reflected on your financial statements. The balance of the purchase price is then deferred.

The theory of some buyers is that your net book value or shareholder equity approximates the liquidation value of your business. The buyer does not want more than that amount invested in cash on the acquisition at closing.

As the seller, your counterstrategy should be twofold: (1) to use different accounting methods in preparing your balance sheet than you use in preparing your tax returns so as to maximize net book value and (2) to reflect undervalued assets on a pro forma statement of your adjusted net book value or shareholder equity.

Your accountant will typically choose accounting principles that minimize your taxable income for tax purposes. However, it is not necessary to use these same principles for financial reporting purposes.

For example, you may use accelerated depreciation of your equipment for tax purposes to reduce your taxes. However, you should use straight-line depreciation of equipment in preparing the financial statements given to the buyer, with a footnote disclosing the different depreciation method for tax purposes.

The effect of using straight-line depreciation will typically significantly increase your net book value, because your equipment can be reflected at a high book value. Other accounting changes can be suggested by your accountant to increase your net book value.

It is preferable not to adopt new accounting methods on the eve of a sale. Therefore, good advanced planning should include adopting such accounting methods many years before the sale.

After you have exhausted using favorable accounting methods to increase your net book value, you should supplement your financial statements with a description of written-off or undervalued assets and add the value of these assets to your net book value or shareholder equity on a pro forma basis. These off-balance-sheet assets can add significantly to the value of your business.

For example, you may in the past have purchased $1 million worth of machinery that has been fully written off through depreciation charges. The machinery may still be worth $500,000, but it does not appear anywhere in your financial statements. Add this $500,000 to your net book value as shown on your financial statements in a column called Pro Forma Adjusted Net Book Value or Pro Forma Adjusted Shareholder Equity. You may have purchased land years ago for $100,000 that is now worth $500,000. The $400,000 appreciation should be added to your pro forma net book value or shareholder equity.

Many businesses expense small tools—that is, they run the cost of tools through the income statement and do not capitalize them as an asset. Under some accounting conventions, a small tool could be one costing less than $500. Determine the market value of these small tools and increase your pro forma net book value or shareholder equity by this figure.

Comb through your business assets to be certain that you have reflected them all at their market value.

REMOVING UNPRODUCTIVE ASSETS
FROM YOUR BUSINESS

Once you understand the method most likely to be used to value your business, consider removing, prior to sale, assets from the business that do not affect its value. Each dollar of asset value that you can remove from the business prior to sale without affecting the buyer's valuation is an additional dollar in your pocket. This is an excellent way of increasing your overall sale consideration.

For example, if you owe your business money, your debt is an asset of the business. However, if the buyers use the EBITDA or discounted cash flow valuation method and do not include interest income on the debt in computing your valuation, they have assigned a zero value to your debt. Accordingly, you should be able to remove your debt from the company (or forgive it) prior to the sale without affecting the buyer's valuation. The same may be true of life insurance on your life and your automobile, which is not necessary to operate the business.

However, rather than waiting until you are negotiating with the buyer to remove these assets, it is wiser to remove them at an earlier time so this issue never becomes a point of negotiation with the buyer.

MINIMIZE YOUR WORKING CAPITAL NEEDS

A typical agreement of sale will require the seller to leave a normalized amount of working capital in the company after the sale closing. If the amount of working capital at the closing exceeds this normalized figure, the seller can remove this excess from the company once the buyer's accountants have verified the excess after the closing has occurred. In effect, this ability of the seller to remove excess working capital from the company is a method of increasing the real purchase price to the seller.

On the other hand, if the working capital at the closing is less than this normalized figure, the seller may have to contribute the dollar amount of the deficiency back to the company. This contribution is usually accomplished by having the buyer escrow a portion of the purchase price paid at closing and using the escrowed amount to repay the deficiency. To the extent a deficiency exists, this is in reality a reduction of the seller's purchase price.

The normalized amount of working capital is usually obtained by looking at the average amount of working capital maintained in the business over some time period and negotiating a normalized figure for working capital. The time period could be a few years or, if your business is seasonal, it could be the same fiscal quarter of the year immediately prior to the year in which the closing occurs.

If you minimize your working capital needs during the years prior to the sale of your company, you may be able to convince the buyer to permit you to remove any excess working capital from the company, thereby increasing your effective purchase price. You can minimize your working capital by a variety of methods, including aggressive collection of accounts receivable and maintenance of minimum cash and inventory levels.

PROTECT YOUR INTELLECTUAL PROPERTY

One of the specific factors in the valuation of your business is whether you have legally protected intellectual property assets, such as patents, trademarks, and copyrights. Your intellectual property assets will assist the buyer in protecting the business from competition and, therefore, makes the business more attractive to the buyer.

Most businesspeople do not know that they even have intellectual property assets to protect. For example, even if you have a nontechnology business, you may still be able to obtain a business method patent on some process or methodology that you use in conducting your business. Likewise, you may have trademarks, service marks, and trade dress that you use in your business that should be legally protected.

Long before your sale target date you should hire a patent or intellectual property attorney to help you identify your intellectual property assets. The process of obtaining patents can take three or four years; it is never too early to begin such a review.

MAKE YOUR FINANCING ASSUMABLE

If you receive bank or other financing for your business, you can make your business more valuable to a buyer by inducing the lender to agree in advance that the financing will be assumable if your business is sold. This is particularly valuable if you have long-term indebtedness at favorable interest rates and terms and is less valuable if your indebtedness is all short term. The buyer's ability to assume long-term financing will increase the value of your business to the buyer.

Most lenders will resist assumability clauses in the financing documents unless they are properly hedged. For example, the bank may require the potential buyer to have a minimum net worth or satisfy other financial tests set forth in the financing agreement, in order to allow the automatic assumption of the debt by the potential buyer. The bank may also require you to remain liable on the debt.

BIGGER IS GENERALLY BETTER

Larger businesses tend to sell for higher multipliers of EBITDA (for EBITDA valuations) and lower discount rates (for discounted cash flow valuations). You cannot analogize a business worth less than $5 million with a business in the same industry worth more than $50 million. The business worth over $50 million always sells for a higher multiplier and lower discount rate. Likewise, you cannot analogize a business worth $50 million with one worth $500 million in the same industry.

This is understandable because buyers prefer larger sized businesses, which are more dominant in their field, and financial buyers are typically not interested in businesses worth less than $10 million.

What this suggests is that a good way for you to build your valuation prior to your target date is to yourself engage in strategic mergers. By building up your business during the presale years through mergers and other acquisitions, you will be a much more attractive target when it comes time to sell.

Eliminating deal killers and impediments to the sale will also increase your business valuation, as discussed in Chapter 3.

VALUATION VERSUS NET SALE PROCEEDS

The appraised valuation of your business is only a starting point in determining your net proceeds from the sale of your business. Different buyers have different methods of appraising businesses and that appraisal could significantly differ from your appraisal.

Even assuming that the buyer is willing to accept the appraised value of your business and use that appraised value as the purchase price, the net sale proceeds you actually receive from the sale will be reduced by the following (as explained in subsequent chapters):

- federal, state, and local income and transfer taxes (see Chapter 11)
- provisions of the sale agreement that require the seller to retain all liabilities other than those specifically identified (see Chapter 18)
- provisions in the sale agreement that require the seller to indemnify the buyer post-closing for events or circumstances that occur before closing (see Chapter 18)

Chapter Three

ELIMINATING DEAL KILLERS
AND IMPEDIMENTS

Once you have made a decision to sell, you should immediately examine your business, with the help of your M&A attorney, to determine whether you have deal killers or other impediments to a sale. These deal killers or other impediments may require many years to resolve successfully. Again, it is important that you make these evaluations many years before your sale target date.

If you have a business of any significant size, a potential buyer will likely hire a law firm and an accounting firm to perform due diligence on your business, as more fully discussed in Chapter 7. Any discovery of defects in your business will be used by the possible buyer to reduce your valuation. A smart seller will hire an M&A attorney and an accountant to identify such defects and attempt to correct them well before attempting to market his or her company. This will avoid embarrassment to the seller in the negotiation process and will help increase the ultimate purchase price of the company.

DEAL KILLERS

The following are typical examples of deal killers if the resulting contingent liability is large in relation to the value of your business:

- employment-related liabilities
- environmental liabilities

- litigation liabilities
- federal, state, and local tax liabilities, including sales and income taxes
- unfunded pension obligations and multiemployer pension plan liabilities
- product warranty obligations of unreasonable scope or length

No buyer is going to assume these liabilities willingly if they are of a material indeterminable amount. Even if you do not require the buyer to assume these liabilities, they may still prevent the sale of your business.

For example, if the property on which your plant is located is environmentally contaminated, the purchase by the buyer of the property subjects the buyer to environmental liability as the owner. This is true even though the buyer did not cause the pollution.

If your business has large, unresolved litigation liabilities, the buyer may be concerned about purchasing your assets because, at least under some state laws, liabilities can be imposed upon the buyer even though the buyer never agrees to assume them. This is particularly true if the buyer continues the same business under the same name and products of the business that caused personal injury.

Many businesses misclassify employees as independent contractors. The resulting liability for payroll taxes, interest, and penalties can, if this practice is carried on long enough, create a very large contingent liability.

The existence of large, unresolved contingent liabilities that could potentially exceed your assets may indicate that your business is insolvent. If so, a sale of assets to the buyer at less than its fair market value could be legally challenged by creditors in the future.

It is, of course, possible to wait to resolve these deal killers until a buyer is found. However, by the time you clean up your environmental contamination or even get a firm estimate on the cost, the buyer may have disappeared. Therefore, it is wiser to handle these issues prior to the potential sale of your business.

If you cannot get rid of the deal killers prior to the sale of the business, it may be possible to set up escrow arrangements for the protection of the buyer and nevertheless proceed with the sale. These escrow arrangements would typically require objective proof of the largest amount of the contingent liabilities, and the buyer would undoubtedly require that same amount of the sale proceeds to be escrowed.

If you handle your deal killers prior to the sale, it is likely that you would spend much less money to resolve these contingencies than the buyer would require in an escrow. By waiting until the point of sale to handle these problems, you will create a high escrow to give the buyer a significant margin for error in its estimate of the cost of cleaning up your problems. Therefore, it behooves you to clean up these problems prior to sale.

However, do keep in mind that some deal killers cannot be escrowed away. These must be resolved well before you proceed with the sale of your business.

OBTAIN AUDITED OR AUDITABLE FINANCIAL STATEMENTS

It is advisable to obtain an audited financial statement for at least the year in which your company will be valued. This is typically your last full fiscal year.

It is also advisable to obtain an audit for the two prior years as well. This is especially true if your business will likely be valued on an EBITDA basis, if your business trends are important to the buyer, or if you may sell to a public company.

An audited financial statement provides the buyer with a greater assurance of your financial results. This is particularly true if your auditor is a large international auditing firm. However, even if your auditor is a one-person office, that audit report is better than giving the buyer an unreviewed financial statement or a so-called compilation report.

Using a prestigious auditing firm tends to reduce the buyer's due diligence. It also creates a certain aura about your company that is conducive to a sale. Large buyers are particularly enthralled by a prestigious auditing firm, as their own audits are usually performed by these firms. They incorrectly view the auditing firm as having some liability to them if the financial statements are wrong. In most states, your auditor has no such liability unless he or she was negligent and actually knew that you intended to furnish the financial statements to the buyer. However, you need not mention that fact to your buyer.

If you normally use a good regional accounting firm, there is probably no need to change auditors on the eve of sale.

Your decision to save money on an audit may reduce the number of potential buyers for your company, particularly public company buyers. Even if you do not obtain an audited financial statement, you should at least obtain an auditable financial statement for the three years prior to sale. An auditable financial statement permits you to complete the audit retroactively at the time of sale.

Public Company Buyers

Public company buyers will generally require audited financial statements from your company if the acquisition is significant (over 20 percent) to them in terms of assets or income or if their investment and advances to your company exceed 20 percent of their total consolidated assets.

If any of these tests yield a result greater than 20 percent but less than 40 percent, one year of your audited financial statements is required by the Securities and Exchange Commission (SEC). If the impact is over 40 percent but less than 50 percent, two years of audited financial statements are required. If the impact on assets or income is over 50 percent, three years of audited financial statements are required. These requirements are relaxed for buyers that are small-business issuers.

Because the public company buyer must abide by these SEC rules, your failure to obtain an audited financial statement can be a deal killer.

It is not a good idea to go to your brother-in-law's auditing firm. The SEC requires that your auditing firm be independent as defined in their rules.

CREATE A TAX–FRIENDLY BUSINESS ENTITY

If you have a C corporation and sell its assets, you will have two levels of tax obligations. The first is a tax at the corporate level on the corporation's gain from the sale. The second is a tax at the shareholder's level on the net proceeds received by the shareholder. As discussed in Chapter 11, this could result in paying more than 50 percent of the sale proceeds to the U.S. Treasury and to state and local taxing authorities.

An S corporation that sells its assets will significantly reduce the tax bite, as the S corporation generally does not pay a corporate-level tax.

If you have a C corporation, you can switch to an S corporation and, provided you do not sell corporate assets within ten years after the conversion, you can avoid a corporate level tax. If you sell corporate assets within the ten-year period, you can still avoid corporate-level tax on the increase in your company's valuation after the conversion.

If you have a limited liability company, you should be aware that your entity will not qualify for a tax-free stock-for-stock merger, consolidation, or similar tax-free reorganization. For example, if General Electric was willing to acquire your business in exchange for its stock, the stock would be taxable to you.

Therefore, unless you are positive that you would never consider a stock offer from a buyer, consider transferring the business assets of your limited liability company to an S corporation well before your projected exit date. If you wait to form an S corporation until the eve of your sale, the IRS could collapse the transaction and ignore your S corporation. This will result in your taxable stock transaction, which could mean that you owe more taxes than you have cash to pay them.

Some consultants argue that you can always sell stock of a C corporation or equity interests of a limited liability company, so why bother to convert to an S corporation? Many buyers will not purchase stock or equity interests because of the fear of hidden or unknown liabilities and the less favorable tax result to the buyer. Even if a buyer is willing to purchase stock or equity interests, the buyer will usually discount the price because of the extra risks and the less favorable tax results.

MAKE YOUR ASSETS TRANSFERABLE

Some of your most valuable assets may be nontransferable without the consent of a third party. For example, most leases are not transferable without consent of the landlord. Neither are most licenses, such as those for patents, trademarks, and other intellectual property.

Good advance planning would suggest that you attempt to make these leases and licenses assignable to a buyer of your business well in advance of the actual sale. If you wait until the agreement to sell your business is signed, the lessor or licensor may well demand additional consideration from you because this individual is aware that you need his or her consent to consummate the sale.

However, if you obtain such consent within the normal course of negotiating or administering the license or lease, the landlord or licensor will be less likely to try to negotiate additional consideration, as you are not under the gun.

Some sellers seek to avoid these consents by selling the stock of their business or by using direct or triangular mergers. This works only if the lease or license does not contain a change-of-control clause and if the buyer is willing to engage in a stock purchase or reverse merger (see Chapter 10). A change-of-control clause in a lease or license is a clause that treats a change in control of your company as a direct assignment of the lease or license.

Most lessors and licensors will resist any blanket permission to transfer your lease or license unless you remain liable for the performance by the transferee. Even then, they may not agree in advance to the transferability of the lease or license. This is particularly true if the lease or license has nonmonetary obligations on your part that will not necessarily be performed satisfactorily by an unknown transferee (for example, a clause in a license requiring the licensee to promote sales of the licensed product).

At a minimum, you should attempt to have the lessor or licensee agree not to withhold their consent to a transfer unreasonably.

SIMPLIFY CORPORATE STRUCTURE

Some businesses are organized with an unusually complex corporate structure. The complexities of the corporate structure can delay and sometimes impede the sale of the business. It is best to have an M&A attorney review your corporate structure to determine if there are methods of simplifying it to facilitate a potential sale.

AVOID BURDENSOME LONG-TERM COMMITMENTS

If you expect to sell your business within a year or two, you should carefully consider the effects on the sale of entering into long-term contracts that will have to be assumed by the buyer. For example, a five-year contract tying you to a particular supplier may make your business less valuable to a potential buyer. Likewise, committing your company to purchase very expensive equipment shortly before the sale could also reduce the value of your business to a potential buyer and impede the sale.

◆

CHAPTER FOUR

PROTECTING YOUR BUSINESS

You must carefully consider how you will protect your business and your proprietary information during the sale process. You should begin thinking well before your target sale date.

MAINTAINING CONFIDENTIALITY OF YOUR DECISION TO SELL

The process of selling your company can last from several months to several years. It is important that you maintain confidentiality of your decision to sell throughout the process.

The sale of your company may have adverse effects on your key employees, customers, and suppliers. Competitors may use your decision to sell as a tool to obtain your customers. It is best that your decision to sell not be publicly disseminated until absolutely necessary.

There are three methods to maintain the confidentiality of your decision to sell:

- Limit the information to trusted advisors, such as attorneys, accountants, investment bankers, or business brokers.

- Require your professional advisors to approach only potential buyers who are approachable on a no-name basis and who will likely maintain the confidentiality of your sale's decision once your name is revealed.

- Require potential buyers to sign confidentiality agreements.

It is important that your professional advisors institute their own internal procedures to protect the confidentiality of the sale process. For example, you may receive a bill from an attorney that specifies exactly what legal services the attorney performed for you and contains the following notation: "Advice concerning sale of your business." Once that bill is submitted to your bookkeeping department for payment, you have effectively blown your confidentiality; your accounts payable clerk now knows your secret and it will not be a secret for long.

Early in the process your professional team should use a code name for the project that will not cause suspicion. The use of terms such as *consultation concerning project X* merely invites suspicion. It is better to use a code name that does not invite suspicion, such as *business planning* or a similar nondescriptive name.

Secretaries and assistants of your professional advisers must be brought in on the secret because they may be talking to secretaries at your place of business. Require your professional advisors to sensitize their own employees to avoid having them inadvertently disclose your sale intentions.

At some point in the sale process, you will no longer be able to maintain the confidentiality of your decision to sell. The ideal is to maintain such confidentiality until the closing of your agreement. However, that is not always possible. Leaks may occur, and rumors may be started.

Long before it is no longer possible to maintain complete confidentiality, you must plan how and to whom the disclosures will be made. It is important that you control the process.

For example, key employees will have to be informed of the secret at an early stage as serious buyers will want to talk with them. How to give incentives to key employees is discussed later in this chapter.

In addition, you may wish to personally visit a few key customers before making any general announcement. You must carefully think through when and how you will approach such customers.

PROTECTING YOUR PROPRIETARY INFORMATION

Maintaining your decision to sell as confidential is not sufficient. You must also make advance plans as to how you will protect the confidentiality of proprietary information of your business from potential buyers who are performing due diligence. Your proprietary information includes customer lists, trade secrets, methods of marketing, and so on.

There are three methods of maintaining the confidentiality of proprietary information:

- Give potential buyers only enough information to permit them to make a purchase decision, but no more.
- Require potential buyers to sign confidentiality agreements.
- Require buyers to agree to refrain from hiring your key employees.

Several methods can be used to limit the information available to what potential buyers absolutely need. For example, if names and addresses of your customers are sensitive information, the potential buyer may initially be satisfied with obtaining the list of the top twenty-five customers without receiving their actual names and addresses. Rather, the list could identify each customer with a code name (e.g., customer A), indicate the state in which the customer is located, and specify the amount of revenues attributable to that customer during the last fiscal year. Your customers' zip codes could also be revealed without stating their actual names or addresses.

Obviously, at the time of signing the agreement of sale, and certainly no later than closing, the buyer will want the actual names and addresses of the customers.

Certain unscrupulous potential buyers use the due diligence process to gain valuable information concerning your business. These buyers do not really intend to purchase your business and are using the due diligence process as a vehicle to obtain a competitive advantage. Sometimes you can identify such unscrupulous potential buyers by carefully checking them out. Potential buyers with unsavory reputations should be avoided.

It is important that you require each potential buyer to sign a confidentiality agreement, which creates a monetary deterrent for using your proprietary information (e.g., liquidated damages) and entitles you to injunctive relief and which includes a clause restricting the hiring of employees. See Appendix 4 for an example of a confidentiality agreement.

Your M&A attorney will assist you in preparing a confidentiality agreement. It is likely that the potential buyer's attorney will have some changes that must be negotiated. You should resist any changes that place an early termination date on the buyer's duty of confidentiality (e.g., one year from the date of the agreement). If you must agree to a termination date, make certain that it is long enough so that the information is probably stale (e.g., two years from the date of the agreement) and be sure that the termination clause contains the following conditions:

- the return to you (or destruction of) all information previously given to the potential buyer
- the assurance that there has been no breach of the potential buyer's duty of confidentiality prior to the termination date

WARNING It is crucial to restrict potential buyers from hiring past, present, and future employees of your business for some period of time—at least one year. Hiring your employees is a simple way of gathering sensitive information about your business. Indeed, as key employees are interviewed by potential buyers during the due diligence process, they may be overtly or subtly solicited for employment with the potential buyer. From the potential buyer's point of view, it is much cheaper to hire an employee to capture a portion of your business than to pay you for the business. Be certain that the potential buyer agrees not to hire employees, even if the buyers are solicited by an employee.

SPECIAL PROBLEMS OF SELLING TO CUSTOMERS, COMPETITORS, AND SUPPLIERS

Selling to a customer, competitor, or supplier creates unusual confidentiality problems.

For example, unless you have a proprietary product, you would not want customers to know your profit margins. They can use this information to reduce the price they pay to you in the future. Therefore, unless you have a method of disguising this information, or a proprietary product, you should refuse to discuss this information prior to closing with a customer.

A competitor would love to know your customer list and the prices they pay, among other things. You should refuse to supply this information prior to closing, whether or not the competitor signs a confidentiality agreement. If you provide such information and the competitor uses it unfairly, you will probably never be able to prove that the competitor ever breached the confidentiality agreement.

Suppliers can also be troublesome buyers, although not as troublesome as customers or competitors. However, you generally would not want a supplier to know your customer list, your resale markup on your purchases from the supplier, or what you pay to competing suppliers, unless the supplier could not possibly harm you with that information.

Occasionally, the problem of selling to customers, competitors, or suppliers is handled by giving the information to an investment banker for the buyer, with the written agreement that it will not be disclosed to the customer, competitor, or supplier until after the closing. However, this can still be a dangerous solution because of your inability to *prove* that the investment banker intentionally or inadvertently leaked the information.

INCENTIVES FOR KEY EMPLOYEES

Potential buyers will want to speak to your key employees prior to signing the agreement of sale as part of their due diligence. Therefore, your decision to sell the company will be brought to the attention of this group of persons at some point in the process.

It is important that these key employees be given the incentive to help promote the sale. If they are not, their natural tendency will be to become concerned about their job security and their future with your company. Moreover, these key employees will begin to think about the full implication of your decision to sell and the effect it will have upon their lives and their futures. This may cause them to think about other possible alternatives for their careers. Keep in mind that whatever bond you may have created with your key employees through the chemistry of your leadership, it may change once you have announced your decision to sell.

The incentive to your key employees must be both affirmative and negative:

- affirmative, in order to align the employees' interest with yours in the implementation of the sale
- negative, in order to disincline the employees from leaving or becoming potential competitors

The affirmative incentives usually consist of some form of termination bonus equal to a meaningful percentage of the employee's base salary. Typically, anywhere from 50 percent to 100 percent of the base salary should be paid. The bonus should be payable only in the event of sale. This affirmative cash incentive can be created immediately, before the potential buyer commences his due diligence with these key employees.

Other types of affirmative incentives must be implemented earlier. One example would be a stock option granted at an early point in time that could be exercised only in the event the company is sold or goes public.

The advantage of a stock option granted several years before the potential sale occurs is that there is no charge against the income of the business for the grant of the option or its exercise, provided that on the grant date the option price is at least equal to the fair market value of the stock at that time.

The disadvantage of a cash termination bonus equal to a percentage of base salary is that in the year of sale, your earnings are reduced by the amount of the bonus. This reduction may or may not be important to the buyer.

In contrast, the exercise of the stock option that had been originally granted years previously does not reduce your year-of-sale earnings. This is true even though the employee could exercise the stock option at a price significantly below the current market value of your stock.

A cash termination bonus is simpler to implement than a stock option plan and should be used in situations where the reduction in the year-of-sale earnings is not material or is unimportant to this buyer.

Negative incentives could take the form of an agreement not to compete or not to solicit customers or engage in other hostile acts in relationship to your company. It may not be possible to obtain this type of agreement on the eve of the sale of your company, as it requires a voluntary act by the employees to execute such a noncompetition or nonsolicitation agreement and some special consideration under state law to make it enforceable.

Therefore, it is necessary to obtain a noncompetition agreement from key employees several years before your sale decision and preferably when the employees are hired. To make such a noncompetition or nonsolicitation agreement enforceable, you should seek counsel from attorneys specializing in this area. Many state laws require some form of special consideration to be given to employees for this purpose if the agreement is signed during the course of employment. For example, in some states you might be able to implement this type of agreement at the same time you are implementing your normal increases or bonuses.

The length of time of the noncompetition or nonsolicitation agreement should be kept sufficiently short so that there is no difficulty in having a court enforce it. Typically, one year is sufficient to protect a buyer and will usually be enforceable if the scope of the limitation is reasonable under the circumstances. Noncompetition or nonsolicitation agreements protect the seller prior to a sale and facilitate a sale to a potential buyer.

Another alternative is to work out a severance plan for employees that requires them not to compete with the company or solicit customers during the period of the severance payments. Severance payments to less-important employees can be limited to one or two weeks, whereas the payments to key employees can last as long as one year. Severance payments can be expensive and therefore should be limited to a period sufficient to permit you or the buyer to cement a new relationship with customers handled by a key employee. Typically, six months to one year is sufficient.

CHAPTER FIVE

PERSONAL CONSIDERATIONS

Personal tax considerations should be foremost in planning the sale of your business. Advance planning will enable you to minimize the following taxes.

MINIMIZING ESTATE AND DEATH TAXES

Long before the target date for the sale of your business, you should consider methods of minimizing estate and death taxes on the transfer of sale proceeds to the next generation. These taxes can be higher than your income tax. The combined federal and state income tax rate can be over 40 percent; in contrast, estate and death taxes can be over 50 percent.

Estate planning to minimize these taxes should take place in the years prior to the sale of your business. It is preferable to make gifts of rapidly appreciating property, such as the stock of the corporation that owns your business. The gift has the effect of preventing the appreciation of stock from being taxed in your estate at death. One common method of minimizing these taxes is by making annual lifetime gifts to your children and grandchildren to take advantage of the annual exclusion. The annual exclusion permits gifts having a value of $11,000 per donee each year ($22,000 if you have a spouse and so elect) without using your lifetime exemption.

You can make gifts above the annual exclusion amount ($11,000 to $22,000 per donee each year) without paying any gift taxes during your lifetime. This can be accomplished by using your lifetime exemption, which permits $1 million of taxable gifts ($2 million for married couples) to be made without paying any gift tax.

To the extent that you make gifts above the annual exclusion plus the lifetime exemption, you will pay a gift tax. However, the elimination from your taxable estate of the future appreciation of the stock that you give away (plus the amount of the gift tax you pay) may result in sufficient estate and death tax savings to be justified.

Before making gifts for which you must pay a gift tax, you should carefully weigh future estate and death tax savings against the following disadvantages: (1) you lose the use of the amount of gift tax you must pay (including interest), and (2) if the stock you gifted would otherwise have been retained by you until your death, there are higher capital gains taxes, which must be paid by your children and grandchildren on their sale of the stock. If you would have otherwise kept the stock until your death, your children and grandchildren would, for federal income tax purposes, have received a step up in their tax bases to an amount equal to the fair market value of the stock on the date of death (or alternate valuation date) and therefore would not pay any long-term capital gain tax except on postdeath appreciation.

Discounts

The value of your stock gift may be significantly discounted by the "minority interest discount" and a "lack of marketability discount" if the stock is of a closely held corporation. The minority interest discount reflects the fact that the minority shares of a closely held business do not have the ability to control the business.

Although the discount depends on the facts and circumstances of each situation, the combination of the minority interest discount plus the lack of marketability discount can result in total discounts of up to 50 percent of the fair market value of the stock on the date of the gift. It is important, however, that the gift not be on the eve of the sale of the company. Rather, the gift should be made over several years prior to the sale.

Gifts of stock of the corporation owning your business should be made sufficiently before the sale so that you can obtain the benefit of a very low valuation for the gifts. This permits you to transfer a greater percentage of your wealth to the next generation while minimizing the estate and death taxes.

For example, if you sell the stock of the corporation that owns your business for $1 million and you give away 10 percent of the stock on the eve of the sale, it is likely that the value of the gifted stock will be $100,000. However, if three years before the sale you fund a trust for your children with 10 percent of the stock, it is likely that you will be able to sustain a substantially lower valuation for the same stock gift. Thus, by making gifts at an earlier point in time, you can increase the percentage of your wealth that can be transferred to the next generation without tax.

If you make gifts of stock, you should contractually retain the right to force the donees to sell the stock if you decide to sell your shares. These contract rights are sometimes referred to as drag-along clauses.

Family Partnerships

The selling shareholder should also consider forming family limited partnerships to reduce estate and death taxes. A limited partnership could be formed in which you would be the general partner and your family would be the limited partners. Stock of your corporation would be given to the limited partnership as a gift.

As general partner, you would continue to control the stock owned by the limited partnership and would have full voting rights and the ability to sell the stock. Your family would hold limited partnership units. It is arguable that the limited partnership units might permit a further discount on the value of the gifted stock over and above the minority interest discount and the lack of marketability discount.

Family limited partnerships do not work with Subchapter S corporations. Instead, you can divide the stock of your Subchapter S corporation into voting and nonvoting stock and give the nonvoting stock to your family.

Recently, limited liability companies (particularly ones formed in Nevada, a low-tax state) have been utilized instead of limited partnerships. In contrast to a limited partnership, a limited liability company affords greater protection for family members against personal liability for debts of the limited liability company and does not require a general partner who is personally liable for such debts.

Charitable Foundations and Charitable Remainder Trusts

If you are charitably inclined, you should consider establishing a charitable foundation or charitable remainder trust and funding it with a portion of the stock of your corporation. The advantage to you is that when the stock is sold, the charitable foundation or charitable remainder trust does not pay any federal or state income tax on the gain resulting from the sale.

In addition, your gift of stock to the charitable foundation or charitable remainder trust produces a federal income tax deduction on your personal tax return. To the extent that you cannot absorb the tax deduction in a single year, your charitable deduction can be carried forward for the next five years.

The charitable foundation permits you to control future charitable gifts by using the gross sale proceeds without diminishment by income taxes. You and/or members of your family can be the trustees of the foundation. However, no portion of the funds can benefit you or your family—except indirectly by relieving you of your future personal charitable obligations.

The charitable remainder trust permits you and your family to receive an annuity for a term of years or for their lives from the trust. At the end of the term of years or upon the death of the noncharitable beneficiaries, the remainder is paid to a charity or charities designated in the trust instrument or chosen by the trustees (which could include you and/or members of your family). Because the charitable remainder trust does not pay federal income taxes on the sale proceeds, the income produced by the gross sale proceeds is approximately 17 percent higher than the income you would have received had you personally sold the stock to the buyer and paid a 17 percent tax on the gain (15 percent long-term capital gain plus an assumed rate of 2 percent state income taxes, net of the federal income tax benefit).

The major disadvantage of both the charitable foundation and the charitable remainder trust is that you lose the ability to receive any portion of the sale proceeds from the stock that you have given away (except that you can receive an annuity from a charitable remainder trust), and hence you have lost ownership of a portion of your wealth. In addition, your income tax deduction for the gift to the charitable foundation or charitable remainder trust will be equal to the fair market value of your stock only if distributions are made from the charitable foundation directly to public charities within fourteen months after the stock is given to the charitable foundation, or if the charitable remainder trust may make distributions only to public charities.

General

It is not recommended that you give away so much of your wealth that you have to depend on your children for your future. Reducing estate and death taxes is not a sufficient reason for jeopardizing your lifestyle.

It is best to make gifts of assets that are passive assets, that is, assets that are not critical to your business. For example, if you lease business real estate from yourself or from a separate partnership that you control, give away a minority interest in that real estate or partnership. Another ideal asset to give away is life insurance on your life that has cash value.

Any wealth transfer of an appreciating asset (such as stock of your corporation) should be accomplished sufficiently prior to the actual sale date so that a low valuation for the gift can be obtained, thereby permitting you to maximize the amount of the wealth transferred.

An excellent time to make gifts of stock is right after a leveraged recapitalization (see Chapter 19). If you engage in a leveraged recapitalization, your business will have taken on a substantial amount of senior debt and you will have withdrawn a substantial amount of equity, thereby depressing the value of your stock.

MINIMIZING STATE INCOME TAXES

The sale of your business will generate income to you that will be taxed at the state and local level. A number of states, including California and New York, have very high personal, state, and local income taxes.

Currently state and local income taxes are deductible for the purpose of computing your federal income tax, except that the deductions are limited for higher income individuals. In addition, some business owners incur federal alternative minimum tax on the sale of their business, and state and local income taxes are not deductible for purposes of computing federal alternative minimum tax. More-over, even after the benefit of the federal income tax deduction, state and local income taxes can still be a significant amount.

For example, if you are a resident of New York City, you are in the 35 percent federal income tax bracket, and you sell your business for a gain of $10 million, the combined federal, state, and city taxes you pay can exceed $4 million (even after considering any benefit of your federal income tax deduction for the state and city taxes). If you are a New York City resident, New York state and city income taxes on the gain can exceed 12 percent of the gain.

One method of avoiding these taxes is to consider changing your state of residence and domicile prior to the sale. For example, both Florida and Nevada have no state personal income tax. If the busi-nessperson in the previous example were to have moved his or her residence and domicile to Florida prior to the sale, he or she could probably save enough taxes, by virtue of the shift of residence and domicile, to purchase a significant-sized house or condominium in Florida. This assumes, of course, you sell stock of your company, rather than the assets located in New York.

You do not necessarily have to change your place of employment in order to change your residence and domicile. You should change your voter registration address, your driver's license, and your bank accounts to Florida. You can still have your business in New York. You should take care to examine the state laws at the time you make your decision because some states, such as New York, California, and Ohio, are carefully auditing this method of avoiding state income tax. Check with your tax attorney before you attempt this maneuver. In addition, if you do not follow correct procedures, you might be con-sidered a resident of more than one state and therefore subject to tax from each state. For a web site that covers state income taxes, see www.taxadmin.org/fta/rate/ind_inc.html.

This procedure is not for everyone. It does not make sense to change your residence and domicile to Florida or Nevada unless you would actually enjoy living in Florida or Nevada. The change should fit your lifestyle and not be driven solely by tax motivations.

CHAPTER SIX

MARKETING YOUR BUSINESS

The effective marketing of your business requires you to put yourself in the place of potential buyers and imagine the characteristics they would find appealing. You must learn to think like a buyer. Many business owners are abysmally ignorant of their competitive position in their own industry. In fact, knowing this is key to effectively marketing your business.

During the years before your target sale date, you must learn as much as possible about the strengths and weaknesses of the competitors in your industry. Potential buyers would expect you to understand your strengths and weaknesses vis-à-vis your competition. Therefore, it is essential that you become more knowledgeable about your competition.

You must also become an expert about your markets and customers. Do you have a special niche in the marketplace? Is your market growing, flat, or declining? If the latter two, what are you doing in order to diversify your markets?

A useful step is to try to prepare a marketing brochure five years prior to your sale target date. See where the weaknesses are in the description of your business.

During the years prior to the sale target date, grow your business with an eye toward eliminating these weaknesses and improving your strengths. The maximization of the ultimate sale price depends upon how successful you are.

SHOULD YOU USE AN INVESTMENT BANKER
OR BUSINESS BROKER?

Just as it is possible (though not always practical) to sell your home yourself, it is possible to sell your business yourself. A few business owners do so successfully, particularly those whose businesses have values of less than $1 million. However, business owners who do not have significant experience in selling a business should consider hiring a reputable investment banker or business broker. This is particularly true of businesses having a value of more than $1 million.

A business broker is used for smaller businesses, usually those below $10 million in total value. Some business brokers specialize in selling businesses worth less than $1 million. An investment banker is used for larger businesses, with the minimum size depending upon the size and prestige of the investment banking firm.

The larger New York Stock Exchange firms (Goldman Sachs, Merrill Lynch, etc.) will typically not handle transactions below $50 million to $100 million. Local and regional investment banking firms will usually handle transactions in which the consideration is at least $5 million to $10 million or more. Transactions between $1 million and $10 million are usually handled by either larger business brokers or smaller investment banking firms.

The advantages of using an investment banker or business broker are as follows:

- An investment banker or business broker experienced in your industry has a greater knowledge of potential buyers for your business than you do.

- Even if you know one obvious buyer for your business, an investment banker or business broker may be able to find one or more other prospects, thereby permitting an auction to occur, which tends to maximize the sale price (see Chapter 8).

- The investment banker or business broker can help screen your potential buyers and prevent you from wasting your time on financially unqualified buyers.

- An investment banker or business broker can assist you in maintaining the confidentiality of your decision to sell by soliciting buyers anonymously.

- An experienced investment banker or business broker can devote a significant amount of time and attention to selling your business and has better methods of contacting potential buyers than you do.

- An experienced investment banker or business broker can assist in negotiating the sale, smoothing rough spots, and protecting you from unrealistic demands.

Some business owners foolishly refuse to retain an investment banker or business broker because they know at least one potential buyer for their business and do not want to pay an investment banker or broker a commission on the sale to this buyer. It is far wiser merely either to exclude this one potential buyer from the commission arrangement or to provide for a lower fee and to use the investment banker or business broker to seek out other purchasers.

The disadvantage of using an investment banker or business broker is that you have to pay a fee based upon a percentage of the sale consideration. In the case of business brokers, for businesses worth less than $500,000, the fee can be 10 percent or even more. The high commission percentage is the result of the relatively low valuation for the business and the fact that the business broker has certain fixed costs of marketing the business. For businesses worth less than $500,000, for which you are unable to negotiate a fee lower than 10 percent, you might consider using a business broker only as your last resort.

For larger businesses, the fee is usually based on the so-called Lehman Formula: that is, 5 percent of the first $1 million, 4 percent of the next $1 million, 3 percent of the next $1 million, 2 percent of the next $1 million, and 1 percent on the rest of the sale consideration. These commission percentages are usually negotiable.

In some cases, you may also have to pay a fixed consulting fee, which is due regardless of whether the business is sold. This is particularly true if your investment banker or business broker intends to prepare a brochure to describe your business in order to better market the business to potential buyers.

Finding an Investment Banker or Broker

How do you find a reputable and experienced investment banker or business broker? You should start with recommendations from an experienced M&A attorney.

If other companies in your industry have been sold recently, inquire as to whom they used for the transaction.

WARNING Make your inquiries discreetly and indirectly so that you do not tip off competitors, customers, suppliers, or employees that your business is for sale.

Obtain recommendations from trusted friends and business acquaintances who can keep a secret. Your accountant can also be a good source for referrals.

You should ask all potential investment bankers or business brokers about their experience in selling companies in your industry. Some investment bankers or business brokers represent only buyers. Try to obtain the names of persons whom they have previously represented in selling their businesses and seek to interview these persons. Take care not to identify yourself as a potential seller.

Many persons who call themselves investment bankers or business brokers are either inexperienced or disreputable. Unemployed executives who have an MBA degree may call themselves investment bankers even if they have never sold a business. A number of investment bankers and business brokers are less than reputable.

In some states, such as New York, business brokers must be licensed. However, state licenses are no guarantee of either competency or reputability.

Once you have selected the investment banker or business broker, you must negotiate an agreement with this individual, setting forth the terms of the arrangement, including the transaction fee. You will need the help of your experienced M&A lawyer to negotiate this agreement. There are many pitfalls.

WARNING State laws may require you to pay a commission once a ready, willing, and able buyer is located and signs an agreement, whether or not the transaction closes, unless you have a specific agreement to the contrary. In effect, you may be legally liable to pay a commission for aborted sales. The fee agreement should be in writing and be specific that no fee is due unless and until the sale closes.

Many other issues are involved in negotiating an agreement with an investment banker or business broker. Here are some examples:

- If a purchase price is payable in installments, the fee should be paid in similar installments and should not be paid in full when the sale closes.
- If the deferred payments to you are reduced by indemnification claims of the buyer, the fee payments should likewise be reduced.
- If the purchase price is payable in whole or in part in stock, try to pay the fee in stock in the same proportion.
- Some forms of agreement require you to pay a commission on the amount of your long-term debt assumed by the buyer. The assumption of long-term debt does not necessarily put money into your pocket, so you should resist paying a fee on such debt assumption.

You must control whom your investment banker or business broker approaches as a potential buyer to purchase your business. Advance approval of such approaches helps you control the sale process and preserves the confidentiality of your decision to sell.

WARNING Be extremely careful how you approach direct competitors. Do so very carefully and on a no-name basis. Otherwise, your competitors may use your sale decision as a competitive weapon.

SELLING THE BUSINESS YOURSELF

If you decide to sell the business without an investment banker or broker, you must maintain the confidentiality of your decision to sell in two ways: by not specifically identifying your business in letters to prospective buyers and in advertisements, and by designating your attorney, accountant, or a friend to be the initial contact person with potential buyers.

To discover buyers, you might consider having your attorney, accountant, or friend do the following:

- Consult investment bankers and business brokers who represent potential buyers.
- Advertise in trade journals.
- Advertise in business papers, including the *Wall Street Journal.*
- Send letters to companies that you think would be interested in your business.
- Send letters to companies that have the same SIC code as yours.

Various Internet sites purport to assist owners to sell their businesses, including eBay. Other sites include www.business4U.com, www.businessnation.com, and www.bizbuysell.com. Caution should be exercised in using these web sites to avoid public disclosure, and the reputation of each web site should be carefully checked in advance.

PREPARE A MARKETING BROCHURE

Whether you use an investment banker or business broker to sell your business or sell it yourself, prior to commencing the selling of your business you should have a marketing brochure, which should contain a description of your business, including a package of financial information.

The marketing brochure will be a key selling tool and should be carefully prepared. If you prepared a marketing brochure many years before the target date, be sure to update your existing brochure.

A good marketing brochure will take several months to prepare. Your attorney, accountant, and other advisors will be helpful in its preparation. It is important to highlight the strengths of your business and to present the weaknesses in the best possible light. You must take care to identify off-balance-sheet assets and assets that your balance sheet undervalues. (See Chapter 2.)

If your business has favorable special valuation factors (see Chapter 2), emphasize these in the brochure. You should also discuss customer relationships and market identification. Your competitive strengths should be carefully noted and explained.

The marketing brochure should not be provided to a potential buyer until appropriate confidentiality agreements have been executed. (See Chapter 4.)

A well-prepared, detailed, and thoughtful market brochure will reduce the buyer's due diligence and expedite the sale. More importantly, a good marketing brochure will enhance the valuation of your business to a prospective buyer, particularly to a large corporate buyer.

If a marketing brochure emphasizes the parts of your business that have higher valuation multipliers, it will assist you in negotiating a higher sale price. The marketing brochure also is useful in assisting corporate development personnel of large corporate buyers to justify to their management and board of directors why they should be purchasing your business at the proposed sale price.

> **WARNING** When hiring someone to prepare your marketing brochure, it is not necessarily wise to choose the low bidder. The marketing brochure is the most important document you can use to enhance the sale value of your business. It does not make sense to save $15,000 by using the low bidder only to have the business valued at a $1 million less than its true worth. Carefully check the credentials of the person you choose to prepare the marketing brochure and review the quality of other marketing brochures prepared by that person.

SETTING THE SALE TARGET DATE

Some business owners wait until they are too old or too sick to sell their business. Some let their executors sell their business after their death.

A great deal of energy is required to market your business properly. Your active participation is necessary in the sale process. Who better can market your business than you?

If you wait to sell until you lack the energy to run the business, potential buyers will sense your weakness. Potential buyers also like to purchase a business from an estate that is under pressure to sell.

To maximize the sale price, you must attract financial buyers, if possible, to compete with strategic and other buyers. A financial buyer will generally want you to continue to operate the business until new management can be trained.

All of these considerations dictate that your target sale date should be several years before you really have to sell. Of course, no one knows when their health will fail them. Therefore, unless you have trained management that is able to carry on without you, prudence would dictate a target date that will make it likely that you can actively participate in the marketing of your business.

The best time to sell your business is when your business is doing well, your industry is growing, and the overall economy is healthy. This may not coincide with your preferred exit date. Therefore, you must be flexible about your exit date.

A good time to sell is after a company in your industry has had an initial public offering (IPO), particularly if the Use of Proceeds section of their IPO prospectus contemplates further acquisitions. The IPO company will be under pressure to effect acquisitions to maintain their credibility to the public market.

You may market your business and discover that there are no buyers or only buyers at fire-sale prices. In this situation, you must be prepared to withdraw your business from the market and, if necessary, operate it for a year or two longer before trying to market it again. If you have a flexible exit date, you will have a greater potential for ultimately maximizing the sale price for your business.

PART II

PRELIMINARY NEGOTIATIONS

CHAPTER SEVEN

SURVIVING THE BUYER'S DUE DILIGENCE

F ew buyers will purchase a business without conducting an extensive investigation, generally called due diligence. The key to surviving the buyer's due diligence is understanding what areas of your business the buyer is likely to investigate and being prepared for that investigation.

Due diligence has similarities to the dating process prior to marriage. If you really want to get married (i.e., sell your business), you'd better dress well and otherwise look as attractive as possible for your date. You want your date (i.e., the buyer) to fall in love with you.

That does not mean that you should hide your defects. The buyer will probably discover them anyway. Rather, once the buyer falls in love with you, your defects become less important. Therefore, it is important for the buyer to fall in love with you before you reveal your defects.

If you have a major defect, consider at least hinting at (but not discussing in depth) the defect early in the due diligence process. While the buyer is flattering you about what a wonderful business you have, this is a good time to be modest and mention your main defect very obliquely and casually and without detail.

It is important that the buyer not feel that he or she has been misled by you when the true extent of your major defect is revealed. The buyer must at all times have confidence in your integrity. Who wants to marry a liar?

STANDSTILL AGREEMENTS

It is increasingly common for a buyer to insist that the seller agree to not shop the business (i.e., actively continue to seek other buyers) after the date the buyer has expressed an interest and an acceptable purchase price and prior to signing a definitive sale agreement. The justification for these no-shop or standstill agreements is that the buyer must make significant expenditures to perform and complete its due diligence and to pay attorneys to draft a definitive sale agreement and, therefore, the buyer does not want the seller to find a rival buyer during this period. In larger acquisitions, the cost of buyer due diligence alone can run into the hundreds of thousands of dollars and in many cases, it can exceed $1 million. Therefore, it is not entirely unjustified for the buyer to ask for some protection during the due diligence period.

In many cases, the standstill agreement is contained in a letter of intent (see Chapter 9). However, standstill agreements can also be separate documents if the seller is unwilling to execute a letter of intent.

Although sellers are naturally reluctant to take their businesses off the market until they know that they have a definitive sale agreement, a properly structured standstill agreement with a proposed buyer will not significantly harm the seller and may actually facilitate the transaction. A properly structured standstill agreement should contain an expiration date that is as short as possible, typically not more than thirty days. Thus, at the end of the standstill period, the seller can continue to negotiate with other potential buyers. If the proposed buyer needs an extension of the standstill period, the seller would be in a position to make a decision as to whether a short extension is justified based upon what has happened during the standstill period.

A properly structured standstill agreement should not prevent the seller from receiving unsolicited offers, as long as the seller does not negotiate with the person making the unsolicited offer during the standstill period.

Many proposed buyers will request a long standstill period (e.g., 90 to 120 days). Such a request should normally be resisted because a motivated buyer should be able to complete due diligence on a faster timetable.

Standstill agreements can actually facilitate transactions. The buyer may have to invest substantial funds to complete the due diligence and that investment may itself motivate the buyer to continue the transaction to completion. In addition, during the standstill period the buyer may fall in love with the business.

It is extremely difficult to negotiate meaningfully with a buyer unless they have completed their due diligence. If you resist any standstill agreement, the buyer may well look elsewhere. It is in your interest to have a potential buyer complete the due diligence and thereby have some investment in the sale process. The buyer's completion of the due diligence process creates a psychological momentum to the transaction and helps facilitate the completion of the sales transaction.

Appendix 5 contains sample standstill agreements, one of which favors the seller and the other favors the buyer.

DATA ROOM

In larger sale transactions, it is customary to maintain a data room in which all relevant documentation about the seller can be inspected by the potential buyer or buyers who are performing due diligence. It is preferable to have this data room off your premises in order to maintain confidentiality and prevent interference with your operations. Your M&A attorney's office is an ideal site.

SPECIFIC DUE DILIGENCE

A recent publication for buyers lists the following four general due diligence rules for buyers:

- Do wine and dine customers, employees, and competitors.
- Talk to outsiders.
- Read upside down.
- Don't fall in love.

The first two rules should alert sellers to the scope of the investigation they will face. The third rule, "Read upside down," suggests that sellers keep their desks clean and require that their key employees maintain clean desks during the due diligence process.

The final rule for buyers, "Don't fall in love," suggests that this is exactly what the seller should seek.

The intensity and breadth of the due diligence process often surprises unprepared sellers. It is important that you anticipate what the potential buyer is likely to look for.

Here are some of the many questions that must be answered by the seller during the due diligence process:

- What makes the company and/or its principal products unique?
- Where or how is the company positioned against competition?
- What is the company's place in the industry (rank, recent growth history, reputation, etc.)?
- What principal advertising messages has the company used successfully and unsuccessfully in the past?
- Are there any major developments in the company, competitive companies, or the industry that could have long-term effects on the company?
- Are there any legal, moral, social, or ethical issues with regard to the business or the industry that could have future impact?
- Generally, how is the business regarded by customers, competitors, vendors, the press, and the industry at large?
- In detail, what has industry growth during the past five years been, and what is the outlook for future years? Attach trade association, published data, and government data if available.
- Does the company give key customers holiday gifts or other presents? Does the company's management entertain extensively? (Be sensitive to clues that indicate inappropriate gifts.)
- What are some major new accounts sold during the past year, and why did they take on the product line?
- What are some major accounts lost during the past two years, and why are they no longer customers?
- Who is responsible for product development?
- What long-range plans are under consideration?
- What limitations exist in product development (e.g., people, capital, technology, outside vendors, tooling time, etc.)?

- What technology or proprietary knowledge is significant to the business?
- What companies possess similar or related knowledge?
- Is the company dependent upon outside resources for any of its technology? If so, describe what and upon whom.
- What resources has the company dedicated to improving product and process technology? What plans are in place (e.g., timetables, budgets, etc.)?
- What quality control systems are in place, and what management tools monitor their performance?
- What are the purchasing terms (e.g., payment terms, shipping, payment of duties, etc.) for each vendor?
- Are foreign purchases made in dollars? If not, in what currency? Are there exchange rate sharing agreements? Does the company hedge foreign purchases?
- Who owns tooling for component parts, packaging, etc.?
- Are tooling costs amortized in piece part prices, or are they purchased and depreciated?
- Is the company a licensee for any brand names, patents, technology,and so forth?
- Are any vendors critical to success? What contingency plans are in place in case a vendor cannot supply for any reason?
- Could any materials used become in short supply?
- Who has principal purchasing responsibility? Is anyone else involved?
- How is inventory financed?
- How did the book inventory vary from the computer reports and from the physical inventory? That is, what adjustments were made?
- What kind of computer hardware is used? Describe fully, including age, lease agreements, special features, and so on.
- What software packages are used?
- How customized are the software packages? Are they written in a commonly used language?
- Does the company have the source code for the software?

- Have vendors been in business a long time, and do they have a large number of similar users?

- What are the sales trends by month for the past two years? Are there seasonal patterns? Are sales affected by major shows or promotions? Does the industry have its own sales cycle? Are sales affected by competition?

- How is sales forecasting done? By whom? How formally? How often? How is it reviewed and validated? How accurate have forecasts been? Does the forecast drive purchasing and production, or are they driven by other decisions?

- What are standard payment terms by division, product line, channel of distribution, and so on?

- What nonstandard terms are granted? When? Why? Who approves them?

- Are reserves for returns or other after-sale adjustments made?

- Are standard, actual, or estimated costs used in estimating and general reporting? How often are standards updated? Who sets the standards?

- How are promotional budgets determined? Evaluate each advertising and promotion account by year in total and as a percentage of sales.

- How are expenses budgeted and controlled? Evaluate all G&A expenses from year to year and as a percentage of sales. Note significant increases or reductions.

The following are suggested to buyers in performing their due diligence among your key employees:

- Ask each key manager what major problems are faced:
  - by his or her department
  - by other departments
  - by the company as a whole
  - by the industry
- Ask each key manager to list the company's strengths and weaknesses.
- Ask each key manager to describe outside threats to or vulnerabilities of the company.

- Ask each key manager to describe the company's major opportunities as it moves forward, especially under new ownership.
- Ask each key manager to assess the risks faced in a change in ownership.
- Ask each key manager to evaluate the impact of the current owner/top manager no longer serving in the present role or being as active. What will future relationships be like?

CHAPTER EIGHT

AVOIDING NEGOTIATION TRAPS

The effectiveness of your negotiating strategy plays a major role in your ultimate success in selling your business. The following are strategies that will enhance your negotiating position and help you avoid common pitfalls in the process.

TYPES OF BUYERS

One way of classifying potential buyers is by whether they are considered financial buyers, strategic buyers, or neither. If you expect to work for the buyer after the sale, it is particularly important that you understand the buyer's culture and motivations.

Financial Buyers

A financial buyer is a purchaser who is motivated solely by financial considerations in acquiring your business and who is not engaged in a business that could be integrated with yours or could otherwise strategically benefit from the acquisition. The financial buyer looks only to your projected financial results and is uninterested in any synergy with an existing business. Financial buyers typically finance their business with money from institutional investors who are looking for large returns over a five-year period. These institutional investors typically are interested in exiting at the end of the five-year period through a sale or public offering.

However, it is not always true that a financial buyer will pay less than a strategic buyer. If capital is very available, as in the late 1990s, financial buyers may have pressure from their investors to consummate transactions and to show a financial return. This pressure can cause a financial buyer to outbid a strategic buyer at times when capital is overly plentiful.

Because the financial buyer does not have any business with which your business has synergy (other than the ability in the case of a consolidator to lay off your back-office personnel), you will typically get a lower valuation from a financial buyer.

The presence of financial buyers in the marketplace permits a broader range of potential buyers for your business and tends to set a floor on the price of your business.

You should take great care in selling to financial buyers who have received their capital from an institution and are still private. These buyers tend to use a portion of the purchase price as equity for purposes of their balance sheet. For example, they may offer you $10 million for the business but only permit you to receive $6 million in cash, with the remaining $4 million subordinated to their institutional lenders on a long-term note. Effectively, you have $4 million added to the equity base of the buyer because their institutional lenders will treat your $4 million note as equity. You are at risk because if the buyer defaults to its institutional lenders, your note will never get paid.

Today, many financial buyers are also strategic buyers because they have a portfolio company engaged in the same business.

Strategic Buyers

A strategic buyer wants to purchase your business because of the synergy with its existing business. For example, if your products have penetrated a particular market that the strategic buyer would also like to penetrate, the strategic buyer may acquire your business to achieve that market penetration.

The strategic buyer must compute how much it would cost to penetrate the same market. Strategic buyers might be willing to pay you a much higher figure than your earnings would indicate, based upon the cost savings to them of market access that your business gives them.

Your financial results are less important to strategic buyers because they are interested in the financial results of their business combined with yours. The strategic buyer tends to take a longer view of their investment than the financial buyer and is less concerned about exiting in five years.

An example of a strategic purchase is the recent acquisition by IBM of LOTUS Development Corp., which gave IBM access to the huge software inventory of LOTUS.

Some strategic buyers express interest in your business in order to discover important competitive information. You should take care with strategic buyers to prevent so-called fishing expeditions.

Other Buyers

Some buyers, sometimes called special-purpose buyers, are neither financial nor strategic buyers. For example, a father may purchase a business for his son or daughter. A businessperson who previously sold a business may decide to purchase another business.

Regardless of what category your buyer is in, it is important to understand your buyer's motivations. Doing so will help you to better structure your negotiations with the buyer and maximize your chances for a successful sale.

NEGOTIATION STRATEGY

It is important that you do not become the principal negotiator for your company. (That is why you assemble your team of professional advisors.)

The reasons for not becoming a principal negotiator for your company are as follows:

- Typically, you will have less experience than your professional advisors in negotiating such sale transactions.
- You will want to remain above the trench warfare that sometimes occurs in negotiations.
- The principal negotiator for your potential buyer will probably

be a second- or third-level management person or his or her lawyer. You do not want to put yourself at their level.

There are two types of negotiators:

- A cooperative negotiator is a negotiator who recognizes mutual problems and comes up with cooperative, creative solutions.

- A competitor negotiator is a negotiator who puts demands on the table, indicating that if his or her demand is not met, the negotiation will be over.

If competitor negotiators are attorneys for the potential buyer or second- or third-level managers, it is possible to handle them by going over their heads. However, if they are CEOs of potential buyers, you have a serious problem, and it may be smart to look elsewhere to sell your business. This is especially true if you are going to have an employment agreement and you will end up reporting to a CEO who is a competitor negotiator.

You should consider using your investment banker or business broker as the lead negotiator. If you have selected an experienced M&A lawyer, that person may also be a good choice to negotiate the sale. Be certain that your attorney has good business sense as well as good technical abilities.

ESTABLISHING A SALE PRICE

Sam Goldwyn, the legendary Hollywood producer—the same Sam Goldwyn who allegedly uttered the immortal lines "any man who goes to a psychiatrist ought to have his head examined" and "a verbal contract isn't worth the paper it's written on"—was negotiating a deal one day with a certain actor. The actor declared, "I'm asking fifteen hundred a week." Snapped Goldwyn, "You're not asking fifteen hundred a week. You're asking twelve, and I'm giving you a thousand."

If you are not really interested in selling your business unless you receive a ridiculously high price, set a ridiculously high price. On very rare occasions you might actually receive it. At worst, you will just drive off potential buyers. If you are not really interested in selling anyway, this is not a great loss.

Some potential sellers establish a sale price that is not realistic and assume that this provides them with the flexibility to negotiate a high price. In general, an unrealistically high sale price merely drives away potential buyers. If you believe that the highest price will be obtained by having competing buyers (such as at an auction), it is not in your interest to discourage potential buyers. Moreover, your high-ball price merely encourages buyers to offer you lowball prices in return.

You are not required to set a sale price for your business. You may just wait for offers from buyers.

Your value to a strategic buyer may be significantly higher than your value to other possible buyers. For example, in valuing your business, the strategic buyer may consider what it would cost them to reproduce your customer base and skilled workforce, and the cost savings to them may make your business extremely valuable. Occasionally, you might receive offers from strategic buyers that exceed your wildest dreams. Therefore, it is not normally in your interest to establish a sale price as your company's value may depend upon who is making the offer.

If you must establish a sale price for your business, it is recommended that it be set at the highest level that could be justified by any of the valuations you have received (see Chapter 2) plus at least an additional 20 percent to give yourself some bargaining room. You will need the help of an investment banker or business broker to compute that valuation, because the value can be higher for one buyer than another, as previously noted.

If your motivation for selling is to obtain a specific amount of money that will keep you comfortable for your lifetime, it is a judgment call as to whether to reveal that information to the buyer. If that amount of money is less than the maximum amount you can reasonably ask for the business, it may be a good negotiating plan, in appropriate circumstances, to reveal to the buyer both the price you want and the reason you have established that price. However, you should not reveal that information until late in the negotiations, when you are comfortable that the buyer is serious. The advantage of revealing that information is that it creates credibility for your asking price. By tying the figure to your future lifestyle, you indicate to the buyer the importance of the asking price to you personally.

If you own real estate that is leased to your business, you have to make a decision as to whether you want to sell the real estate or continue to lease it to the buyer. In some businesses, the primary value of the business is in the real estate. Therefore, when setting a sale price for your business, you should make it clear whether or not that price includes the real estate and, if not, what your lease terms will be. In many negotiations, the buyer may be willing to overpay for the real estate to make up for the fact that the seller was unhappy with the price offered for the business.

Dos and Don'ts for Effective Negotiation Strategy

The following are some general negotiation suggestions:

- Use questions to establish the buyer's needs, to clarify issues, and to advance creative alternatives.
- Listen carefully to the buyer's lawyer. Evaluate the information you have received before you respond.
- Be open-minded about your strategies and tactics. Carefully choose the words you use to be sure they are essentially neutral. The way you use them will determine how successful you are in establishing a positive climate. Don't use them as fixed rules that determine who will be the winner. Instead, use them to move the negotiation forward toward a mutually satisfactory solution.
- Be sensitive to the meaning of the buyer's gestures. They give you valuable information about the progress of the negotiation, even if the buyer is trying to manipulate you.

Table 8.1 shows various buyer negotiation strategies and possible seller counters.

The Public Offering Alternative

If your business has only one or two potential buyers, you might consider the public offering alternative to gain leverage in your negotiations. If your company can qualify for an initial public offering (IPO), see if you can get a letter of intent from a potential underwriter. The letter of intent is typically a nonbinding letter expressing the willingness of the underwriter to participate in your IPO.

The letter of intent shows that you have an alternative to the sale

TABLE 8.1   STRATEGIES AND POSSIBLE
                   COUNTERSTRATEGIES

BUYER'S STRATEGY	SELLER'S POSSIBLE COUNTERS
Buyer starts by making a lowball offer.	Don't rise to the bait. Counter high and wait it out.
Buyer sends someone who has to answer to others for most decisions.	Find out how and when employee will get approval from superiors. Try to meet head person alone. Ask how negotiations are expected to be successful with this approach.
Buyer presents demands as unalterable.	Change focus to other issues. Bring in associates to strengthen side. Suggest mediators and arbitrators.
Buyer pretends to be personally insulted, even if the seller hasn't done anything to deserve it.	Deny attempt to personalize. Ask forgiveness. Call a caucus.
Buyer takes an unexpected approach while maintaining original objective.	Spring surprises in return. Delay in taking action.
Buyer leaves the room and stops the negotiation.	Cut off the negotiations temporarily. Start at preparation stage again. Call a recess. Spring surprises in return.
Buyer pretends a matter is already settled and agreed on in hopes that the other side will go along.	Reject this ploy. Get others to verify that no such matter was settled.

of your company. It strengthens your bargaining position. Moreover, the letter of intent demonstrates to the potential buyer that once it has acquired your business, the buyer can do its own IPO or, if the buyer is already public, do a spinoff of some of your stock to its public shareholders.

Conducting an Auction

It is generally agreed that an auction produces the highest price for a business. Generally, you need two or more bidders to conduct an auction. However, an auction can be conducted with only one bidder if the auction is a closed auction, that is, no one knows who else is bidding.

To induce potential buyers to bid at an auction of your business, you must assure them that the business will be in fact sold to the highest bidder and that the auction will be conducted fairly.

If you have not made a decision whether or not you really want to sell your business, you will not be able to hold an auction effectively. Likewise, if you favor one bidder over another and want to give your favored bidder the last bid, it is unlikely that you will be able to induce other potential buyers to participate in the auction.

The most suitable businesses for an auction are businesses with good financial results and a strategic market position. If neither of these characteristics is present, the auction may not be as successful but should still be considered if there are competing buyers.

The auction must be conducted by a person in whom bidders have confidence and pursuant to written rules and procedures that are uniformly applied to all bidders. Your investment banker or attorney can fulfill this role.

Bidders are generally turned off by open auctions—in other words, auctions where their bids are disclosed to all other bidders—and by auctions in which there are innumerable rounds of bidding.

Auctions can also be classified as controlled auctions and uncontrolled auctions. In a controlled auction, the company initiates contact only with selected buyers, whereas in an uncontrolled auction (also sometimes called an open auction), there is no limit on the number of potential bidders. Uncontrolled auctions potentially attract the largest number of buyers, but may be highly disruptive to the company and its employees. Many companies prefer a controlled auction, which is less disruptive.

To induce bidders to participate in your auction, bids should be submitted in writing and maintained in confidence. Cutoff dates for bids should be advertised and adhered to.

It is preferable from the seller's point of view to have at least two rounds of bidding, with the second round of bidding confined to the highest two bidders. If there are more than four bidders, you may wish a third round of bidding.

It is essential that you provide all bidders with the same agreement of sale form, which will be prepared by your counsel. Each bidder should be requested to state any changes in the agreement of sale form when submitting his or her bid. In determining who is the highest bidder, the legal terms must be considered along with the price.

For example, suppose one bidder bids $15 million and a second bidder bids $14.5 million. If the $14.5 million bidder is willing to cut off any indemnification rights against you after the closing, but the $15 million bidder is unwilling to do so, you may consider the $14.5 million bid to be higher. As noted in Chapters 11 and 18, the important question is how much will you be left with after the sale is completed and any indemnification rights of the buyer have terminated.

To make the bids meaningful, the agreement of sale should provide for a forfeitable deposit upon signing and eliminate any due diligence out. Otherwise, the high bidder could use the auction as a vehicle to postpone making a final purchasing decision to the detriment of the seller, who has lost the other bidders.

The agreement of sale form should contemplate a quick closing after the signing. If the sale to the high bidder does not close quickly, the other bidders will have lost interest by the time the seller realizes that the sale to the high bidder will not be consummated.

WEEDING OUT POTENTIAL BUYERS

It is important that you quickly weed out potential buyers with the following characteristics so that you do not waste your valuable time:

- The buyer is merely on a fishing expedition.
- The buyer does not have a strong commitment at the CEO level to purchase your business.
- You always negotiate with second- and third-level management, never the CEO.
- The buyer has no prior record of making acquisitions.
- The buyer does not have the financial resources to acquire your business.
- The buyer's culture is not acceptable to you, and you want to continue to run the business.

CHAPTER NINE

LETTERS OF INTENT: A RECIPE FOR LITIGATION

A letter of intent (also called an "agreement in principle") is a document signed by both the buyer and the seller that expresses the intention of the parties to sell/buy the business but is not legally binding. The purpose of the letter of intent is to set forth the major business terms of the transaction and to confirm these terms in writing to prevent any misunderstanding. Typically, the letter of intent will state that it is not legally binding and that the only legally binding document is the definitive agreement of sale. Appendix 6 contains a sample letter of intent.

The problem with letters of intent is that sometimes they are legally binding even though the parties say that they are not. For example, the $11 billion judgment against Texaco, Inc. in the Getty merger was based upon a letter of intent signed by Getty with Pennzoil that was not supposed to be legally binding. The reason the $11 billion judgment was obtained against Texaco (the ultimate buyer) rather than Getty's shareholders (the seller), was an indemnification agreement Texaco had executed with Getty that protected Getty against suits by Pennzoil. This famous case and its repercussions are discussed in the articles at the end of this chapter.

Another problem with the letter of intent is the fact that many securities lawyers believe that a public company buyer must disclose a proposed material acquisition once a letter of intent is signed. The public disclosure of the letter of intent with your company effectively tells the world about your decision to sell sooner than you might prefer.

A final problem with letters of intent is the tendency of the lawyers for the buyer and seller to use the letter of intent to negotiate terms. This may result in expensive and protracted negotiations over the words of a document that is not intended to be legally binding. It also holds up the drafting and execution of the final agreement.

Therefore, it is preferable to avoid a letter of intent and proceed directly to the final agreement.

GETTY LETTER OF INTENT

The most dramatic example of the sometimes binding nature of letters of intent is the jury verdict in Texaco-Pennzoil involving the battle for the Getty Oil Company.

Pennzoil had prepared a five-page single-spaced memorandum of agreement that was signed by Gordon Getty, as sole trustee of the Sarah C. Getty Trust; Harold Williams, as president of the J. Paul Getty Museum; and Hugh Liedtke, Pennzoil's chairman. That memorandum of agreement spelled out in considerable detail the terms of the transaction and provided for approval by the Getty Oil board. After lengthy meetings and negotiations, the Getty board rejected the terms of the transaction as spelled out in that memorandum. Ultimately, Pennzoil and the Getty Oil board agreed on a proposal that contained some revised and, from Getty's standpoint, improved terms. Although the Getty board clearly voted to reject the terms of the initial memorandum of agreement, at the trial there was conflicting testimony as to whether the Getty board ever voted on approving the memorandum of agreement with revised terms.

The jury returned an $11 billion verdict against Texaco based on its finding that the Getty Oil Company, the Sarah C. Getty Trust, and the J. Paul Getty Museum, which controlled about 11.8 percent of that stock, had entered into a binding agreement with Pennzoil pursuant to which Pennzoil was to become a three-sevenths owner of Getty Oil. The jury found that the "agreement in principle" between the parties was binding even though no definitive agreements had been reached, and even though the parties contemplated negotiating and entering into such agreements.

In reading the subsequent articles on the Getty letter of intent, remember that the $11 billion judgment would have been the responsibility of the seller's major shareholders but for the indemnification agreement executed by Texaco.

CAUTION TALKS: TEXACO-PENNZOIL CASE MAKES FIRMS CAREFUL ABOUT MERGER MOVES; JUST WHAT IS AN AGREEMENT STIRS MUCH UNCERTAINTY; A RISK IN SHAKING HANDS—BUT THE PRECEDENT MAY FADE

Earlier this year, Michel Zaleski consummated a day and a half of tough negotiations by doing what he always does upon reaching an agreement in principle. "I looked the guy in the eye, stuck out my hand and said, 'Let's shake on it,'" the New York investment banker recalls.

But across the table, the opposing attorney looked back askance. "We can't do that," he told Mr. Zaleski, with an uncomfortable smile.

As Mr. Zaleski pulled back his hand, he could feel the Texaco chill. "I never thought a handshake was anything more than a moral commitment," he said. "But now people are afraid to make even a moral commitment for fear someone will use it against them."

Four months after a Texas jury delivered an $11.12 billion verdict against Texaco Inc. for thwarting Pennzoil Co.'s agreement in principle to buy part of Getty Oil Co., the largest civil-damage award in history is casting a long, cold shadow across American business. Deal makers say the huge verdict, by undermining time-honored assumptions on Wall Street about what constitutes an enforceable agreement and what doesn't, is forcing people to be much more cautious.

"The lesson learned is that the most general of writing can be construed as an agreement," says Jay Grogan, an attorney who researched the Texaco case for his Dallas law firm of Jackson, Walker, Winstead, Cantwell & Miller. "It's really pretty scary."

Adds another Dallas lawyer, Robert Profusek of Jones, Day, Reavis & Pogue: "Today, an agreement is in the eyes of the beholder."

This "post-Texaco" climate of uncertainty is having a chilling effect on bidding competition. Some companies, accustomed to vicious bidding wars in the mergers and acquisitions market, have grown gun-shy in the wake of the Texaco verdict, especially when a potential target has entered any type of agreement with a third party. Some boards of directors, meanwhile, have had to grudgingly accept lower bids for

(continues)

Caution Talks *(continued)*

their companies' assets rather than risk being sued for breach of contract by an angry bidder.

"No longer can we say, 'We stole a deal fair and square,'" says Alen E. Rothenberg, a San Francisco investment banker. "Now, there's a new constituency out there. In addition to shareholders and employees, now we have to worry about rejected suitors."

By discouraging companies from aggressively competing for acquisitions, the Texaco verdict has provided management, in effect, with a new lockout tool. For example, in a news conference two days after directors of Eastern Airlines agreed to sell the carrier's assets to Texas Air Corp. for what many analysts termed a very low price, Eastern's chairman, Frank Borman, dismissed the possibility that a rival bid for Eastern could succeed "even if someone offered more." He added, "You probably have heard of Texaco and Pennzoil."

Lawyers and investment bankers also say the Texaco case is one of several factors—including cost—that have hastened the pace of deal making. These observers note that "letters of intent" and "agreements in principle" are becoming less common today as negotiators try to reach final terms faster to freeze out any higher bidders or interlopers.

"Now, instead of relying on a handshake and two months of due diligence, the lawyers fly in immediately, lock the door, and sign everybody up in a few days with conditional outs," says Michael Halloran, a securities lawyer for Pillsbury, Madison & Sutro in San Francisco.

Much of the Texaco chill, however, may be due to psychological overreaction. The case didn't make any new law in the areas of contracts and fiduciary duty; it determined only that an agreement existed between Pennzoil and Getty and that Texaco had wrongly interfered with it. "That's an important distinction legally, and most business people don't understand it," says Mr. Profusek, the Dallas attorney.

Moreover, many legal experts consider the case an aberration whose significance they expect to be whittled away on appeal. Daniel J. Good, a mergers and acquisitions specialist with E. F. Hutton & Co., says, "The most sophisticated legal talent on Wall Street are incredulous that this decision was decided on the facts."

Many companies say the case has had no effect on their business practices. International Business Machines Corp., for example, says its standing policy, spelled out in its Business Conduct Guidelines, remains unchanged. The guidelines instruct IBM sales representatives that letters of intent, additional agreements "and the like" are "usually not firm orders" and are thus fair game for competing bids.

Other judges, meanwhile, have already signaled disagreement with the thinking in the Texaco verdict. Last month, Nebraska's Supreme Court, in a 4–3 decision, overturned a lower-court judgment against the Minneapolis-based commodities giant, Cargill Inc., for thwarting a merger agreement between its rival, ConAgra Inc., of Omaha, NE, and MBPXL Corp., a Wichita, KS, meatpacker. The case, which closely resembled Pennzoil's suit against Texaco, focused on the question of whether Cargill had "tortiously interfered" with ConAgra's written agreement to buy MBPXL by offering a higher price for the meatpacker's assets.

But in contrast to the Texaco case, the Nebraska high court rejected the notion that a merger agreement could be used to lock out interlopers. The court held that MBPXL's directors acted in accordance with their fiduciary responsibility, as stipulated in Delaware law, by reneging on the ConAgra agreement in favor of Cargill's higher bid. Board of Directors, wrote the court's majority, cannot use agreements to "infringe on the voting rights of shareholders or chill the bidding process."

After the decision, ConAgra's chairman, Charles M. Harper, said the company's shareholders "would be much better off if we were in Texas, where a contract is a contract."

The ConAgra-Cargill case, in fact, probably better reflects prevailing legal doctrine on contractual interference than the Texaco verdict does. In a major decision in January 1985, the influential Supreme Court of Delaware ruled in the case of *Smith v. Van Gorkam* that directors can be held personally liable if they approve a takeover agreement at an undervalued price. The Van Gorkam decision suggests that a board's obligation to shareholders may well supersede an agreement with a suitor.

Says J. Tomilson Hill, a mergers and acquisitions specialist at Shearson Lehman Brothers Inc.: "The Texaco decision hasn't changed a board of directors' fiduciary responsibility with respect to price—a basic tenet of both Delaware and [federal] securities law."

Nonetheless, the Texaco case has clearly affected some recent agreements. Texas Air's $600 million proposed acquisition of Eastern

(continues)

Caution Talks *(continued)*

stands out as a case in point. After Texas Air's takeover announcement, at least two other carriers were said to have considered offering higher bids for Eastern: Pan American World Airways and Braniff Inc.

Although a Pan Am spokesman said the Texaco verdict didn't figure in the carrier's decision not to bid on Eastern, one Braniff official close to Jay Pritzker, whose family holds a majority stake in Braniff, says Mr. Pritzker would have made a bid but was dissuaded by, among other impediments, his concern that Mr. Borman's public invocation of the Texaco case indicated that the two parties wouldn't tolerate any interlopers.

"The Texaco case was used as a negotiating tool to stop the bidding process," observes this official, who declined to be identified, "and it was used to the detriment of shareholders."

In the Eastern Airlines case, one key union, the machinists, refused to agree to new labor concessions unless Mr. Borman resigned. The board wouldn't go along with that and instead signed with Texas Air. But insiders critical of the pact say Eastern should have sought a higher bid once it became clear that all three of the company's unions were willing to take sizable wage cuts if Mr. Borman resigned. Mr. Borman hasn't resigned, but Eastern's pilots and flight attendants agreed to new wage concessions; its machinists have refused.

Some industry analysts say the ultimate deterrent to other suitors was economic, not legal. The Texaco case "was a factor," says Robert J. Joedicke of Shearson Lehman Brothers, but with $2.5 billion of debt and severe labor problems, "Eastern was not an outstanding candidate for a takeover."

The Texaco case also affected a recent bidding war between two jet-engine makers, Pratt & Whitney, an East Hartford, Connecticut, unit of United Technologies Corp., and Rolls-Royce Inc. of Greenwich, CT, a unit of Rolls-Royce Ltd.

In December, the Greenwich-based United Parcel Services of America Inc. ordered 20 refitted Boeing Co. jets, starting a competition between Pratt and Rolls for the $400 million engine contract. At first, according to a source privy to the negotiations, Rolls seemed in the lead, but then Pratt made price concessions. United Parcel gave Pratt a handshake agreement for the order.

While lawyers were writing the final contract, however, Rolls came back with another bid, some $25 million below Pratt's price. At that point, Pratt representatives raised the Texaco decision in a conversation with executives of United Parcel, and the Pratt accord sailed through, the source says.

Spokesmen for Rolls, Pratt, and United Parcel declined comment.

In another recent transaction, the closely held Miraflores Co. of San Francisco declined to entertain potentially higher bids for its assets after entering into a preliminary takeover agreement with Guest Supply Inc., based in New Brunswick, NJ. Although the two companies had exchanged letters explicitly stating that their merger agreement was non-binding, advisers to Miraflores, a supplier of hotel amenities with 1985 revenue of $7.1 million, recommended against considering subsequent bids for fear that Guest Supply might sue.

"In the Texaco case, even though the parties were not legally bound to go forward, pulling out at the last minute offended the jury's sense of justice," Miraflores' chairman, John Chapman, contended. "That turned out to be more important than the law."

If nothing else, most lawyers agree that the Texaco verdict is a chastening reminder of how capricious the legal system can be. "The Texaco case is a textbook illustration of the dangers of ever getting involved in the American judicial system," says Rodgin Cohen, an attorney with the New York law firm of Sullivan & Cromwell. "The courts can do wild and unpredictable things."

Insofar as the Texaco verdict has contributed to an increasingly prevalent lockout mentality, it may be costing shareholders money. Companies that try to limit bids are less likely to receive the fullest price. In 1983, for instance, the family that owned a large stake in Stokely–Van Camp Inc. tried to buy the company for $55 a share. An unsolicited suitor, Quaker Oats Co., launched an offer, however, and eventually bought Van Camp for $77 a share.

Ultimately, the principal issue raised in the Texaco verdict—whether a director's fiduciary responsibility to seek the highest price takes precedence over contract law—may have to be more clearly resolved in the courts before many deal makers will feel comfortable entering bidding wars. Utilicorp United Inc. is asking a Houston federal court to do just that.

(continues)

Caution Talks *(continued)*

In a suit against Energas Co., of Amarillo, TX, the utility is contending that Energas unlawfully interfered in January with Utilicorp's preliminary agreement to buy Trans Louisiana Gas Co., of Lafayette, LA. Utilicorp is arguing that TransLa's directors repudiated their agreement, just two days after it was reached, to take a higher offer from Energas. Each side has accused the other of trying to either duck or exploit the Texaco verdict by "forum shopping" for a favorable court.

An Energas spokesman, who says the case belongs in Louisiana courts because the target company is situated in that state, charges Utilicorp with trying to "capitalize on the hysteria following the Texaco verdict" by bringing suit in Texas.

Utilicorp's president, Richard C. Green, Jr., counters that both the suit and the Houston venue have "substantial merits," but he concedes that "clearly, the Texaco-Pennzoil example was there and seemed to be the best path to follow."

THE GAMBLER WHO REFUSED $2 BILLION: PENNZOIL'S J. HUGH LIEDTKE, FIGHTING TEXACO, MADE A HISTORIC BET

The whole amazing story is beyond anyone's previous experience in business or law. Pennzoil's celebrated suit arose from Texaco's takeover of Getty Oil, which allegedly wrecked a planned Pennzoil-Getty deal. A Texas jury decided in November 1985 that Texaco owed Pennzoil $10.5 billion—the largest award in history. A higher court later reduced it to $8.5 billion, but by mid-April interest and penalties had brought it up to $11 billion. Texaco offered to pay Pennzoil around $2 billion if Pennzoil would drop its claims. Pennzoil Chairman J. (for John) Hugh Liedtke—in what must be the biggest turndown of cash ever—looked that ten-figure sum in the eye and said no. The next day Texaco filed for bankruptcy protection, the biggest company ever to do so.

Liedtke (pronounced LID-key), the man who turned down Texaco's $2 billion settlement offer, in mid-April still held out his hand for more. Asked by *Fortune* whether he is the greediest man in the world or simply in need of psychiatric help, Pennzoil's barrel-bellied chief executive chuckled and replied, in a voice so gravelly and deep you practically have to drill for it, "Maybe both." Then he adds, "I don't think 'greed' is fair, I really don't." Liedtke, 65, refuses to accept what he calls a "shotgun settlement" on Texaco's terms. "Pennzoil is unmoved by Texaco's dramatic gesture," he says. "Maybe now we should sit back awhile and see how they like bankruptcy—the euphoria should wear off in about a week. We will not take an unreasonably low settlement, whether it takes six months or four years."

This pugnacious gambler may never have expected to pocket the whole $11 billion, but Liedtke still insisted on a settlement in the $3 billion to $5 billion range—roughly twice as much as Texaco's equally intransigent leaders would pay.

The man who runs Texaco is adamant that his company has done nothing wrong. "I am interested in settling this thing," says James W. Kinnear, 59, a trim, personable marketer who became Texaco's chief executive only last January. "But I believe we are absolutely right under the law."

That obstinate attitude is reminiscent of John K. McKinley, 67, who was Kinnear's predecessor and got Texaco into this bind. Combined with the arrogance for which Texaco is famed in the oil patch, stubbornness contributed to the devastating series of setbacks the company has suffered in courts from Delaware to Texas to Washington, D.C. McKinley, an overbearing Alabamian who looks like Lyndon Johnson, failed to take Pennzoil's suit seriously enough at first and then lost big. He and Kinnear reluctantly tried to settle the case, but their efforts accomplished nothing. Now the company, long criticized for flat-footed management, will be run under the cumbersome rules of Chapter 11 bankruptcy, perhaps for years. Only three units, accounting for 4% of Texaco revenues, are in Chapter 11, but since they are the parent company and finance units, their uncertain prospects cast doubt on all Texaco operations.

The inability of Liedtke and Kinnear to reach a compromise for so long proved horribly costly. The day after Texaco's bankruptcy filing, the market value of Pennzoil's stock dropped $631 million, prompting outraged shareholders to wake Liedtke in the middle of the night with

(continues)

The Gambler Who Refused $2 Billion *(continued)*

angry phone calls to his home. Texaco's stock, already priced far below estimates of the company's intrinsic value, fell a bit further. Security analysts believe that if asset-rich Texaco had paid a settlement as high as $3 billion instead of going bankrupt, relieved investors would probably have pushed Texaco's market value up by more than $3 billion. Kinnear does not think much of that argument, and he is sticking to his guns: "Whatever we offer now will be less than our last settlement proposal."

For all the allure of a timely settlement, none seemed likely as long as the leaders of the two companies refused to sit down and negotiate seriously. For months, backed up by squads of expensive lawyers and investment bankers, they did little more than lob unacceptable proposals at one another like hand grenades.

When Liedtke and Kinnear individually discuss their negotiations, one likely reason for their lengthy impasse emerges: these men genuinely do not seem to understand or respect one another enough to communicate effectively. Both talk; neither listens. For 16 months Texaco threatened to file for bankruptcy if pushed too hard. Liedtke pushed anyway, and Texaco eventually made good its threat.

Asked why he continued to push, Liedtke offers this story: "When my daughter Kristie was a little girl, she'd threaten to hold her breath until she died if she couldn't have her way. She'd turn red and scare her mother and me half to death. On our pediatrician's advice, one time we just let her hold her breath till she keeled over. She never did it again. She has a very sweet disposition now." Counters the exasperated Kinnear: "The truth is he was holding our head under water. You better hold your breath."

Liedtke and Kinnear have almost nothing in common to help bridge the $2-billion-wide gulf that divided them. Liedtke is an entrepreneur and a rebel who named his first major company, Zapata Petroleum, after the famous Mexican revolutionary. Kinnear, by contrast, is an Annapolis-trained company man who toiled in Texaco's rigid bureaucracy for 33 years before winning his place atop it just six years before his mandatory retirement. Liedtke's suits don't always fit; Kinnear dresses for success, Texaco style, with French cuffs and a tie clip. Each man is convinced he is fighting for a principle and the other fellow is wrong.

The bankruptcy filing came on a Sunday, after days of intense settlement negotiations in Houston between Texaco and Pennzoil. Kinnear, whose earlier offers had reportedly been somewhere around $500 million, finally made his top offer of about $2 billion if Pennzoil would acknowledge that amount as full settlement of the court's award. "Texaco was in a hostage situation," says Frank Barron, a Cravath partner. "It's analogous to paying ransom to kidnappers. You don't do it because the kidnappers deserve the money but because you want the hostage back."

Liedtke refused the offer, and Kinnear returned to White Plains for a Texaco board meeting on Saturday. That day Liedtke sent a counteroffer to Kinnear by corporate jet, using Pennzoil's pilot as courier. Liedtke says he offered to settle for something between $3 billion and $5 billion. The next day he flew to New York for meetings with Kinnear. But, relates Joseph Jamail, chief lawyer for Pennzoil in its suit against Texaco, "They filed for bankruptcy while he was still in the air. It kind of made him wonder whether they were talking in good faith."

Liedtke says he had to turn down Texaco's $2 billion offer. Having won $11 billion, he argues, he has a fiduciary duty to Pennzoil's stockholders to collect as much of that money as possible. His advisers told him that a settlement in the $3 billion to $5 billion range would be fair. If he were to accept a settlement much smaller than his advisers have suggested, says Liedtke, Pennzoil's shareholders might have grounds for a successful lawsuit.

Kinnear and his fellow Texaco board members—who include such business heavyweights as former IBM chairman Frank Cary and Capital Cities/ABC chairman Thomas Murphy—have a similar problem. Texaco shareholders have already filed 15 suits against them, arguing that the directors should be liable for an act—the Getty takeover—that resulted in an $11 billion judgment against the company. A settlement with Pennzoil could give those suits extra power by appearing to be an admission of wrongdoing by directors, and the dollar amount of the settlement might be seen as a measure of the damage done to Texaco's

(continues)

The Gambler Who Refused $2 Billion *(continued)*

shareholders. Says Frank Barron: "That possibility never entered into the board's deliberations."

Tulsa-born Liedtke, a big friendly galoot with a face as droopy as a basset hound's, definitely does not look or talk like a wizard of high finance. But be warned: the blood in his veins is Prussian, and this good old boy is a graduate of Amherst, where he majored in philosophy, and of Harvard Business School and the University of Texas Law School. He is smart, tough, unconventional, and lucky—a combination that makes him a fearsome adversary.

Liedtke got lucky early in life. After navy service on an aircraft carrier during World War II, he settled down to practice law in Midland, Texas, which sits atop one of the biggest pools of oil in the continental U.S. According to Robert Green of Merrill Lynch, who had been Liedtke's Amherst roommate and is now Pennzoil's lead investment banker, Liedtke quickly tired of the divorces, estate cases, and wills that constituted the bulk of his practice. So Liedtke teamed with his younger brother, William, also a Midland lawyer, to invest modest sums in oil exploration.

In 1953 they joined with George Bush—now vice president of the United States—to form the exploration company called Zapata. They invested $2,500 each, raised $1 million, and had the good fortune to drill one successful well after another, amassing Texas-size fortunes while still in their early 30s. Though they severed their business ties in 1955, Liedtke and Bush remain good friends. "George isn't a wimp, I can tell you that," says Liedtke. "I think he'd make a whale of a president."

Liedtke was a corporate raider and bust-up artist decades before those terms were invented. His first big move was a friendly takeover of South Penn Oil Co. in the early 1960s. Once part of the Standard Oil trust, South Penn made the popular lubricating oils sold under the Pennzoil brand name. The company owned plenty of valuable assets but produced paltry profits. The brash young Liedtke figured South Penn would do better if he were running it. When Liedtke arrived on the scene, the company was controlled by J. Paul Getty, the oilman then called the richest American. Getty installed Liedtke as chief executive, and a few years later Getty sold out to him. Liedtke merged the exploration business into South Penn and renamed the company Pennzoil.

His fascination with hidden asset values led Liedtke into the fight with Texaco. In late 1983 he noticed that shares of Getty Oil Co. were selling for considerably less than the per share value of Getty's vast reserves of oil and gas. Liedtke started buying. Soon he formed an alliance with Gordon Getty, one of the late J. Paul's sons. A gifted musician and an amateur businessman, Gordon headed a family trust that owned 40% of Getty oil.

He and Liedtke cooked up a deal that would greatly increase Getty's market value. Early in 1984, Pennzoil and Getty Oil announced a detailed agreement in principle for Pennzoil to buy three-sevenths of Getty's shares for $3.9 billion, or $112.50 per share, $40 more than the market price of a month before. Several days later, however, Getty accepted a Texaco offer to buy all of its shares for $125 each, a price later raised to $128. The total came to more than $10 billion, a record at the time. Pennzoil sued, arguing that Texaco had illegally interfered with a binding contract between it and the Getty interests. Far from being intimidated by the lawsuit, Texaco's McKinley went ahead with the purchase.

In retrospect he should have been much more cautious. Martin Lipton, the renowned takeover lawyer who represented the Getty Museum—a principal owner of Getty Oil—had insisted that Texaco indemnify the Getty interests against lawsuits arising from the deal. Texaco management considered the risks and agreed, scarcely imagining how vast the consequence would be. When the Texas jury ruled in Pennzoil's favor to the tune of $10.5 billion, Texaco had no one with whom to split the bill. And while Texaco, along with many objective observers, regards that damage award as absurdly high, the company did not present its own theory of damages during the original trial. To advocate a different way of figuring damages, the company's lawyers reasoned, would only dignify Pennzoil's claim.

The Texas appellate court that reduced the damage award nevertheless sustained the jury's verdict. As of mid-April, Texaco still intended to appeal to the Texas Supreme Court and then, if necessary,

(continues)

The Gambler Who Refused $2 Billion *(continued)*

the U.S. Supreme Court. But neither tribunal was obliged to hear the case. G. Irvin Terrell, an attorney with Baker & Botts, one of Pennzoil's law firms in Houston, estimated that exhausting the appeal process could take as little as nine months if neither court accepts the case, or as long as 18 months if both do. Some independent lawyers and security analysts think presenting appeals to both courts could take much longer, perhaps three or four years.

The only way Texaco could escape the judgment entirely would be to win on appeal—possible but unlikely. At worst, if Texaco refused to settle it could end up having to pay Pennzoil the whole $11 billion it owed the day it went into bankruptcy—also unlikely. But as of mid-April each of those extremes represented a serious risk for one of the two warring CEOs, and an opportunity for the other. Since neither man had won a decisive advantage, settlement still seemed in the interest of both. Although the sum of roughly $2 billion that divided them seemed impossibly large, the financial risks each man faced if he did not settle were even larger. Splitting the difference—arriving somewhere between $2.5 billion and $3.5 billion, say—might have made sense for everyone concerned.

Bad management by both Texaco and Pennzoil transformed an awkward dispute into a disaster of historic proportions. Managers hoping to avoid making epic messes of their own are finding this miserable saga a rich source of lessons.

Lesson Number 1: Even the most learned and famous lawyers and investment bankers that money can buy may give imperfect advice.

Lesson Number 2: Before you agree to indemnify people, ask yourself why they need indemnity in the first place. Marty Lipton's request that Texaco indemnify the Getty interests could have alerted Texaco's McKinley to the considerable risk he faced.

Lesson Number 3: Never engage in a jury trial if you can avoid it. If you can't avoid it, treat even the silliest-seeming jury trial with life-and-death seriousness. No one knows what a jury will do.

Lesson Number 4: Corporate shareholders do not require their fiduciaries to fight for matters of principle, but they get very testy when their financial interest is threatened. It is often wiser to settle, even if you are right.

Lesson Number 5: If you're going to negotiate at all, you must be prepared to respect your opponent's position. As of mid-April, that was a lesson that Hugh Liedtke and James Kinnear apparently still had not learned.

PART III

THE SALE PROCESS

CHAPTER TEN

STRUCTURING YOUR TRANSACTION

The structure of a sale is important to the seller because structure: (a) affects the after-tax sale proceeds, (b) can significantly increase or decrease the seller's legal fees, and (c) can adversely affect the very feasibility of the sale itself. For example, if you have assets that cannot be transferred without the consent of a third party (e.g., a below-market lease) or a government agency (e.g., a license), an asset sale may not be feasible.

The following are the most common sale structures:

- sale of assets
- sale of stock
- mergers (direct, reverse, triangular, and forward)
- consolidations
- management agreements, licenses, leases, joint ventures, and the like

If at all possible, you should avoid management agreements, licenses, leases, and joint ventures with the potential buyer if you really want to sell your business.

Management agreements with the buyer, with no guarantee that a sale will ultimately occur, are particular "no-nos," unless you are desperate. A management agreement permits the buyer one long look at the seller's business in which the buyer will inevitably find warts to help drive down the ultimate selling price.

ASSET SALES VERSUS STOCK SALES

A sale of your assets is one of the most common forms of structuring. Buyers prefer this structure since they can pick and choose what assets they want to acquire. A buyer may decide not to purchase your cash or accounts receivable and thereby reduce the buyer's financing requirements. Even more important, buyers can assume only certain disclosed liabilities of the seller and not assume any other liabilities.

This contrasts with a sale of stock in which the buyer in effect acquires, indirectly through stock ownership, all of your assets (both desired and undesired) and all of your liabilities (both known and unknown). Although it is possible to escrow a portion of the sale consideration to protect the buyer from unknown liabilities, many buyers are concerned that the escrow may not be sufficient to cover the potential unknown liabilities. There may also be tax advantages to a buyer of an asset sale over a stock sale, which are discussed in Chapter 11.

A stock sale is the preferable structuring from a seller's viewpoint. The seller can (with minor exceptions) obtain long-term capital gains treatment on the gain resulting from the sale of stock. The sale is less expensive to effectuate because there is no requirement to transfer individual assets and there is no potential sales tax (as is the case in some states on asset sales). All that is required is to assign the stock certificates to the buyer.

From the seller's viewpoint, an asset sale is probably the least desirable structure (assuming that the seller is not remaining in business). After the selling entity (the target) receives cash or other consideration for its assets, the selling entity must pay (or make provision to pay) all remaining unassumed liabilities (including taxes resulting from the sale) prior to any distribution to shareholders. If the board of directors of the selling entity distributes the sale consideration and any remaining unpurchased assets to its shareholders without paying (or making provision to pay) unassumed liabilities, the directors may have personal liability to these unpaid creditors. The distribution of the full sale consideration from an asset sale could be held up for many years until litigation against the selling entity is set-tled and other contingent liabilities are resolved.

Under most state laws, if the selling corporation is formally dis-solved, the unpaid creditors only have a short period of time (typi-cally two years after formal dissolution) to assert their claims. Therefore, it is best to dissolve the selling corporation as soon as pos-sible to start this statute of limitations on creditors.

Upon liquidation or dissolution, the sale consideration and any remaining unpurchased assets would be distributed to a liquidating trust of which you could be the trustee. The liquidating trust would pay all claims once they were resolved and distribute its remaining as-sets to shareholders.

> **WARNING**   If the selling corporation fails to formally dissolve, there is, depending upon state law, no short time limit on the assertion of claims by unpaid creditors against directors and shareholders. Therefore, after an asset sale (assuming you are not remaining in business), dissolution should occur as quickly as possible to commence the running of the statute of limita-tions.

Other disadvantages of an asset sale as opposed to a stock sale may exist. As noted, in some states (such as California) an asset sale can trigger sales tax. However, many buyers insist upon this structure be-cause of its advantages from their viewpoint.

A stock sale is generally preferred by buyers only when there are nontransferable assets in the selling entity, such as a nontransferable lease or license that does not contain a change of control clause. Buy-ers may also desire to purchase your stock when you have tax-loss car-ryover (see Chapter 11).

MERGERS AND CONSOLIDATIONS

In a merger, all of the assets and liabilities of one corporation are transferred to the other corporation (the survivor of the merger) by operation of law. The consideration payable to the shareholders of each of the merging corporations is specified in an agreement or plan of merger. The transfer of assets and liabilities automatically occurs when the plan or agreement of merger is filed with the Secretary of State or the Corporation Bureau of the state or states in which the two corporations are incorporated. The plan or agreement of merger may specify an effective merger date that is later than the filing date if state law so permits. An example of an agreement and plan of merger is contained in Appendix 8.

In contrast to an asset sale, which requires specific bills of sale and assignments to transfer title to your assets, the transfer of title occurs automatically by operation of law on the effective date of the merger. No bills of sale or assignments are normally necessary to transfer title. State law specifically provides that the transfer occur automatically on the merger effective date.

The problem with a merger is that it transfers to the survivor all of the assets (known or unknown) of the disappearing corporation and all of its liabilities (known or unknown). The buyer may not wish to acquire all of your assets. More important, the buyer does not want to assume unknown liabilities you may have. Therefore, many buyers avoid mergers and prefer to purchase only specific assets and to assume only specified liabilities.

The following are different kinds of mergers that can be effectuated:

- forward direct merger: buyer survives merger with target
- forward triangular merger: buyer's subsidiary survives merger with target
- reverse direct merger: target survives merger with buyer
- reverse triangular merger: target survives merger with buyer's subsidiary

Figure 10.1 gives a pictorial description of a triangular merger.

Consolidations are identical to mergers except that a newly formed third corporation survives the merger between the target and the buyer or between the target and the buyer's subsidiary.

Under most state laws, all of the shareholders of each party to the merger or consolidation can be forced, by a majority vote, to exchange their shares for the consideration specified in the agreement or plan of merger or consolidation. This includes any of the following:

FIGURE 10.1 A TRIANGULAR MERGER

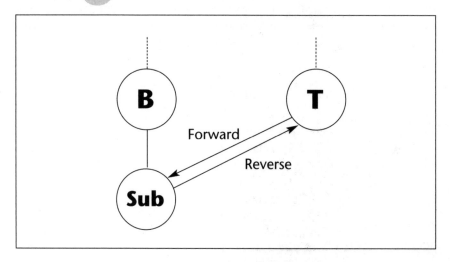

- cash
- stock or other equity securities of the surviving entity or of a parent corporation of the surviving entity
- notes of the surviving entity or of a parent of the surviving entity
- an earnout payable in cash, stock, or notes
- any combination of the foregoing

Any objecting minority shareholders are usually given dissenters' rights of appraisal in these transactions. Dissenters' rights of appraisal entitle the dissenting minority shareholders to receive cash equal to the fair value of their stock in one of the parties to the merger or consolidation. This is true even though the plan or agreement of merger specifies that the shareholders of the same corporation are to receive stock or notes. The fair value of the stock of the dissenter is determined by the court under a statutory procedure specified by state law, if the parties cannot otherwise agree.

Selected portions of an agreement and plan of merger are contained in Appendix 8. It specifies the consideration to be received by the shareholders of the target (the disappearing corporation), which is merged into the buyer in a forward merger. The consideration to be received by the target's shareholders is either common stock of the surviving corporation (the buyer) to the merger or cash as elected by each of the target's shareholders, subject to limits set forth in the agreement and plan of merger.

SUMMARY

The following sections summarize the major advantages and disadvantages of each of the most common sale structures. Target refers to the entity that operates your business.

Sale of Assets

Primary advantages: Step up in tax basis for buyer; no hidden liabilities acquired by buyer (but may have some carryover liabilities)

Primary disadvantages: Nonassignable assets; potential sales tax; target's shareholder may pay double taxes and/or taxes at ordinary income rates (see Chapter 11); greater expense; target must be dissolved

Sale of Stock

Primary advantages: Long-term capital gains to target's shareholders; mechanically simpler and less expensive; avoids problems of nonassignable assets (provided there is no "change-of-control" clause); avoids potential sales tax; retains target's unemployment tax rate (if favorable)

Primary disadvantages: Hidden liabilities acquired by buyer including tax, tort, and contract liabilities; retain target's unemployment tax rate (if unfavorable)

Mergers and Consolidations

Advantages: All assets and liabilities transferred to survivor by operation of law; minority shareholder can be forced to sell by vote of majority shareholder (in contrast to a stock sale)

Disadvantages: Unknown and contingent liabilities transferred; unwanted assets transferred (like a stock sale)

USING STRUCTURING TO SOLVE PROBLEMS

The following are four different problems that are common in sale transactions and how each can be solved by the structuring of the transaction.

Problem Number 1

Target has below-market rate on leased property, and lease prohibits direct assignment by operation of the law.

Solution

Provided there is no "change of control" clause in lease, a stock sale, reverse direct merger, or reverse triangular merger

Problem Number 2

Target has minority shareholders who are opposed to sale.

Solution

Merger or consolidation or asset sale

Problem Number 3

Target has large contingent liability.

Solution

Asset sale (does not work if specific assets sold are environmentally contaminated or if deemed fraudulent transfer)

Problem Number 4

Target has large federal income tax loss carryover that buyer wishes to preserve.

Solution

Purchase target's stock or reverse merger (direct or triangular), but normally limited yearly use of carryover post closing to long-term federal interest rate multiplied by target's value at closing. (See Chapter 11.)

THINK AFTER TAXES: CASH FLOW TO YOU*

The combination of federal and state income taxes can take approximately 37 percent or more of taxable income resulting from the sale of your business. Therefore, you should give careful consideration to methods of minimizing these taxes.

You must learn to think in terms of after-tax cash flow to yourself. To illustrate: Suppose you had a $10 million cash offer and a $9 million cash offer for your business. Which should you take?

If you automatically answered the $10 million cash offer, you are wrong. You are thinking in *pretax dollars* instead of *after-tax cash flow*. The correct answer requires you to determine the after-tax cash flow to you of each offer.

A $9 million offer for your stock is better than a $10 million cash offer of which $3 million is for stock and $7 million is for a noncompete covenant and consulting agreement.

To prove that the $9 million offer is better, make the following assumptions:

- Assume a 17 percent combined federal and state tax rate on long-term capital gains.
- Assume a 37 percent combined federal and state tax rate on ordinary income.
- Assume you have no tax basis for your stock.

---

*The federal income tax rates used in this book are based on rates in effect in January 2005 and do not reflect federal income tax changes effective thereafter.

The computation in Table 11.1 demonstrates that the $9 million cash offer creates after-tax cash flow to you of $7.47 million, compared with after-tax cash flow of only $6.9 million (ignoring the additional cost of self-employment taxes) from the $10 million cash offer.

C CORPORATIONS VERSUS S CORPORATIONS

Most businesses to be sold are conducted through corporations, although limited liability companies are becoming increasingly popular. Your after-tax cash flow from the sale of your business depends in part on whether your corporation is a so-called C corporation or a so-called Subchapter S corporation.

If your business is conducted as a sole proprietorship, general or limited partnership, limited liability company, or other tax flow-through entity, skip this section.

C Corporations

If you are unlucky enough to have a C corporation, you have two levels of tax that you will have to pay if you sell the assets of the corporation. The first is a tax at the corporate level on the gain the corporation has on the sale of the business assets. The second is a tax at the shareholder level on the net assets of the corporation received by the shareholders.

Assuming that all of the corporation's assets were sold and all of its liabilities assumed by the buyer, the assets distributed to shareholders would equal the gross sale proceeds to the corporation, less federal and state income taxes paid by the corporation. Combined

TABLE 11.1 COMPUTATION FOR THE $9 MILLION
VERSUS THE $10 MILLION OFFER

COMPUTATION	
$9.0 MILLION	**$10.0 MILLION**
Less 17%, or $1.53 million	Less 17% of $3 million, or $0.51 million
	Less 37% of $7 million, or $2.59 million
Net $7.47 million	**Net $6.9 million**

federal and state income tax at the corporate level can be as high as 40 percent or more on the gain to the corporation.

To illustrate: Assuming that the gross sale proceeds for the corporation assets are $1,000, and that the gain on the assets sold is taxable at ordinary income rates, the corporation will be left with $600 (assuming a 40 percent combined federal and state corporate income tax rate). When the $600 is then distributed to the shareholders, and again assuming the receipt of the $600 by the shareholders is all taxable as long-term capital gain at a 17 percent rate, the shareholders are left with $498. Effectively, between the tax at the corporate level and the tax at the shareholder level, over 50 percent of the $1,000 gain on the sale is paid in income taxes.

Your first reaction may be to say, "Well, why should I sell corporation assets? Let me just sell the stock of my C corporation and only pay a 15 percent federal long-term capital gains tax on the gain."

That is fine if you can get the buyer to agree. However, the buyer may not wish to acquire the stock of your corporation and be subjected to its hidden liabilities. Moreover, the buyer generally does not get a step-up in the tax basis of depreciable assets of your C corporation if they buy your stock. If the buyer purchases your stock and then elects to step up the tax basis of your assets to equal the purchase price for your stock plus the corporation's liabilities, the buyer will have to pay the tax on the gain resulting from the step-up (unless the C corporation possesses utilizable net operating losses for prior tax periods which may offset such gain).

The net result is that buyers either will not purchase stock of C corporations or will reduce the purchase price for the stock to equal the loss of tax benefits. Either way it comes out of the seller's pocket.

To avoid a double tax, sellers of C corporations are increasingly asking that a significant portion of the consideration be paid to them in the form of consulting fees or an employment contract. This reduces the amount of the consideration actually paid for the assets of the C corporation and effectively reduces the large income tax bite resulting from two levels of tax. However, consulting fees and salary are still subject to ordinary income tax rates as well as employment taxes. It should also be noted that amounts designated as consulting fees may be treated as the equivalent of goodwill to the extent that such fees are excessive in relation to the services to be provided.

Any allocation of the purchase price to a covenant not to compete, as opposed to a consulting fee or an employment contract, may cause the buyer to reduce the purchase price, because the buyer cannot obtain a current tax deduction for a covenant not to compete. These payments are treated similar to goodwill and are amortizable by the buyer over a fifteen-year period.

Fifty Percent Exclusion

If you sell stock of your C corporation and your stock was "qualified small-business stock" issued after August 10, 1993, and held for five years, you can be taxed at a 14 percent federal income tax rate (50 percent of 28 percent). The limit on the exclusion is the greater of $10 million or 10 times the aggregate adjusted basis for all "qualified small-business stock" issued by the corporation and disposed of by you during a tax year. Although 14 percent is not much of a saving over a 15 percent rate for long-term capital gains, it is likely that the 15 percent rate will at some point be increased.

"Qualified small-business stock" refers generally to a corporation engaged in manufacture, wholesale, or retail whose aggregate gross assets do not exceed $50 million (subject to qualification and exceptions). The corporation must meet active business requirements during substantially all of the period you held the stock.

In order to qualify for this special rate, the stock must be initially issued to you *after August 10, 1993 and held for five years.*

Even though an effective 14 percent overall federal income tax rate might be applicable for regular income tax purposes, a higher rate could be applicable for alternative minimum tax purposes.

S Corporations

The major advantage of the S corporation is that it is not subject for federal income tax purposes to a double tax upon sale of its assets. There is typically no income tax at the corporate level (subject to certain exceptions) when the S corporation sells its assets. The only federal income tax is at the shareholder level on the gain realized by the corporation, which is then allocated to the shareholders in accordance with their proportionate shareholder interests.

Some states do not recognize S corporations, and in those states a double tax will apply for state income tax purposes upon the sale of your assets.

The nature of the gain allocable to the shareholders on the sale of the S corporation's assets depends upon the character of the assets that are sold. Capital assets held for more than one year will produce long-term capital gain, whereas items such as inventory and accounts receivable will produce ordinary income.

Allocating the Purchase Price to Lower Seller's Taxes

Let us assume that the buyer wants to purchase your corporation's assets and is not interested in purchasing your corporation's stock. The proper allocation of the purchase price to these assets can significantly reduce your income tax resulting from the sale. Therefore, it is important to understand the differing tax interests of you and the buyer.

It is in the buyer's interest to allocate the purchase price consideration to those assets that produce the most immediate tax benefit to the buyer. Accordingly, the buyer will want to allocate as much as possible to your inventory and to your accounts receivable, as these allocations reduce the buyer's taxable income, and hence taxes, at the earliest point in time.

For example, assume that you have on your books inventory that has a book value and a tax basis of $1.1 million, but that inventory has a retail market value of $2 million. It is in the buyer's interest to allocate as much as possible of the purchase price to your inventory because when the inventory is sold for $2 million (presumably within the next year), this allocation will reduce the buyer's taxable income and taxes.

Although the buyer may desire to allocate $2 million of the purchase price to the inventory, the buyer's tax advisor will probably tell the buyer that the IRS would challenge such a high allocation, as it is unusual to pay retail for a bulk purchase of inventory. However, the buyer may well place a figure as high as $1.8 million on the inventory purchase so that when the inventory is sold for $2 million, the buyer will have only $200,000 in taxable income.

If the buyer allocated only the seller's book value of $1.1 million to the inventory and the buyer resold the inventory within one year, the buyer would have $900,000 of taxable income on the inventory resale.

A public company buyer might allocate only $1.1 million to the inventory in order to show higher accounting earnings. However, most buyers are interested in reducing income taxes and would use the higher allocation.

Table 11.2 illustrates the discounted present value to the buyer of

TABLE 11.2 **DISCOUNTED PRESENT VALUE* OF EACH $1 TAX CASH FLOW TO BUYER**

Allocation to inventory and receivables (1-year return) = $0.91
Allocation to goodwill (average 8-year return) = $0.47
Commercial real estate (average 20-year return) = $0.15

*Assuming 10 percent per annum compounded annually

the allocation of $1 of purchase price consideration to different assets you may sell.

It is in the seller's interest to allocate as much of the consideration as possible that is in excess of the tax basis to items that produce long-term capital gain to the seller. Under law, the long-term capital gain is taxed generally at a maximum combined federal and state rate of approximately 17 percent. In contrast, the top combined federal and state rate on ordinary income can be 37 percent or more.

The following are some of the capital assets of the corporation that normally produce long-term capital gain when sold and are not subject to so-called recapture of depreciation deductions at ordinary income rates:

- land
- buildings not depreciated by use of accelerated depreciation
- patent rights
- copyrights
- trademarks
- goodwill

Assume that the above assets do not have an aggregate fair market value that is sufficient to absorb the full purchase price (including any liabilities assumed by the buyer). The seller should next be interested in allocating the remaining purchase price consideration (including any liabilities assumed by the buyer) to the following group of depreciable assets, even though a portion of the allocation over your tax basis may be ordinary income to the extent of depreciation deductions previously taken:

- buildings depreciated by use of accelerated depreciation rates
- machinery and equipment
- furniture and fixtures

Stock is a capital asset. Therefore, if the seller is able to persuade the buyer to purchase the stock of his corporation, all of the gain would be generally taxed at long-term capital gains rates.

As noted previously, the buyer may not want to purchase stock of the corporation because the buyer is thereby assuming hidden liabilities of the corporation. Even an escrow by the buyer of a portion of the purchase price may not be sufficient to protect the buyer from such hidden liabilities, which could exceed the amount of the escrow and might even exceed the full purchase price.

Occasionally, buyers must purchase the stock of a corporation (or use a reverse merger) because of nontransferable assets in the corporation, such as a long-term lease or other nontransferable contracts on very favorable terms (provided such leases or other contracts do not contain a change-of-control clause). However, in these situations, buyers typically seek to lower the purchase price to compensate themselves for the smaller tax benefits they receive and to reflect the higher tax benefits received by the seller.

If the buyer is successful in the negotiations in allocating the purchase price (including assumed liabilities) to assets that produce immediate tax benefits to the buyer, such a concession by the seller should add to the value of the business to the buyer. This is true because the buyer's after-tax future cash flow will be increased as a result of the seller's concession. Therefore, the seller should negotiate additional consideration to compensate him- or herself for this concession. This is particularly true if the allocation favoring the buyer increases the seller's taxes.

A typical allocation clause is contained in section I(D) of the agreement of sale contained in Appendix 7, involving the sale of the assets of a physical therapy center.

TAX-FREE EXCHANGES

A seller cannot have a tax-free exchange with the buyer unless the seller is willing to accept stock of the buyer for at least 50 percent of the total consideration. Although tax-free treatment is possible when less than 50 percent of the total consideration constitutes stock, the IRS, for ruling purposes, will not give you a favorable ruling unless the 50 percent test is satisfied. Unless you would like to litigate with the IRS, you should avoid transactions that are intended to be tax free unless at least 50 percent of the consideration is in stock.*

If you receive cash or other forms of consideration other than stock of the buyer above the 50 percent threshold, the portion above 50 percent is taxable. To be 100 percent tax-free, you will need 100 percent of the consideration in the form of stock of the buyer.

An example of a partial tax-free exchange is contained in Appendix 6. See Chapter 12 for tax-free exchanges with a public company.

A limited liability company does not qualify for a tax-free reorganization under Section 368 of the Internal Revenue Code of 1986 ("Code") (as amended). However, it may be possible, in limited situations, to structure a tax-free exchange under Section 351 of the Code. This would occur, for example, if both the buyer and the seller are willing to transfer their assets (or equity interest) to a new corporation in exchange for its stock, which would be owned jointly by equity holders of the buyer and seller. Although it is possible to structure this type of transaction in limited situations, it is not typical. Therefore, if your business is a limited liability company, consider transferring your assets to an S corporation long before your exit date if your exit might include a tax-free exchange.

VALUING TAX-LOSS CARRYOVERS

Businesses that have an operating tax-loss carryover should consider this carryover as an asset of the business. Under the Internal Revenue Code of 1986 (as amended), the buyer cannot acquire your tax-loss carryover if the transaction is structured as a sale of assets or is deemed to be a sale of assets (e.g., a forward merger). The buyer must structure the transaction as sale of stock or a reverse merger (see Chapter 10).

---

*To the extent that the acquiring entity is taxed as a partnership for federal income tax purposes, however, the transaction may generally be structured as a tax-free exchange, in part, notwithstanding that the portion of the consideration in the form of equity may be less than 50 percent of the total consideration paid.

Even if the transaction is structured to obtain the tax-loss carry-over, the buyer's ability to use the seller's loss carryover is generally subject to significant limitations if the buyer acquires more than 50 percent of your stock (or if the buyer's acquisition, in conjunction with certain other stock acquisitions in the three-year period ending on the date of the buyer's acquisition, results in an ownership change of more than 50 percent of the corporation's stock). Under these circumstances, the buyer is limited to using such portion of the tax-loss carryover that equals (1) the long-term tax-exempt rate multiplied by (2) the value of your business on the date of closing.

The "long-term tax-exempt rate" is the highest of the adjusted federal long-term rates and is based on the average market yield on outstanding marketable U.S. debt instruments with remaining periods to maturity exceeding nine years. This rate is determined monthly by the Internal Revenue Service.

For example, assume that your business is being purchased for $10 million, that you have a $30 million loss carryover, and that the federal long-term interest rate is 5 percent per annum. The buyer is limited to using $500,000 of your tax-loss carryover (5 percent times $10 million) in each year to offset the buyer's taxable income. This results in the spreading out of the buyer's ability to utilize the loss and significantly decreases its current discounted value to the buyer.

In addition, tax-loss carryovers cannot extend for more than twenty years after the date that they were incurred. Thus, the twenty years may run out before the tax-loss carryover is fully absorbed by the buyer. In the previous example, the buyer would in twenty years utilize a maximum of $10 million (20 times $500,000 per year) of the $30 million carryover.

As noted above, the 50 percent test is subject to a three-year look-back period. Thus, you cannot avoid the 50 percent test if the buyer acquires 50 percent of your stock in one year and the balance of your stock the next year.

Likewise, giving the buyer options to purchase your stock or securities convertible into your stock does not prevent the tripping of the 50 percent test, because the IRS will treat these options and conversion rights as if they were exercised for purposes of applying the 50 percent test.

The only practical method of avoiding the tripping of the 50 percent test is for the buyer to acquire 50 percent or less of the stock and value of your business and to wait for more than three years to buy the rest of the stock. Few buyers are willing to structure their purchase in this manner.

Some major accounting firms have suggested having the buyer acquire 50 percent or less of the target's (seller's) stock and giving the target a loan for the balance of the purchase price that is due three years and one day after the closing. The theory is that the target would not have the funds to pay the loan and the buyer can receive the balance of the target's stock in payment of the loan. Again, it takes a very aggressive buyer to engage in this type of transaction.

CHAPTER 11 BANKRUPTCY

The 50 percent test does not apply in a Chapter 11 bankruptcy proceeding, provided the shareholders of the old loss corporation and qualified creditors own at least 50 percent of the voting power and value of the stock of the new loss corporation. *Qualified creditors* refers to persons to whom the corporation was indebted provided either (1) the indebtedness was held by the creditor at least eighteen months before the Chapter 11 filing or (2) the indebtedness is held in the ordinary course of the trade or business of the old loss corporation and is held at all times by the same person.

If your company is in Chapter 11, the potential buyer can acquire the debt from your creditors who held their indebtedness for more than eighteen months before your filing and can then receive your stock in exchange for that debt in a Chapter 11 plan of reorganization, all without tripping the 50 percent test.

This area is very complex, and there can be some minor loss of tax attributes (including loss carryovers). However, Chapter 11 does provide an interesting vehicle to permit the preservation of tax-loss carryovers. Only sophisticated buyers will consider this type of transaction.

CHAPTER TWELVE

SELLING TO A PUBLIC COMPANY

Public companies are ideal buyers. This is particularly true of companies that have just had a public offering and need a home for their cash.

Unlike private companies, public companies are under pressure from securities analysts and from the public market to increase their current earnings. Consequently, they will make decisions that will maximize their future reported accounting earnings, even though this may cost them additional income taxes.

Because tax benefits are less important than accounting earnings to a public company, it is easier for the seller to negotiate a more favorable after-tax cash flow from the purchase price when selling to a public company. For example, it is not unusual for public companies to suggest larger allocations of the purchase price to capital assets with a long useful life. Capital assets that can be depreciated by the buyer over long periods of time produce very low depreciation charges to reduce the buyer's reported income. Obviously, the seller prefers these allocations because the seller obtains the benefit of long-term capital gain for all or a portion of the allocation.

ACCEPTING PUBLIC COMPANY STOCK

If you accept the public company's stock for all or a portion of the sale price, you have made a major investment decision. Because a large percentage of your wealth will likely be tied up in the buyer's stock, you will not want to accept stock consideration unless it has the following characteristics:

- The buyer must be a publicly held company that is sufficiently well capitalized and has sufficient growth prospects so that you will not be taking major economic risks in accepting the buyer's stock.
- There must be a liquid market for the stock—in other words, the stock is publicly traded in a recognized marketplace and is freely tradable.

WARNING Many stocks traded on the Pink Sheets, the NAS-DAQ Bulletin Board, the Small Cap NASDAQ, the NASDAQ National Stock Market, and other exchanges have inadequate trading activity. The market for these stocks is so thin that any significant sell order reduces the market price. Avoid these stocks.

Even if the buyer is a large New York Stock Exchange company, you may wish to consider whether it is wise having so much of your wealth in one specific stock. The principle of diversification would suggest that it is not.

Even if the buyer looks like it will do well in the future, no one can tell. Likewise, if the buyer's industry or the stock market as a whole does poorly, that can have disastrous results on your personal wealth.

Many public companies use their stock to make acquisitions because of its high price-to-earnings multiplier. For example, if the public company's stock is selling for 25 times their trailing twelve-months'

WARNING A favorite negotiating ploy of public companies is to value your business at a high price and then give you their stock, which is overly inflated in value, as the sale consideration. If their stock price subsequently drops before you can sell it, you may have severely undervalued your business.

earnings, and they can purchase your company with stock for 10 times its earnings, their stock price would presumably be increased by the fact that your earnings are now multiplied by 25, whereas they only paid you a multiplier of 10.

If you become a large shareholder of the buyer, you may be required to hold a substantial portion of the buyer's stock for an extended period in order to preserve the tax-free status of the exchange. If you decide on a tax-free exchange, make certain that the buyer's stock is fully registered and freely tradable at all times after the closing of the sale.

If the stock is not freely tradable at all times, the stock is not worth its current price. Indeed, any valuation expert would require a significant discount from the current trading price in computing the market value of restricted stock. Depending upon the nature of the restriction, this discount can be as much as 33⅓ percent to 50 percent of the trading price and even more than 50 percent if the stock is very volatile.

Unless you receive fully registered stock at the closing of the sale or you can demand registration of your stock, you will generally have to wait two years before selling the stock under Rule 144 of the Securities Act of 1933. Even after one year, your ability to sell under Rule 144 is restricted by the availability of current information about the buyer, and there will be limitations on the amount you are allowed to sell and the manner in which you sell.

After two years from the closing, and provided you have not become a director of the buyer or assumed any other control relationship with the buyer, you may sell even unregistered stock without restriction.

Under Rule 144, every three months you may sell the greater of 1 percent of the outstanding buyer's stock or one week's average trading volume during the preceding four weeks.

WARNING Sellers who take 100 percent of the purchase price in buyer's stock and who do not have freely tradable stock are taking a huge risk with their personal wealth. Avoid these transactions like the plague. The only possible exception is if you receive a "market floor" clause, which gives you more stock if the trading price falls. However, receiving more of the buyer's stock under a market floor clause does not adequately protect you from the buyer's bankruptcy or from dramatic trading price drops during the period the stock is not fully tradable.

PURCHASE ACCOUNTING

If the buyer is a public company or expects to become part of a public company in the future, the valuation placed on your company by the buyer can be significantly affected by the buyer's proposed accounting for the acquisition. Remember, public companies are more interested in their reported earnings under generally accepted accounting principles than tax results, so a higher sale price can generally be negotiated with a buyer if the acquisition has a favorable impact on their future reported earnings. Therefore, it is important to understand what factors can create such a favorable impact.

Under Financial Accounting Standards 141 and 142 and International Financial Reporting Standard 3, all acquisitions must be accounted for using purchase accounting. Under purchase accounting, the acquisition consideration plus any assumed liabilities are allocated to the assets of the acquired corporation in accordance with the fair market value of these assets. To the extent that the acquisition consideration plus any assumed liabilities exceed the fair market value of the acquired assets, the excess is treated as goodwill. For purposes of the buyer's income statement, under purchase accounting the assets are deemed acquired on the date of closing, and income earned by the buyer prior to the date of closing is not considered part of the buyer's income.

Goodwill is defined as the excess of the cost of an acquired entity over the net of the amounts assigned to acquired assets and assumed liabilities. Other acquired intangible assets are to be separately recognized if: (1) they arise from contractual or other legal rights, regardless of whether those rights are transferable or separable from the acquired enterprise, or (2) in cases where they do not arise from such contractual or legal rights, only if they are separable, that is, capable of being separated or divided from the acquired enterprise. A lengthy list of illustrative intangibles, which are deemed to be distinguishable from goodwill, has been compiled by the Financial Accounting Standards Board. Among the listed intangible assets are:

- Trade or service marks
- Trade dress (unique color, shape, or package design)
- Customer lists
- Order or production backlog
- Licensing, royalty, or standstill agreements
- Lease, construction, or franchise agreements
- Use rights such as drilling, water, mineral, timber cutting, and route authorities
- Servicing contracts such as mortgage servicing contracts
- Trade secrets
- Patented and unpatented technology
- Internet domain names
- Computer software and mask works
- Core deposits (for financial institutions)
- Artistic-related intangibles including books, magazines, newspapers, musical compositions, or photographs

In general, public company buyers prefer to purchase assets whose costs do not have to be amortized or depreciated. The requirement to amortize or depreciate the cost of an asset reduces the public buyer's post-acquisition financial earnings. Goodwill and other intangible assets that do not have definite lives do not require any amortization, but are tested annually for impairment. Intangible assets that have definite lives must be amortized over those lives.

Therefore, the greater the amount of the goodwill and intangible assets that do not have definite lives resulting from your acquisition, the higher the post-acquisition financial earnings of the buyer. If you are able to identify to the buyer the specific intangible assets of your business that do not require any amortization, you may be able to use this information to increase the purchase price for your business. However, this is easier said than done, as it is difficult to obtain information as to how the seller is going to value your intangible assets.

You should also be aware whether any so-called "negative goodwill" is recognized by the buyer. If the total of the purchase price paid by the buyer plus the value of the liabilities assumed by the buyer is less than the fair value of the acquired assets, the buyer has negative goodwill. Negative goodwill is beneficial to buyers because it permits them to proportionately reduce the cost of the acquired assets (with certain exceptions) and could even permits them to recognize an extraordinary gain (or additional income under IFRS 3).

Negative goodwill means that you sold your business too cheaply. If you obtain a hint that the buyer expects to have negative goodwill, raise the sale price if possible. Of course, you may not find out that the buyer had negative goodwill until after the closing or until after you are legally bound to sell your business, in which case the presence of negative goodwill gives you no or little leverage. However, the presence of negative goodwill could be used in negotiating a disputed working capital adjustment clause after the closing or to amicably resolve other issues with the buyer.

In negotiating the sale price for your business, it is helpful to understand the effect of the combination on the buyer's post-acquisition financial earnings, as this information can assist you in negotiating a higher sale price.

RECAPITALIZATION ACCOUNTING

Recapitalization accounting produces a similar result to pooling accounting (which was abolished effective June 30, 2001). In other words, it avoids the necessity of revaluing the assets of your business and also avoids the creation of goodwill, the amortization of which depresses future earnings of the buyer. To achieve recapitalization accounting, the buyer will require you to continue to own a small percentage of the surviving entity, typically less than 10 percent. It is likely that many buyers who are either public or expect to go public will structure transactions to achieve recapitalization accounting in order to maximize their future reportable accounting earnings per share.

CHAPTER THIRTEEN

SELLING A PUBLICLY HELD COMPANY OR A CONTROL BLOCK

I f your company is already publicly held, special issues will apply to its future sale. These unique considerations are as follows:

- Any leak of your sales decision to the trading markets will usually result in a run-up of your market price. This is because speculators will be anticipating the receipt of a control premium over the normal trading price as a result of the potential future sale. If the leak is attributable to the company or its directors, officers, or employees, you will be forced to issue a press release to inform the trading markets of your sale decision—even though you would prefer not to announce it.

- Any run-up in the market price of your stock as a result of a leak may discourage potential buyers who are not willing to pay a price that equals the overall market value of your company. However, some of these discouraged buyers might otherwise be preferable buyers from your company's cultural or other perspective.

- Once a sale decision is made, some states, such as Delaware, may require the directors to act as auctioneers to maximize the price, especially if there are competing bidders. This auctioneer duty may not be in your interest if you would prefer, for cultural or other reasons, a particular buyer who does not offer the highest price. One solution is to reincorporate your company well in advance of the target sale date in a state that does not impose an auctioneer duty (e.g., Pennsylvania).

- Delaware, where many public companies are incorporated, imposes a duty of candor on the directors. The full parameters of this duty of candor are unclear in a sale situation; however, this duty may force directors to make disclosure of the sale decision and major events in the negotiations prematurely, thereby interfering with the sale process. A possible solution is to reincorporate outside of Delaware well in advance of the target sale date.

- Any decision to withhold information from the trading markets of the negotiation of a potential sale can create Rule 10b-5 liability for the directors under the so-called probability/magnitude test adopted by the U.S. Supreme Court. This test requires the directors to weigh the magnitude of the event against the probability of its occurrence in making disclosure decisions. In view of the vagueness of this test, it is wise to maintain a substantial amount of director and officer liability insurance coverage before commencing the sale process.

CONTROL PREMIUMS

The law in most states generally permits the holder of a control block to receive a premium for the block over and above the price paid to all other shareholders. This is true whether the company is public or private.

The American Law Institute has articulated this rule and its exceptions in the following statement contained in section 5.16 of the 1994 version of the American Law Institute's *Principles of Corporate Governance: Analysis and Recommendations:*

> A controlling shareholder . . . has the same right to dispose of voting equity securities . . . as any other shareholder, including the right to dispose of those securities for a price that is not made proportionally

available to other shareholders, but the controlling shareholder does not satisfy the duty of fair dealing to the other shareholders if:

(a) The controlling shareholder does not make disclosure concerning the transaction . . . to other shareholders with whom the controlling shareholder deals in connection with the transaction; or

(b) It is apparent from the circumstances that the purchaser is likely to violate the duty of fair dealing . . . in such a way as to obtain a significant financial benefit from the purchaser or an associate.

It is clear that 51 percent of the outstanding stock is a control block. It is not clear how much less than 51 percent of the outstanding stock will constitute a control block for purposes of permitting you to receive a control premium. Nor is it clear that you can receive a control premium if you own 30 percent and your spouse owns 21 percent. Therefore, it would be in your interest to be certain that you have 51 percent of the outstanding stock registered either in your name alone or in your name and your spouse's name as tenants by the entireties. (This is a form of ownership that only a husband and wife can enjoy in most states. It prevents creditors of either spouse from attaching the assets for debts of any single spouse.)

The SEC's so-called "all holders rule" requires that a buyer making a tender offer for the stock of a publicly held company (i.e., a company whose stock is registered under section 12 of the Securities Exchange Act of 1934) offer the same price to each shareholder. However, the all holders rule does not prevent the buyer from privately negotiating with you for a price that includes a control premium and then launching a tender offer at a lower price.

Any control premium that is received in a public company acquisition is usually subjected to litigation. Therefore, great care should be exercised in structuring this type of transaction.

CHAPTER FOURTEEN

SELLING TO YOUR OWN EMPLOYEES OR TO AN ESOP

I t is not unusual during the sale process to receive an expression of interest from a group of key employees. Indeed, you may, through feelings of loyalty and camaraderie, prefer your key employees to be the buyer, even though they are not necessarily the highest bidder.

The primary difficulty in selling to key employees is that they usually lack the capital and require you to finance them. Moreover, once your key employees become active bidders, they will not necessarily be as cooperative with other potential buyers who are willing to pay a higher price and do not need you to finance them.

MBO AND LBO

If your business has the cash flow or assets to support a leveraged recapitalization (see Chapter 19), your key employees can probably find institutional financing for a management buyout (MBO) or a leveraged buyout (LBO). The only practical difference between the two is that in an MBO, the management receives much more equity and generally leads the transaction. Even in an LBO, it is not unusual for management to obtain at least 5 percent to 10 percent of the equity. An equity position of 30 percent or more is not unheard of in an MBO.

For your employees to locate institutional financing for an MBO or LBO, your business must be large enough to attract institutional lenders and investors. Typically, these institutional lenders and investors will not want to structure a transaction involving less than $5 million to $10 million in senior debt. Senior debt is unsubordinated debt, which may or may not be collateralized.

Federal income tax law changes adopted in 1991 have made MBOs and LBOs that require annual interest payments of more than $5 million (subject to reduction) less attractive by denying interest deductions for these excess interest payments. These MBOs and LBOs typically involve $40 million to $50 million or more in order to create an annual interest payment of approximately $5 million.

As discussed more fully in Chapter 19, the senior institutional lenders will typically lend on an asset or cash flow basis to your company to permit the repurchase of your stock with the proceeds of the loan. If your company has excellent growth prospects but does not have the assets or cash flow to satisfy senior institutional lenders, mezzanine lenders (typically, unsecured lenders and subordinated lenders), or private equity funds or investors might be interested in financing the MBO or LBO.

Make sure that your company has enough cash after the repurchase of your stock to pay its debts in the ordinary course of business and that it is adequately capitalized. If not, in the event of a subsequent bankruptcy, the trustee in bankruptcy or trade creditors will challenge the transaction as a fraudulent transfer.

If your key employees are able to obtain institutional financing for an MBO or LBO, this probably means you could obtain institutional financing for a leveraged recapitalization. In a leveraged recapitalization, as discussed in Chapter 19, you retain control of your company and receive some cash for some of your stock from the money supplied by the institutional lenders and investors. Of course, thereafter you must work in a highly leveraged environment and with significant restrictions on your operations.

If you are not willing to work under these conditions, an MBO or LBO with your key employees would be a reasonable choice, because, unlike in a leveraged recapitalization, you could receive cash for 100 percent of your stock.

On some MBOs and LBOs, the senior lenders and investors may require you to accept a portion of the purchase price for your stock in deferred payments, with the balance paid in cash at the closing. Typically, these deferred payments are evidenced by a note that is specifically subordinated to the senior lender's debt. Consequently, in the event of a default on the senior debt, you may never be paid your note.

The usual reason for requiring you to accept a subordinated note for a portion of the purchase price is that otherwise there will not be enough cash flow to satisfy the senior lender cash flow coverage ratios (see Chapter 19).

To protect yourself under these circumstances, you may try to negotiate the following:

- a right to resume control of the company in the event of a default until any defaults are cured
- a right of first refusal on any sale of the company by the senior lenders
- a lien on all assets and stock subordinate only to the senior lender

ESOP FINANCING

If you have a large annual payroll, an employee stock ownership plan (ESOP) might be used to purchase your stock. An ESOP is a type of qualified retirement plan that invests primarily in your company's stock.

From your viewpoint, the primary advantage of an ESOP is that a qualifying sale is free of any federal income tax and you can roll the cash you receive into a diversified portfolio of investments. Here is how it works.

- You sell anywhere from 30 percent to 100 percent of all outstanding stock to the ESOP (including any shares previously owned by the ESOP).
- Your company must not be publicly traded and must be a C corporation.
- If you held your stock for three or more years prior to the sale, there is no federal income tax on your gain if you use the cash to purchase securities of most U.S. corporations.

For example, you can use the cash from the ESOP sale to purchase a diversified portfolio of blue-chip corporate debt securities, preferred stock, or common stock. Thus, you can acquire debt securities of the baby-bells (for example, Bell South), preferred stock of Exxon, and common stock of Microsoft—all without paying any federal income tax on the sale and rollover into the diversified portfolio.

The only limitation on your portfolio is that all of the investments must be in U.S. corporations that derive not more than 25 percent of their gross receipts from passive investment income (e.g., a mutual fund) and that use more than 50 percent of their assets in the active conduct of a trade or business. Most of the blue-chip companies will qualify under this standard.

A qualified cash sale to an ESOP is thus far more advantageous to you than a cash sale for the same price to an unaffiliated buyer or even a tax-free merger. For example, in a tax-free merger you receive stock of only one company—all of your eggs are in that one basket. In order to diversify yourself, you must sell that stock and pay a tax and then reinvest the after-tax money into a diversified portfolio. In contrast, the qualified ESOP sale permits you to achieve a diversified portfolio without ever paying any federal income tax.

If your company is a Subchapter S corporation, or elects Subchapter S status after a tax-free rollover, the ESOP has other advantages. The ESOP does not pay federal income taxes on the income earned as a shareholder of a Subchapter S corporation. This means that the ESOP could borrow money from a bank to purchase your stock and repay the bank loan with the federal income tax savings. Thus, instead of using the dividend from your company to the ESOP to pay federal income taxes, the ESOP could use the dividend to repay its indebtedness to the bank.

It should be noted, however, that special rules apply to S corporation sponsored ESOPs where the S corporation stock is not widely held. Specifically, if through the application of constructive ownership rules certain "disqualified persons" (that is, certain individuals and their families treated as directly or indirectly owning certain threshold percentages of stock in the S corporation) own in the aggregate at least 50 percent of the outstanding S corporation stock for a particular plan year, (1) a significant excise tax may be imposed upon the S Corporation and (2) income of the S Corporation attributable to shares allocated to disqualified persons may be treated as having been distributed by the ESOP and will become taxable in the hands of the disqualified persons.

In general, the company's contribution to an ESOP is deductible for federal income taxes, but the deduction is limited to 25 percent of your annual payroll (including other qualified plans and assuming all employees are plan participants) plus interest on the ESOP loan. Thus, if your company's annual payroll is $10 million and your company has no other qualified plans, your company can contribute $2.5 million a year to the ESOP (plus any interest on ESOP loans).

This means that the principal amortization on the bank loan to the ESOP loan can equal as much as $2.5 million per year. If the ESOP repurchased your stock for $12.5 million, the ESOP could finance the purchase with a five-year level principal amortizing loan requiring principal paydown of $2.5 million per year. This assumes, of course, that your business has the cash flow to make contributions to the ESOP sufficient to permit the ESOP to pay principal debt service of $2.5 million per year plus interest. Because the contributions to the ESOP are deductible by the company for federal income tax purposes, including the amount used to pay the principal of the ESOP loan, the cash flow of the company is increased by the benefit of these tax deductions.

The only limit on the duration of the ESOP loan is what lenders are willing to provide (assuming stock collateral is released from the loan in proportion to principal and interest payments). If you could obtain a ten-year level principal amortizing loan in the previous example, the ESOP could repurchase your stock for $25 million, provided it was worth that much.

If you pay dividends on your stock, the dividend paid to the ESOP on the stock it holds may be tax deductible for federal income tax purposes if certain conditions are met.

From your viewpoint, an ESOP sale is ideal if the following are true:

- You sell 100 percent of your stock.
- The sale is all cash.
- The ESOP sale price is the same price that an unaffiliated buyer would pay.

If any of the previous conditions are untrue, the advantages of selling to the ESOP must be balanced against the disadvantages.

For example, if you sell only 30 percent of your stock to the ESOP, rather than 100 percent, you may wind up some day with minority shareholders. Generally, when your employees retire they have the absolute right to receive their portion of the ESOP's stock ownership in your company. They also will have a right to "put" the stock to your company or the ESOP, thereby forcing the company or the ESOP to repurchase it for cash. Your company or the ESOP might not be able to afford the repurchase, particularly if a large group of employees retire at the same time and puts all of their stock.

Most employees who retire will not want to keep your stock. Those who do keep the stock can be prevented from selling the stock to outsiders without giving your company a right of first refusal. You can also adopt a bylaw preventing nonemployees from holding stock.

If you do not receive all cash from the ESOP upon the sale of your stock and instead take a note, you are still at the risk of the business. The ESOP funding to pay the note depends upon the cash flow of the company. Moreover, unlike a note that you receive from an unaffiliated buyer, you will probably not be able to obtain a guarantee of repayment from anyone other than your own company. The stock you sold to the ESOP can also serve as collateral for the note.

An ESOP can also be costly to maintain because of the bookkeeping and the necessity for yearly (or at least frequent) appraisals. Typically, an ESOP appraisal can be obtained for $5,000 a year if you are not too picky about the appraiser. The bookkeeping costs can easily run another $5,000 to $10,000 per year.

Even if you do not sell 100 percent of your stock to the ESOP, the ESOP can still be used by an unaffiliated buyer to sweeten your after-tax cash flow. For example, an unaffiliated buyer might purchase 70 percent of your stock and have you sell the remaining 30 percent to an ESOP with a tax-free rollover.

INTERNAL CASH FLOW ACQUISITIONS

If you want to sell to key employees and they cannot obtain outside financing, you may structure a sale that permits them to use internally generated cash flow to pay the purchase price.

You could sell your stock to your company in exchange for deferred installments of the purchase price. Your employees would be given the right to purchase small amounts of stock with their own funds, through payroll deductions, or both. You have to protect yourself against default through liens on the stock you sold and on the assets of your business.

If your company is an S corporation and has never been a C corporation, you can sell your stock back to your company slowly until your key employees' stock constitutes a majority of the outstanding stock. The price paid to you would be treated as long-term capital gains (assuming that you held the stock for more than one year).

However, if your company is or was previously a C corporation, a slow sale of your stock may produce ordinary income to you equal to the earnings and profits of the C corporation. To avoid this and to obtain long-term capital gain, you may have to sell all of your stock at once back to your company or at least create a "substantially disproportionate redemption."

To create a substantially disproportionate redemption, after the redemption you must own less than 50 percent of the combined voting power of all classes of stock entitled to vote, and the ratio of your voting stock to all voting stock after the redemption must be less than 80 percent of the same ratio before the redemption. Thus, if before the redemption you owned 100 percent of all voting stock, you must own not more than 49 percent after the redemption. If you own 60 percent before the redemption, you must own less than 48 percent after the redemption. In computing these percentages, you are deemed to constructively own the stock of other related persons and entities, including your spouse and children.

Selling to your key employees who use internally generated cash flow to pay the purchase price is a dangerous method of selling your business. You are still at the risk of the business to receive your full purchase price. Such a sale should only be attempted if you have no ability to sell to outsiders or you feel such loyalty to your key employees that you are willing to assume these risks.

PART IV

SALE TERMS

CHAPTER FIFTEEN

DEFERRED PURCHASE PRICE PAYMENTS: HOW TO BECOME THE BUYER'S BANKER

Although it is preferable to have the full purchase price paid at closing in cash, it is not unusual for the buyer to insist upon deferred payments of a portion of the purchase price. In effect, you are lending your money to the buyer. If this situation occurs, you must think like a banker.

Bankers do not lend money without obtaining all of the collateral and guarantees that they possibly can. That should also be your attitude as a seller lending your money to the buyer.

When the buyer asks you for a deferred payout, ask the buyer why he cannot borrow the money from a bank. The buyer's answers may give you some insight into the risks of the buyer's business.

Bankers want to make certain that the borrower has a significant equity stake in the business, which will be lost if there is a default. Therefore, you should insist upon a substantial down payment by the buyer. If you finance 100 percent of the purchase price, the buyer has little to lose if there is a default. Moreover, as discussed subsequently, if there is a default, you may have to pay more in income taxes to reacquire your corporation than you received in cash from the buyer.

COLLATERAL

If you cannot avoid accepting deferred payment terms, ask initially for an irrevocable bank letter of credit to secure the payout. Retreat from this position only reluctantly.

At a minimum, you will want a lien and security interest on whatever assets you sold to the buyer. If you sold stock, you will want a lien and security interest on the stock, as well as all of the assets of the entity whose stock you sold. You may have to subordinate your lien to the lien of the buyer's bank, but it is still worthwhile to obtain the lien.

Likewise, you would want to have a guarantee by the buyer and, if the buyer is an individual, by his or her spouse. It would also be helpful to obtain a lien on the buyer's assets.

PRINCIPAL AND INTEREST

Payments of principal and interest under any note should be made frequently, at least monthly or quarterly. Avoid notes that balloon at the end of a long period of time. Frequent payments can give you early warning of the buyer's financial problems. Preferably, the interest rate should equal the buyer's cost of borrowing from banks under comparable terms. If the interest rate is less than this figure, the buyer has no incentive to prepay the note. The interest rate should at least compensate you for your loss of use of the money. If any payment of principal or interest is missed, the note should provide for the acceleration of all future payments of principal and interest.

NOTES

Like a bank, you should request a note to show evidence of the deferred payments. If possible, the note should be negotiable and not subject to be set off by amounts you owe the buyer.

Negotiation permits you to transfer the note to a holder in due course (such as by pledging the note to your bank for a bank loan to you). Such a transfer has the legal effect of cutting off most of the buyer's legal defenses to payment under the note. The pledging of large installment notes, generally over $5 million in principal amount, can produce advance tax consequences (see "Tax Issues," later in this chapter).

WHO IS LIABLE UNDER THE NOTE?

Many buyers form special-purpose subsidiaries to acquire new businesses. These special-purpose subsidiaries typically have minimal capital. Consequently, you will want this note not only to be signed by the special-purchase subsidiary but also to be guaranteed by the parent corporation buyer and, in appropriate cases, the principal shareholders of the buyer and their spouses.

If the originator of the note and the other guarantors do not have adequate net worth to pay the note (other than the assets you sold them), you have entered into what is in effect a nonrecourse sale. You are permitting the buyer to acquire your business, and your only effective recourse is against the assets you just sold.

In some circumstances, this is the best deal you can get. This situation tends to happen if you are selling to an employee or group of employees. In any situation in which your only real recourse is to the assets you just sold, you should negotiate an additional premium over the selling price to compensate you for the risk you are assuming.

AFFIRMATIVE AND NEGATIVE COVENANTS

You should also request affirmative and negative covenants from the buyer similar to what a bank would demand of the buyer. If the covenants are violated, you should have the right to accelerate and collect the deferred payments.

Examples of affirmative covenants include the following:

- requiring the buyer to maintain an adequate amount of insurance on its business
- requiring the buyer to conduct its business in a lawful manner and consistent with past practices
- requiring the buyer to pay all taxes due

If possible, you should request negative covenants pursuant to which the buyer will not permit certain things to happen to itself or to its subsidiaries.

Examples of negative covenants include the following:

- requiring the buyer not to permit its working capital amount to fall below a certain figure or a certain ratio
- requiring the buyer not to permit its debt-to-equity ratio to exceed a certain figure
- placing restrictions on the buyer's capital spending
- placing restrictions on insider transactions and distributions, including dividends, salaries, leases, purchases, and sales

DEFAULTS

If there is a default by the buyer on other debt, you will want this event also to be a default on your note. This will enable you to accelerate the deferred payments and immediately foreclose.

If you have an employment or consulting agreement with the buyer, or a real estate lease, a default under these agreements by the buyer should also constitute a default on your note. You will also want the buyer to be required to pay all of your attorney's fees and costs in any collection effort.

I was once able to negotiate a provision in a note permitting the seller to vote the stock sold to the buyer in the event of a default. The effect of this clause was that it permitted the seller to regain control of the board of directors of the company in the event of a default. This clause was negotiated in the case of a sale to employees of the company who were backed by a venture capitalist, and may not always be obtainable in negotiations.

FORECLOSURES

If the buyer defaults, your misery will be compounded by the difficulties of reacquiring your business and by the adverse tax consequences.

If the buyer defaults, you can foreclose on the stock or other collateral you received. However, you must go to the expense of holding a public foreclosure sale to permit yourself to become a bidder in it. In a private foreclosure sale, you cannot be a bidder.

You can avoid a foreclosure sale and just take back the stock or other collateral for your note only if the buyer does not object and you give up any rights against the buyer for a deficiency judgment (i.e., a judgment for the excess of your note over what the returned collateral is worth).

At a foreclosure sale, you can use your unpaid note to bid for the stock or other collateral. If you are the successful bidder in a foreclosure, the value of the stock or other collateral you acquire is deemed to be taxable to you as if you received cash in an equal amount. The same is true if you just take back your collateral without objection from the buyer and give up your rights to a deficiency judgment.

The effect of being subjected to federal income taxes on your collateral recovery is that you must use some of the cash you previously received from the buyer (less the tax you already paid) to pay the tax on your collateral recovery. This adds insult to injury.

If the buyer voluntarily agrees to a purchase price "adjustment" in lieu of a foreclosure, which reduces the purchase price to the amount you actually received, you may be able to avoid these adverse tax consequences. However, this requires the cooperation of the defaulting buyer, and you will have to pay a price for such cooperation.

WARNING If you finance 100 percent or close to 100 percent of the purchase price and the buyer defaults, you may be taxed on foreclosure or other recovery of your collateral for the entire value of your business on the date you recover it. You may not have received enough cash from the buyer to pay for your federal income taxes and consequently will be required to pay the taxes out of your own pocket.

Never sell a business on a deferred payout of 100 percent or close to 100 percent of the purchase price. Always insist on receiving in cash at least the amount of taxes you will have to pay on a subsequent foreclosure.

In general, if you sell stock, insist on receiving 17 percent of the purchase price (less your tax basis) in cash. If you sell ordinary in-

come assets, insist on receiving 37 percent of the purchase price (less
your tax basis) in cash.

> **WARNING**   A number of technical requirements for install-
> ment reporting must be satisfied. For example, if you receive a
> note from a person other than the purchaser or the note is
> payable on demand or is issued by a corporation and readily
> tradable, you will lose installment reporting. Thus, the seller
> will have to pay federal income tax on the value of the note or
> deferred payments in the year of sale even though the seller
> has not received any cash from the sale.

TAX ISSUES

A selling shareholder who receives part or all of the purchase price in
notes or deferred payment obligations and who recognizes gain on
the sale will generally be taxed on the installment method of reporting for federal income tax purposes. This means that you will report
a proportionate part of your total gain on the sale each time you collect a part of the note or deferred purchase price.

You must be certain that your note or deferred payment obligation qualifies for installment reporting. If not, your gain is all taxed
at closing even though you have not received all of the cash.

A 1988 amendment to the Internal Revenue Code limited the
benefits of the installment method for larger sales to stock. An annual interest charge on the seller's tax liability deferred by the installment method is imposed for certain sales of property to the
extent that the aggregate amount of installment receivables that
arose from such sales during the year and that are outstanding at the
end of the year exceeds $5 million. In addition, there are antipledg-
ing rules that provide that any pledge of these large installment notes
triggers taxable gain to the extent of the net proceeds from the
pledge. Therefore, carefully review with your tax consultant your en-
titlement to the full benefit of installment reporting prior to signing
any sale agreement.

There is only one significant advantage of a note over cash. If the
purchase price was entirely cash, you would only be able to invest the

after-tax portion of the purchase price. To the extent that the note allows you to defer taxes because of installment reporting, the buyer will be paying you interest on these deferred taxes.

POST-CLOSING WORKING CAPITAL AND PURCHASE PRICE ADJUSTMENTS

If you have excess working capital over your normalized working capital at the sale closing date, many sale agreements will permit you to withdraw this excess once the buyer's accountants have verified its existence as of the closing date. However, as noted in Chapter 18, it may take a long time after closing until a decision is made as to how much excess there is. Also, the ultimate distribution to you of this excess working capital may be further delayed by virtue of an arbitration or other dispute resolution mechanism contained in the sale agreement.

Because it is possible that there will be a significant delay in the payment of the excess working capital to you, you should treat this payment obligation as a loan to the buyer and as a deferred purchase price payment. Accordingly, you should insist upon the receipt of interest, collateral, covenants, default clauses, and so forth in the same manner that you would negotiate with the buyer if the buyer insisted upon a long-term payout of your purchase price.

Some sale agreements have an estimated purchase price paid at the closing that is then adjusted subsequent to the closing based upon the actual closing date balance sheet. Again, it may take a significant period after closing until you receive any increase in the purchase price resulting from the actual closing date balance sheet. These post-closing purchase price adjustments, to the extent favorable to the seller, should also be viewed as loans to the buyer and treated accordingly.

If your negotiating position is strong, you might consider requiring the buyer to deposit a certain amount of money in escrow at closing. This should be an estimated amount that is equal to the highest amount of working capital and other purchase price adjustments that would most likely be due to you as the seller under the sale agreement.

CHAPTER SIXTEEN

EARNOUTS: ANOTHER LITIGATION RECIPE

An earnout is a method of paying the seller for her or his business based upon the performance of the business after the date of closing. An earnout is a useful method of reconciling the buyer's and seller's conflicting valuations of the business.

The buyer may say to the seller that if the seller's projections of future income come true, the seller should be paid the seller's asking price. The seller should, of course, counter that if the seller's projections become true, the seller should receive an even higher amount than originally asked to compensate the seller for the risk being assumed in the earnout. Through negotiations, the parties ultimately arrive at a formula.

Sellers should generally avoid 100 percent earnouts. They should insist that a high percentage of the purchase price consideration be fixed. When the seller does not have the bargaining power to negotiate a high fixed consideration, it may be wise to decide not to sell the business because in effect, the seller would be giving up ultimate control of the business to the buyer without being assured of any control premium.

CONTROL

Earnouts do not work very well unless the seller continues to control the business. If the buyer controls the business, the buyer can make certain decisions that effectively undermine the earnout.

For example, if the buyer controls the business, the buyer may decide to step up marketing or research and development (R&D) in the years in which the earnout is measured. The buyer will get the benefit of the additional marketing or R&D in the years after the earnout is over. However, that does not help the seller.

LEGAL PROTECTIONS

Even if the seller maintains managerial control, the buyer will almost never give up potential legal control of the business. Therefore, the seller needs legal protection to permit the maximization of the earnout. Some of these protections are summarized as follows:

- The seller must protect him- or herself from being forced to hire new employees during the earnout period. New employees increase costs and decrease earnout payments.
- The seller also needs protection from having unwanted marketing or R&D costs imposed upon the business.

Sometimes the issue of unwanted marketing costs, R&D, and employees is reconciled by permitting the buyer to force the seller to incur these costs but eliminating these costs from the seller's income for the purpose of computing the earnouts. Even if the buyer accepts this solution, care must be taken to ensure that the cash necessary for these buyer-imposed costs is paid by the buyer and does not reduce the cash available to operate the business. Otherwise, the earnout will be reduced by interest costs on loans that must be incurred to fund these buyer-imposed costs.

- Any purchases, sales, or other transactions between the earnout business and the buyer or its affiliates must be at arm's-lengths prices and terms. If you do not obtain this legal protection, you may find yourself selling to the buyer without profit or at a loss.
- The buyer must also be obligated to supply the cash needs of the business during the earnout period. A cash-starved business cannot grow in a manner to maximize the earnout.
- Care must be taken to prevent the buyer's general and administrative (G&A) and overhead from being charged against the

business. A large buyer will typically have much higher G&A and overhead costs than the seller. If these costs can be charged to the business during the earnout period, the earnout will be substantially reduced, if not eliminated.

• Likewise, the methods of accounting practiced by the seller prior to the closing should be continued during the earnout period. For example, if the seller was taking straight-line depreciation on equipment prior to the date of closing, you do not want the buyer to impose an accelerated depreciation after the closing, thereby artificially decreasing accounting income for earnout purposes.

Earnouts require a very careful negotiation of the terms. Your lawyer and accountant are very valuable during these negotiations.

NEGOTIATING EARNOUT AMOUNT

Earnout negotiations typically revolve around determining what is a home run with the bases loaded and what is a single. Earning levels that will make the buyer smile should give the seller the maximum earnout earnings; levels that are barely passable should give the seller the minimum earnout.

If the seller understands the buyer's valuation formula, it should not be too hard to figure out what constitutes a home run with the bases loaded. For example, suppose your business sells between 4 and 8 times EBITDA. The buyer offers you 4, and you counter with 8. The buyer says that he or she will not go beyond 5 times EBITDA unless it is in the form of an earnout.

In this example, the earnout should, at a minimum, give the seller the opportunity to earn back the 3 times EBITDA that was lost in the negotiations. The buyer may be willing to accede to that demand if during the earnout period, the higher EBITDA when multiplied by 5 equals the earnout figure demanded by the seller.

NEGOTIATING MEASUREMENT PERIOD
FOR AN EARNOUT

After negotiating the amount of the earnout, the buyer and seller then negotiate the measurement period for the earnout. The measurement period should be long enough to permit the seller to maximize the earnout amount. Sellers must determine in what future years their earnings will likely be maximized and then provide some room for slippage.

For example, if the earnout goal is likely to be achieved in year 2, the seller should negotiate to permit the goal to be achieved in year 3 and still maximize the earnout.

If the earnout is measured by setting specified goals for years 1, 2, and 3, the earnout should permit the seller to miss the goal for year 1 and be able to make up for it in a subsequent year. Likewise, if year 1 is a super year, but year 3 is poor, the seller should be able to seek the right to apply excess earnings from year 1 to year 3.

In effect, the seller should retain the right to sprinkle earnings throughout the measurement period in a manner that will maximize the earnout amount.

PROTECTING PAYMENT OF THE EARNOUT

Because an earnout is really a method of deferring some of the purchase price payments, you need to have the same protections as if you accepted a note for a portion of the price. If all of the earnout payments are due in five years, this is no different from a balloon note due in five years, which should be avoided.

In general, earnouts have less risk of nonpayment than notes because they are payable only if there are earnings. Nevertheless, you should take care to protect your ability to collect earnout payments by using the following:

- early payments of earnout amounts
- prohibiting distributions or loans to the parent buyer corporation until all earnout payments have been satisfied
- escrowing of excess cash for the benefit of earnout recipients

EARNOUT LITIGATION

Because earnouts are a form of deferred payments, the seller who accepts an earnout needs the same protections as the seller who accepts a buyer's note.

Earnouts breed litigation because of their complexity. It is common to have serious disputes as to the amount of the earnout that has actually become earned by the seller. Therefore, you should exercise great caution before agreeing to an earnout.

It behooves the seller to negotiate a clause in an earnout that requires the buyer to pay the seller's attorney's fees if there is a dispute concerning the earnout and the seller is successful in the litigation. A typical negotiating response to this request is that the buyer would like a similar clause if the seller sues on the earnout and loses.

Although this reciprocal clause is not desirable from the seller's viewpoint, regarding attorneys' fees in general, the seller is better off with a winner-take-all clause, especially when dealing with a large, wealthy buyer. These buyers typically have more financial resources than the seller can afford. They can engage in scorched-earth litigation tactics that the seller may not be able to afford and may thereby force the seller to settle cheaply.

If there is a winner-take-all litigation clause, the seller may be able to engage an attorney to represent him or her in the earnout litigation but will work on a partial or whole contingent fee basis. This permits the seller to level the playing field in any litigation with a wealthy buyer.

IMPUTED INTEREST

A portion of each of your earnout payments (whether payable in cash or stock) will be deemed to be imputed interest taxable to you at ordinary income rates. This is true even though you sold stock to the buyer, which normally produces capital gain. The only way to avoid this is to require the buyer to pay interest to you on the earnout payment at least equal to the minimum rate necessary to avoid imputed interest.

If you cannot negotiate such a minimum interest payment from the buyer, you should attempt to negotiate an increase in the amount of each earnout payment to compensate you for the fact that it is not all taxed to you as a long-term capital gain.

For example, a very significant portion of the earnout payment due in the fifth year of a five-year earnout will be imputed interest taxable to you as ordinary income and not as long-term capital gains, even though you sold stock to the buyer. Assuming that the fifth-year earnout payment was $10 million and the imputed interest rate was 7 percent per year, approximately $3,287,900 ($10 million discounted at an 8 percent per annum rate, compounded monthly) would be taxed at ordinary income tax rates as imputed interest, and the remaining $6,712,100 (less tax basis) would be taxed as long-term capital gain.

Earnout payments in the form of stock are also subject to the imputed interest rules. Imputed interest income is deemed to be realized when you receive the earnout stock and, in some cases, even earlier. This is true even though you are not taxed on the receipt of the earnout stock because of a tax-free reorganization.

If you receive a stock earnout, you will need to have the cash necessary to pay the income tax on the imputed interest income portion of the stock earnout payment. As noted in the previous example of a $10 million fifth-year earnout payment, this could be a substantial sum. Therefore, you should, if possible, negotiate for the buyer to pay a minimum interest rate on the stock earnout payment or be prepared to pay the tax out of your own pocket.

CHAPTER SEVENTEEN

NEGOTIATING EMPLOYMENT AND CONSULTING AGREEMENTS

T he buyer may wish to retain your services after the sale and want you to execute an employment or consulting agreement. Likewise, you may wish an employment or consulting agreement for either of the following reasons:

- A significant part of the consideration for your business is being paid to you pursuant to an employment or consulting agreement.

- You have an earnout and need assurance that you will be in control after closing.

The legal protections provided to the seller by employment or consulting agreements are often misunderstood. For example, if the seller has a five-year employment contract at $200,000 per year, is the seller assured of receiving $1 million?

The answer is "not necessarily."

First, the payments under the employment or consulting agreement are just another form of deferred payment. The seller needs all the same protections as if he or she were given a note for $1 million, including protections from buyer's bankruptcy, and so on. The seller also needs collateral, acceleration rights, and other protections afforded to a seller who is taking back a note from the buyer.

Of course, if the seller can easily get another job for $200,000 a year, the seller does not need these protections. However, even if the seller's prospects are bright for such a job at closing, will they be equally bright three years later? Because few sellers can be certain of the answer, caution would dictate that most sellers should obtain some security from the buyer that the payments be made under the employment or consulting agreement.

Second, under most employment or consulting agreements, if the buyer breaches the agreement and fires the seller, the seller is obligated to mitigate damages. This means that the seller must look for a new job and the buyer is only liable for the difference between what the new job pays and the $200,000 per year. If the seller immediately finds another job that pays $200,000 or more, the seller has no remedy against the buyer for the breach.

The only method of protecting against this result is to insert into the employment or consulting agreement a no-mitigation clause. Such a clause says that if the buyer breaches the agreement, the seller has no duty to mitigate damages, and any income the seller earns from another job will not offset the damages owed by the buyer to the seller. If your employment or consulting agreement is silent on this issue, the law requires you to mitigate. Therefore, be certain to insist on a no-mitigation clause in your contract.

There are a number of other traps in employment and consulting agreements, described in the following sections.

Problem Number 1

If the contract is silent, the buyer can move the business across the country and require you to change work locations.

Solution

Protect yourself from having to move more than twenty miles from your existing home by a specific clause in the contract.

Problem Number 2

The buyer may retain a very broad right in the contract to terminate you "for cause" and cut off your salary and benefits.

Solution

Limit for-cause terminations by narrowing the language as to what constitutes cause (e.g., criminal convictions). Also, require the seller in the contract to give prior written notice of any event that can trigger a for-cause termination, together with an opportunity to cure that event (if a cure is possible).

Problem Number 3

The contract is not specific about your fringe benefits or contains language that permits the buyer to change your fringe benefits.

Solution
Spell out specifically what fringe benefits you require and eliminate the right of the buyer to change them unless the change gives you greater or equivalent value.

Problem Number 4

The agreement of sale or the employment or consulting agreement forbids you to compete with the buyer even if your employment is terminated during the employment period under your employment agreement.

Solution
Make the noncompetition provision conditional on the requirement that you continue to receive your salary and fringe benefits under the employment contract or consulting agreement.

WARNING The buyer may resist this solution because it raises a tax issue for the buyer—that is, whether any part of the consideration paid under the employment or consulting agreement is really not for services (and therefore is not currently tax deductible by the buyer) but is part of the sale price (and therefore must be allocated to the assets or stock purchased or to the noncompetition agreement). If the buyer is unwilling to take this risk, the noncompetition provision should be modified or deleted.

Your employment agreement with the buyer should afford you the right to terminate your employment for good reason. The following are examples of good reason:

• Buyer's material breach of the employment agreement

- Your assignment, without your consent, to a lesser position than you enjoyed at the sale date or the reduction of your authority or responsibilities
- Your relocation without your consent

NONCOMPETITION AGREEMENTS

It is not unusual for the buyer to request you to sign a noncompetition agreement. The noncompetition agreement may be inserted into the employment or consulting agreement or may become part of the definitive agreement of sale, or both.

Although noncompetition agreements are not always enforceable in a pure employment setting, the courts are generally more willing to enforce noncompetition agreements that are negotiated in connection with the sale of a business. Therefore, you should assume that a noncompetition agreement will be enforced against you by the courts.

The attorneys for buyers typically overdraft the noncompetition agreements so that they extend well beyond what the buyer needs for protection. It is the function of your attorney to narrow these noncompetition agreements so that they provide no more protection than the buyer absolutely needs. If feasible, the noncompetition clause should be changed to a nonsolicitation of customers clause.

Particular care should be taken with clauses that restrict your working for a large company that has one division that competes with the buyer, even though you are working in an entirely different division that does not compete with the buyer. Likewise, you should not be restricted from purchasing minor amounts of publicly traded stock of a company that may compete with the buyer.

The noncompetition agreement should require the buyer to notify you in writing of any alleged breach and give you an opportunity to cure the alleged breach before the buyer takes legal action.

The buyer may verbally assure you that you will be released from the noncompetition agreement when it makes sense to do so and that the buyer will not be unreasonable. *Do not accept such assurances.*

Your bargaining power to obtain exceptions from the noncompetition agreement is highest just prior to the signing of the final sale documents. This is the honeymoon period. After closing the sale of your business, your bargaining power is severely diminished. *Therefore, get the exceptions in writing before signing.*

If you are receiving deferred payments of the purchase price, the noncompetition provision should immediately terminate if there is a default by the buyer on the deferred payments.

If your bargaining power is strong, consider offering the buyer a nonsolicitation of customers or employees clause, rather than a noncompetition agreement. A clause preventing you from soliciting existing customers or employees of the business would not prevent you from competing with the business. However, keep in mind that successfully negotiating such a provision is difficult.

CHAPTER EIGHTEEN

AVOIDING TRAPS IN THE AGREEMENT OF SALE

The final agreement of sale typically consists of the following major provisions:

- business terms
- warranties and representations of buyer and seller
- closing date provisions
- covenants (i.e., agreements) imposed on the seller prior to and after closing
- conditions precedent to the buyer's obligation to close
- conditions precedent to the seller's obligation to close
- indemnification clauses
- miscellaneous provisions

A sample agreement of sale involving the sale of the assets of a physical therapy center to a large public company buyer is contained in Appendix 7.

If you have a good bargaining position, it is a good idea to have your attorney, rather than the buyer's attorney, prepare the first draft of the agreement of sale.

PURCHASE PRICE AND OTHER BUSINESS TERMS

The amount and the method of determining the purchase price for the stock or assets of your business are the most crucial issues in the negotiation between you and the buyer. It is in your interest to have a clearly stated purchase price that is payable to you at the closing of the sale of your business. In the case of an asset sale, it is important that all or substantially all of your company's liabilities are assumed by the buyer and all of your company's employees are reemployed by the buyer.

If all of your company's liabilities are not assumed by the buyer in an asset sale, the unassumed liabilities reduce the effective purchase price to you. Your company would receive the purchase price for the assets from the buyer and then have to pay the unassumed liabilities or reserve from the purchase price an amount equal to the unassumed liabilities before distributing the purchase price proceeds to you as an equity holder of your company. For example, if the buyer purchases all of your company's assets and does not reemploy all of your company's current employees and assume all of their accrued benefits, your company may be liable to its current employees who are not reemployed for their accrued vacation and sick pay as well as other termination benefits. The required termination benefits to be paid to these employees by your company effectively reduces the purchase price available to be distributed to you as an equity holder of your company.

On the other hand, buyers generally prefer to have a formulaic purchase price (e.g., 125 percent of net book value), which is determined based upon a closing date balance sheet that is constructed by their accountants subsequent to the closing, with the purchase price thus determined payable to you after the closing. In the case of an asset sale, buyers are very reluctant to assume any liabilities other than the liabilities specifically disclosed to them and they may not commit to hire all of your company's current employees and assume your company's accrued obligations to them. In fact, many buyers insist that you terminate your company's entire workforce effective at the closing, subject to the right of the buyer to rehire them, at its discretion, if they pass drug and alcohol testing required by the buyer.

Even in a stock sale, it is typical for the buyer to insist upon an escrow of a portion of the purchase price for liabilities of the company that are not specifically identified and assumed by the buyer and to insist upon your company's laying off, effective at the closing, certain employees whom the buyer does not wish to retain, with you personally indemnifying the buyer for any termination costs for such laid-off employees.

Because you may not be able to identify or value all of the potential liabilities of your business, you or your company will likely be stuck with the unidentified liabilities (including contingent liabilities that cannot be valued) and liabilities that you were not even aware of when you signed the sale agreement, whether the sale agreement is for your stock or assets.

> **WARNING**   Many sellers naively assume that the purchase price for their business verbally agreed to with the buyer is what the seller will actually receive. In reality, this is the highest price they may receive and it is likely that they will receive less as a result of the provisions of the sale agreement that require the seller to retain all liabilities other than those specifically identified and further require the seller to indemnify the buyer post-closing for events or circumstances that occur before closing.

Post-Closing Determination of Purchase Price

Many sale agreements provide a formula for the purchase price (e.g., 125 percent of net book value on the closing date), so that the purchase price is determined after the closing. If you agree to a post-closing determination of the purchase price, you should insist upon a closing date payment of an estimated amount of the purchase price, which is not refundable to the buyer.

Once title to your stock or assets has been transferred to the buyer at the closing, your bargaining power is greatly diminished. Once title has been transferred to the buyer, your business is owned and controlled by the buyer and, in the event of a dispute concerning the purchase price, your legal remedy is generally limited to money damages as determined by a court or arbitrator after a long and expensive litigation.

If your purchase price must be determined by a formula, it is important that this determination be made before closing, rather than after closing, in order to give you the option to abort the closing if there is a dispute. The sale agreement should provide for this ability to abort the closing if there is a dispute about the purchase price before the closing.

If you are unable to negotiate a purchase price that is fully determinable before the closing, you should attempt to pin down as many elements of the purchase price as possible before you are obligated to proceed with the closing. For example, the buyer may insist that they cannot fully determine the purchase price until their accountants produce a closing date balance sheet, well after the closing, as the purchase price is based upon some percentage of your net book value at closing (e.g., the aforementioned 125 percent). You should insist, before signing the sale agreement, that the buyer's accountant agree with the balance sheet prepared by your accountant as of a date prior to the sale agreement so that you can flush out any disagreements before legally binding yourself to the sale agreement. By having the buyer's accountant sign off on your earlier dated balance sheet, you can effectively limit the number of possible challenges that the buyer can raise post-closing. If the buyer insists that you execute the sale agreement before the buyer's accountant has reviewed the earlier dated balance sheet prepared by your accountant, you can stipulate that the sale agreement specifically say that the buyer's accountant must agree with your earlier dated balance sheet before the closing or you are not legally obligated to close the sale.

Why is it important to limit the number of post-closing challenges that can be made by the buyer? Accounting is an art and not a science. For example, your accountant may have agreed to a bad debt reserve for your accounts receivable or an inventory valuation that the buyer's accountant would dispute. By requiring the buyer's accountant to sign off on your bad debt reserve and inventory valuation in the earlier dated balance sheet, you have limited the post-closing disputes to only events that occurred between the earlier dated balance sheet and the closing date that may have affected the bad debt reserve and inventory valuation.

Another method of pinning down the buyer who insists upon a post-closing determination of the purchase price is to provide a clear formula in the agreement for that determination. Suppose, for example, the buyer insists that inventory must be valued as of the closing date. You should then insist that there be an agreed-upon formula set forth in the sale agreement that would control the valuation. The following is an example of such a formula:

Physical Inventory

A physical inventory of the Inventory shall be taken by representatives of Seller and Buyer as of the close of business on the last business day prior to Closing. The Inventory will be valued as follows: (1) raw materials will be valued at Seller's purchase price, as reflected on Seller's invoice therefor; (2) work-in-progress shall be valued at the lower of (a) Seller's purchase price, as reflected on Seller's invoice therefor; (b) 65% of the lowest selling price that Seller maintains for such products, as provided in Schedule 1.D, or (c) 65% of the lowest market price for such products; and (3) finished goods shall be valued at the lower of (a) Seller's purchase price, as reflected on Seller's invoice therefor; (b) 75% of the lowest market price that Seller maintains for such products, as provided in Schedule 1.D, or (c) 75% of the lowest market price for such products. Any item of Inventory that is unusable, whether due to damage, failure to meet the specifications for which such item as purchased or manufactured, or otherwise, shall be excluded from the Inventory being purchased. In the event of a dispute between Buyer and Seller as to the amount or method of valuing the Inventory, the dispute shall, at the joint cost of Buyer and Seller, be immediately referred to a so-called "Big Four" accounting firm, to be agreed upon by Buyer and Seller, and the decision of such firm as to such valuation shall be final and binding on the parties hereto.

WARRANTIES AND REPRESENTATIONS

The warranties and representations are intended to require the seller to describe the company and serve to allocate risk between parties. These warranties and representations include the following subjects:

- organization and good standing
- authority; no conflict
- capitalization

- financial statements
- books and records
- title to properties, encumbrances
- condition and sufficiency of assets
- accounts receivable
- inventory
- existence of undisclosed liabilities
- legal proceedings, orders, judgments
- absence of certain changes and events
- contracts; no defaults
- insurance
- environmental matters
- employees, labor relations, compliance
- property
- certain payments
- full disclosure
- transactions with related persons
- brokers and finders

Section II of the agreement of sale, contained in Appendix 7, contains the seller's warranties and representations. Each of the numerous warranties and representations must be separately true and correct, even if they cover overlapping areas. For example, the agreement of sale will typically contain a warranty and representation that you have no pending or threatened litigation and a separate warranty and representation that you have no contingent liabilities. A threatened lawsuit is also a contingent liability. Therefore, if you qualify your "no litigation" warranty by reference to a specific lawsuit, you must also qualify your "no contingent liability" warranty by reference to the same lawsuit.

Typically at the end of the document there is a schedule of exceptions that permits the seller to indicate where the warranties and representations are incorrect. For example, if there is a warranty and representation that the seller has no lawsuits or environmental liabilities, this is usually preceded by the words "except as provided in this schedule." If the seller has lawsuits or environmental liabilities, they must be described in these schedules.

WARNING The agreement of sale should make it clear that whatever information is contained in the schedule of exceptions modifies all warranties, representations, and covenants contained in the agreement and cannot be the basis for an indemnification claim against the seller except as specifically provided for in the agreement. If you fail to do this, you may find that you are liable to the buyer even if you made full disclosure in the schedule of exceptions but failed to make reference in the schedule to all of the overlapping warranties, representations, and covenants.

If these schedules are not correct and complete, the buyer has the right to sue the seller (and its shareholders, if they signed the agreement) for breach of the warranty and representation. The buyer also has the right to refuse to close the sale.

If the seller breaches any warranty and representation, the buyer typically has the following options:

- Refuse to close the agreement of sale.
- Close the agreement of sale and seek damages from the seller.
- If the buyer first discovers the breach after closing, rescind the transaction if the breach is material.

It is extremely important to be truthful and careful in making warranties and representations. Even innocent mistakes can result in your having to return a portion of the sale price.

A seller can seek to have all of his or her warranties and representations terminate at the closing in order to avoid post-closing breach claims. However, unless the seller has an excellent bargaining position, most buyers will refuse this request.

RULE 10B-5 WARRANTY AND REPRESENTATION

The following warranty and representation contained in the agreement of sale set forth in Appendix 7 (see Section II[C] of the agreement) deserves special note:

> No representation or warranty made under any Section hereof and
> none of the information set forth herein, in the exhibits hereto or in
> any document delivered by any of the Companies or any of the Share-
> holders to the Purchaser, or any authorized representative of the Pur-
> chaser, pursuant to the express terms of this Agreement contains any
> untrue statement of a material fact by the Companies or the Share-
> holders or omits to state a material fact by the Companies or the Share-
> holders necessary to make the statements herein or therein not
> misleading.

This warranty and representation requires the seller to disclose
any other material facts (particularly adverse facts) about the seller's
business that the buyer ought to know. This disclosure is required
whether or not the buyer has requested the information in the agreement of sale. In effect, the burden is placed on the seller to disclose
other adverse facts about the business that the buyer neglected to
have warranted and represented.

This warranty and representation is sometimes called the Rule
10b-5 warranty, because a portion of the language is based on Rule
10b-5 under the Securities Exchange Act of 1934. However, this warranty differs markedly from Rule 10b-5. Under Rule 10b-5, a seller is
not liable in making material misstatements or material omissions
unless the seller did so intentionally or with reckless disregard for the
truth. In contrast, this warranty does not require the buyer to prove
that the seller intentionally or recklessly deceived the buyer. All the
buyer needs to prove is that the seller in fact failed to provide such
material information. The fact that the seller's error was in good faith
is irrelevant and is not a legal defense against the buyer's lawsuit.

ACCOUNTS RECEIVABLE

The following accounts receivable warranty and representation appears in the agreement of sale contained in Appendix 7 (see Section
II[K]):

> The accounts receivable of each of the Companies that are part of the As-
> sets are in their entirety valid accounts receivable, arising in the ordinary

> course of business. On or before 180 days from the date of the Closing, the Purchaser shall collect at least $160,000 of such accounts receivable.

This warranty and representation requires the seller to guarantee the collection of $160,000 of accounts receivable within 180 days after the closing. This warranty is in addition to representing that all of the acquired accounts receivable are valid and arose "in the ordinary course of business."

A number of variables exist in the accounts receivable warranty. The buyer can have you warrant any or all of the following:

Version 1:   The accounts receivable reflected on your financial statements represent amounts due for products or services you sold in the ordinary course of business in accordance with generally accepted accounting principles.

Version 2:   The accounts receivable are all collectible.

Version 3:   The accounts receivable will in fact be collected.

The seller should have no difficulty with version 1. Version 2 (the accounts receivable are collectible) is ambiguous, because it is not clear whether this warranty means that you are guaranteeing collection. Version 3 (the accounts receivable will be collected) is clear but also the least favorable from the seller's perspective.

CLOSING DATE

From the seller's point of view, it would be preferable to sign the agreement and have the closing the same day. This is true because the agreement of sale in many cases effectively converts the sale into an option given to the buyer to close the transaction.

For example, in many cases there is a so-called "due diligence out" in the conditions precedent that permits the buyer to terminate the agreement if, upon completion of due diligence, the buyer is not satisfied. Likewise, if the buyer discovers even an inadvertent breach by the seller of any material warranties and representations or the buyer cannot get exactly the legal opinion required from his or her attorney, the buyer is not obligated to close.

In some cases, it may be necessary to have time between signing the agreement of sale and the actual closing. This may occur because the buyer does not want to expend the funds necessary to do a complete due diligence investigation until the seller has signed an agreement of sale. It may also occur because certain consents of third parties are needed to complete the sale or there are required government filings, such as Hart-Scott-Rodino filings, which generally apply to the sale of assets or acquisition of voting securities.

When there is time between the signing and closing, the seller should attempt to eliminate as many of the buyer's "outs" as possible at the earliest possible time. For example, if there is a due diligence out, the buyer should lose this out after a certain period of time, such as ten or twenty days after the date of signing, even though the closing may not occur for sixty days after the signing because of the necessity of a third-party consent or some other factor.

If the buyer obtains a due diligence out that extends until the moment of closing, the buyer is really receiving an option to buy the business without ever paying for that option. In addition, during this period of time, your company is removed from the market for other potential buyers.

WARNING   Make certain that the agreement of sale terminates on a specific date if a closing has not occurred by that date. Otherwise, the buyer can indefinitely delay the closing, thereby preventing you from selling to others. If the closing does not occur by the specified date because of your fault or breach, limit the buyer's remedy to damages, so that you can sell to someone else.

CONDITIONS PRECEDENT

Conditions precedent are extremely important. If the conditions precedent to the buyer's obligation are not satisfied, the buyer does not have to complete the sale. The same is true for conditions precedent to the seller's obligation. However, a breach of a condition precedent (in contrast to a breach of a warranty, representation, or covenant) may not necessarily allow the innocent party to sue for damages. Rather, the innocent party's only remedy is typically limited to walking away from the transaction—in other words, refusing to close the sale.

Buyer's Obligations

The typical conditions precedent to the buyer's obligation to close are the following:

- The seller's warranties and representations must be true and correct as of the date of closing, and all of its covenants must have been complied with.
- Satisfactory legal opinions must be issued to the buyer.
- The buyer's due diligence must be completed satisfactorily.
- All necessary third-party consents must be obtained, including any necessary clearance under the Hart-Scott-Rodino Antitrust Improvements Act of 1976, as amended (generally applicable to nonexempt sales involving more than $50 million in sale consideration).
- There must be no lawsuits seeking to prevent the consummation of the transaction.
- If applicable, approval by the buyer's and/or seller's shareholders must be obtained.

The seller should negotiate the wording of the conditions precedent to the buyer's obligation so as to minimize the buyer's ability to change his or her mind at the last minute. For example, if there are legal opinions that must be given to the buyer to require the buyer to close, have such opinions given by your attorney and not the buyer's attorneys. Likewise, the form and substance of the legal opinion should be negotiated before executing the agreement of sale so that the buyer cannot impose new legal opinion requirements at the last minute.

As noted, any due diligence out for the buyer should have a short time frame so that the agreement of sale does not turn into an option.

If the seller has a good bargaining position, the seller may wish to negotiate limitations on the buyer's right to walk away from the deal once the agreement of sale is signed. For example, if the seller can negotiate a so-called "hell or high water clause," there is no bringdown of the warranties and representations to the closing date and the buyer's walk-away rights are extremely limited. In addition, if a seller warranty or representation is untrue on signing but is true at closing, the buyer should not be able to refuse to close.

The seller should also seek to negotiate a provision requiring the buyer to give the seller prompt written notice of the buyer's discovery of a breach by the seller of one of the seller's warranties, representations, or covenants. The written notice should be accompanied by the buyer's election either to waive the breach and proceed with the closing or to terminate the agreement. In the absence of such a provision, the buyer could discover a breach by the seller and then wait until the last minute to spring this on the seller. In addition, if the buyer discovers a breach by the seller before the closing, the buyer should not be permitted to close the sale and then sue the seller after the closing under the indemnification clause.

If you wish to receive an employment or consulting agreement, this should be added to the conditions precedent to the seller's obligations.

> **WARNING** Be careful that the agreement contains all of the conditions precedent to the seller's obligations. If your employment or consulting agreement is listed as a condition precedent to the buyer's obligations but not the seller's obligation to close, you are required to close whether or not the buyer executes the employment or consulting agreement. The buyer can merely waive the condition precedent to its obligation to close and force you to close.

Seller's Obligations

The conditions precedent to the seller's obligations to close typically include the following:

- The buyer's warranties and representations must be true and correct as of the date of closing, and all of its covenants must have been complied with.

- Satisfactory legal opinions must be issued to the seller.
- The seller's shareholders must be released from personal liabilities for corporate obligations.
- All necessary third-party consents must be obtained, including any necessary clearance under the Hart-Scott-Rodino Antitrust Improvements Act of 1976, as amended.
- There must be no lawsuits seeking to prevent the consummation of the transaction.
- If applicable, approval by the buyer's and/or seller's shareholders must be obtained.

Care should be taken that the conditions precedent to the seller's obligation to close generally parallel the conditions precedent to the buyer's obligation to close.

RELEASE OF PERSONAL GUARANTIES

It is important that you obtain a release from your personal guaranties, corporate bank loans, leases, licenses, and similar obligations and debts of your business to the extent they are assumed by the buyer. The buyer may offer indemnification against these personal guaranties to the extent that they cannot be released at the closing. Indemnification is a poor substitute for a release. Indeed, a post-closing deterioration in the buyer's financial condition may cause such indemnification to be illusory.

Moreover, if the third party (such as the bank whose loan you personally guaranteed) will not release you even if the buyer substitutes its guaranty, this probably means that the buyer is not sufficiently creditworthy. Accordingly, you would be foolish to rely on the buyer's indemnification.

In situations where you do close without obtaining a release of your personal guaranty, you are, in effect, providing a credit enhancement for the buyer. You should request compensation from the buyer for the credit enhancement. The compensation can take the form of an increased purchase price, equity in the buyer, or other forms of compensation.

INDEMNIFICATION CLAUSE

The indemnification clause typically requires the seller and his or her shareholders to indemnify the buyer not only for breaches of warranties, representations, and covenants but also for other kinds of claims (such as tax liabilities or environmental liabilities) that may occur after closing that were not agreed to be assumed by the buyer.

The indemnification clause typically creates liability to the buyer after the date of closing even for matters that the seller had no knowledge of before the closing. For example, a typical indemnification clause may require the seller to indemnify the buyer from any post-closing claim resulting from a pre-closing "act, omission, or event." This indemnification obligation applies even if the seller did not know about the pre-closing "act, omission or event."

Unless the indemnification clause is properly limited, this clause serves as an excellent vehicle for the buyer to readjust the sale price after the closing. The indemnification clause creates liability to the buyer after the date of closing.

Even if there is no indemnification clause as such, a breach of any of the warranties or representations or covenants contained in an agreement to sell assets or stock will also create such liability unless the agreement specifically provides that no lawsuit can be brought after the date of closing.

In a merger or consolidation, in which your entity disappears into the buyer or its subsidiary, the seller's shareholders have no indemnification liability after the closing unless they specifically agree to assume such liability.

It is important to limit claims under the indemnification clause so that they may be bought within only a short period of time or they are barred. Typically a seller can negotiate for short periods of time for certain kinds of liabilities that the buyer should discover very shortly after the closing. Other kinds of indemnification claims, such as tax liabilities, may require a longer claim period. See Section XIII[B] of the agreement of sale contained in Appendix 7.

If the buyer received a tax benefit from the loss that the buyer is asking you, the seller, to pay under the indemnification clause, it should be made clear that the buyer's tax benefit reduces your indemnification obligation. Similarly, if the buyer recovers money from his or her insurance company or from a third party, this should reduce your liability.

Likewise, you should preclude the buyer from any right to undo (or rescind) the transaction after closing because of a material loss subject to indemnification. The buyer's legal remedy should be limited to a price adjustment under the indemnification clause. Likewise, the buyer should agree not to seek punitive damages from you.

If the buyer discovers a breach by the seller before the closing and nevertheless chooses to close, the seller should be able to treat such closing as a waiver of the seller's breach. If there were no such wavier, the buyer could choose to close the purchase with full knowledge of the breach and then seek indemnification. The buyer's right of indemnification thus effectively lowers the selling price after the seller has already sold the business.

If the buyer has a claim asserted against him or her by a third party for which you are responsible under the indemnification clause, you will also be liable for his or her attorneys' fees. The buyer's attorneys typically have no incentive to limit their fees, because you, not their client, are paying for the litigation. Consequently, it is important that you have the right to appoint the attorneys for the buyer, because you thereby will have more leverage to control their fees. You should also give yourself the right to control the defense of the claim.

This will be agreeable to the buyer only if you choose from a list of law firms acceptable to the buyer and there is no doubt as to your ability to pay any adverse judgment. If there is doubt as to your ability to pay an adverse judgment, the buyer will probably require an attorney of his or her choosing to participate in the litigation and will not give you control of the defense.

Section X of the agreement of sale contained in Appendix 7 of this book contains examples of the clauses suggested in this section.

> **WARNING** Be certain that there is a ceiling on your liability under the agreement of sale. The ceiling should apply not only to the indemnification clause but also to your liability for breach of any provision of the agreement of sale. The ceiling figure should, at a maximum, not exceed the purchase price to the extent paid in cash.

(continues)

It is also customary to negotiate a so-called basket clause, which limits your liability for smaller claims. For example, the basket clause may provide that you are not liable for the first $50,000 of claims and are liable only for amounts in excess of $50,000. The theory of the basket clause is that the buyer should have recourse only for more significant claims against the seller and that the buyer probably would have consummated the agreement of sale if the buyer had to pay an additional immaterial amount.

Obviously, what is immaterial depends on the size of the transaction. In general, a basket clause equal to 1 percent of the consideration is usually not objectionable to most buyers. However, in appropriate circumstances, you may be able to negotiate a much higher percentage of the purchase price in the basket clause. Some basket clauses provide that if the total claims exceed the basket clause figure, the entire amount of the claims is collectable by the buyer, not just the amount in excess of the basket clause amount. Thus, in the preceding example, if the total claims were $51,000, the seller would be liable for the entire $51,000, rather than just $1,000.

Limiting the Seller's Indemnification Obligations and Insurance

The indemnification clause should be viewed as causing a potential reduction of the purchase price and should be limited as much as possible in the negotiations with the buyer. The following are several additional methods of limiting your exposure under the indemnification clause:

- Create shorter time limits for certain claims, such as breaches of accounting warranties and representations, so that they must be made within a short time after the first audit is completed by the buyer after the closing.
- Limit the amount for which indemnification may be claimed to a percentage of the purchase price and, in no event should

that percentage exceed the actual amount of the purchase price received by you in cash.

- Give yourself the ability to offset claims under the indemnification clause against unpaid amounts of the purchase price (starting with the longest maturity of any note given by the buyer for a portion of the purchase price).
- Give yourself the ability to offset claims under the indemnification clause with tax or other benefits received by the buyer as a result of the claim, or unanticipated benefits to the buyer from the sale.
- Insure your exposure to the extent possible.
- Require the buyer to insure itself against post-closing claims that are subject to indemnification and waive the subrogation rights of the insurer against you.

Prior to entering into the sale agreement, you should carefully review all of your insurance coverage to determine its adequacy in both scope coverage and amount. For example, if you do not have employment practices insurance, consider buying it, as it will provide coverage for some of the employment practices claims made after the closing, which are subject to indemnification. If possible, require the buyer to maintain adequate insurance after the closing; if the buyer refuses to do so, pay for it yourself.

Be careful to have the insurer waive any subrogation rights against you if you are not the named insured under the policy. If an insurer pays a claim, and you are not the named insured, but the buyer is the named insured, the insurer may come after you for reimbursement under their right to be subrogated to the buyer's rights against you.

INDEMNIFICATION OF SELLER

The seller and its directors, officers, and shareholders need indemnification protection as well as the buyer. For example, if after closing the buyer sells a defective product or service and the seller or his or her directors, officers, or shareholders are sued along with the buyer, they should also be entitled to indemnification.

Therefore, the seller and his or her directors and officers should receive indemnification from the buyer's conduct of the business after the closing. For an example of this clause, see Section X[B] of the agreement of sale contained in Appendix 7.

The seller also needs indemnification from any claims by former employees who were hired by the buyer. It is not unusual for such former employees to join the seller in any lawsuit that they bring against the buyer for wrongful termination after the closing or for other kinds of claims.

In general, the seller should be indemnified from any claims resulting from liabilities that the buyer agreed to assume in the agreement of sale. For example, if the buyer agreed to assume any pension liabilities due to the seller's employees, the seller must be indemnified by the buyer from any claims brought by a former employee resulting from disputes as to the amount of such pension. The same is true as to environmental liabilities, accounts payable, or other liabilities that are specifically assumed by the buyer in the agreement of sale.

INSURANCE

It is important to have the buyer maintain insurance after closing that protects you, the seller, against third-party claims, particularly accident claims. For example, if you sell a defective product or service before closing, that defective product or service could give rise to a claim after closing. You must be insured for that claim, preferably at the buyer's expense.

However, regardless of who maintains or pays for the insurance, you still need protection from such claims. You may have to continue your own insurance for some time after closing to protect yourself. This is particularly true if you sell assets, as the buyer typically will not agree to pay for unasserted claims due to defective products or services that you sold.

Even if the buyer maintains the insurance, you will need an insurance certification from the buyer's insurer, together with the insurer's agreement to notify you of any amendments or deletions of coverage or any terminations of the buyer's policies and, as noted, a waiver by the insurer of any subrogation rights against you.

As noted, you also need protection from any claims resulting from defective products or services sold by the buyer after the closing. At a minimum, you will want indemnification from the buyer for these claims and to be named as an additional insured on the buyer's liability policies, with subrogation rights against you waived.

WHO IS LIABLE UNDER AGREEMENT OF SALE?

In general, anyone who signs the agreement of sale has liability under the agreement unless the agreement specifically provides otherwise. If the agreement of sale provides for the sale of your stock in your corporation to the buyer, you are, of course, liable under the agreement.

Resist any attempt to secure your spouse's signature on the agreement of sale unless your spouse is also a shareholder of the shares or the shares are owned jointly or by the entireties. It is acceptable to permit your spouse to consent to the sale as long as your spouse has no liability under the agreement of sale. By removing your spouse from liability, you can, in many states, insulate personal assets from the buyer if you own such personal assets as tenants by the entireties with your spouse.

If your corporation enters into an agreement of sale to sell assets to the buyer, it is customary for the buyer to require the shareholders of the selling corporation to sign the agreement of sale as guarantors. The same is true if the transaction is structured as a merger or consolidation.

WARNING If there are minority shareholders of your corporation, try to limit your personal liability to your proportionate share of the stock. If you fail to negotiate this limitation, you can be liable for 100 percent of the loss unless you have some kind of contribution agreement with your minority shareholders.

Be warned: You can be personally liable under the agreement of sale even if you did not sign it. For example, securities laws may make you personally liable as a control person if your corporation is otherwise liable under these laws.

You may also incur personal liability if you give a certification to the buyer as a corporate officer pursuant to the agreement of sale and the certification is wrong. You may avoid this liability by making it clear in the certification that you are only acting as a corporate officer and not in a personal capacity.

GENERAL

These legal clauses are really part of the overall business negotiation. For example, the buyer may be willing to trade a small price reduction for the elimination of warranties and representations or other protective clauses to the buyer. Therefore, you must work closely with your attorney to create package proposals in which concessions you are giving to the buyer on business terms are linked with concessions your attorneys want from the buyer's attorney on legal terms.

PLANNING FOR THE CLOSING

At closing you will receive your check or wire transfer and any promissory notes and stock that were part of the purchase price. In return, you must transfer the stock or assets of your business or effectuate any mergers or consolidations.

If the closing involves a plant closing or a mass layoff, there are various federal, state, and local laws that require prior notice, usually sixty days. For example, the U.S. Worker Adjustment and Retraining Notification Act (WARN) requires employers of 100 or more employees (subject to exceptions) to give employees, state dislocated worker units, and local governments sixty days of advance written notice of plant closings and mass layoffs. Whether the sixty days of notice is calculated as working days or calendar days will depend on the jurisdiction in which your company resides. In addition, employers may be subject to state or local plant closing laws that apply more broadly than WARN, in other words, laws that apply to employers with fewer than 100 employees, or those that impose additional notice requirements, such as longer notice periods. You will not want to provide notice under WARN or a state or local statute until you have signed an agreement of sale and any due diligence outs have been waived; therefore, your closing may be delayed until the required waiting period has been satisfied.

Similarly, if your transaction is subject to the Hart-Scott-Rodino Antitrust Improvements Act of 1976, as amended (certain transactions generally involving over $50 million sale consideration), a prior notice and a fifteen- to thirty-day waiting period are required.

There are three planning items for the closing:

- Insist that your attorneys do a preclosing, or dress rehearsal, well before the actual closing date so that the closing is not held up by last-minute issues.

- Request a wire transfer of immediately available funds to your account. Your right to a wire transfer must be contained in the agreement of sale. If a wire transfer is not feasible, request a bank check or a certified check.

- Plan in advance of the closing as to exactly how you will invest the funds you receive at closing.

The last two planning items can best be illustrated by the actual case of a businessman who had received a $25 million check at closing and then stupidly mailed it to himself. The check was lost in the mail and, in fact, was not replaced for thirty days. The loss of interest on the check, at an 8 percent per annum interest rate, was over $164,000.

Prior to the closing, you should know exactly how and where your funds will be invested so that these transactions can be effectuated on the closing date without loss of interest.

PART V

ALTERNATIVES TO SELLING YOUR BUSINESS

CHAPTER NINETEEN

LEVERAGED RECAPITALIZATION

Before you decide to sell your business, you should explore the alternatives of a leveraged recapitalization or going public. Although going public is a familiar concept, leveraged recapitalization is not.

If your motive for selling your business is that you are tired of working, skip this chapter and the next. Leveraged recapitalizations and public offerings (assuming you are the CEO) require you to work harder—not retire.

Likewise, if your motivation for selling is that your business is going downhill quickly, skip this chapter and the next. You are not going to be able to take a declining business public. Also, institutional lenders and investors will not be interested in a leveraged recapitalization.

A leveraged recapitalization typically involves having your company borrow money (without your personal guarantee) from institutional lenders or investors, who receive a senior debt security, possibly with warrants, to purchase your company's stock. Your company then uses the money to recapitalize your company, and you receive cash in the recapitalization for a portion of your stock. You wind up with a significant stock position in your company (usually a majority), plus the cash.

A simple example of a leveraged recapitalization would be to go to your local bank, borrow money on behalf of the business (without a personal guarantee) and then dividend that money to yourself in your capacity as the stockholder of the business. This is only possible if your company is creditworthy and your bank will permit a leveraged recapitalization. Many banks have specialized lending groups that will permit leveraged recapitalizations.

Professional real estate investors typically use leveraged recapitalizations to withdraw equity from their real estate. If the real estate has appreciated, the professional investor re-mortgages the property with a higher mortgage (with recourse on the mortgage loan limited to the property) and withdraws the excess cash resulting from the re-mortgage, thereby withdrawing a portion of the real estate appreciation from the venture.

Many entrepreneurs fail to take advantage of the full borrowing capacity of their businesses and, instead, opt to sell their business to a financial buyer. However, the financial buyer has no reluctance whatsoever in placing maximum debt leverage on the business. The financial buyer uses the proceeds from the debt leverage of your business, together with a much smaller amount of the financial buyer's own funds, to purchase the business from you. This large debt leverage on the business permits the financial buyer to receive potentially high financial returns on the smaller amount of equity which the financial buyer uses, together with the debt proceeds, to purchase the business from you.

Had you engaged in a leveraged recapitalization yourself, rather than selling to a financial buyer, you could have received a substantial amount of funds for your own personal use (as a cash dividend) without selling or losing control of your business, without giving up one share of your equity, and without a personal guarantee.

Many companies cannot qualify for a leveraged recapitalization. They do not have either the assets or the cash flow to support a leveraged recapitalization or the growth prospects necessary to attract mezzanine lenders, an equity fund, or an underwriter of a public offering. These companies really have little choice but to sell to an outsider or to their own employees (including an ESOP). (See Chapter 14.)

Leveraged recapitalizations work only if your company can attract an asset-based lender or a cash-flow lender or has such a high growth potential that you can attract a mezzanine or equity investor.

To attract an asset-based lender, you will need substantial asset values, particularly liquidation values. The following are the normal requirements for asset-based lenders:

- accounts receivable: 70 percent to 85 percent
- inventory: 40 percent to 65 percent
- machinery and equipment: 75 percent to 80 percent of orderly liquidation value
- real estate: the lesser of 50 percent of fair market value or 75 percent of quick auction value
- senior term debt (fixed or adjusted rate; three- to seven-year term)
- working capital revolver (floating rate; one- to three-year term)

To attract a cash-flow lender, your company usually needs cash flow sufficient to cover 2.5 times the debt service on senior debt and 3.5 times all debt service. If your business does not have this kind of cash flow, a cash-flow leveraged recapitalization usually will not work. These figures, however, can vary with banking conditions.

The following are the normal requirements for a cash-flow lender:

- based on cash flow coverages (cash flow or EBITDA, divided by total interest cost), 3.5 times total coverage typical (2.5 times senior interest coverage)
- leverage ratio (funded debt divided by cash flow or EBITDA), a maximum of 3.5 is typical
- senior revolving credit facility (floating rate; one- to three-year term)
- senior term debt (fixed or floating rate; three- to seven-year term)
- mezzanine debt (fixed rate; five- to ten-year term; "equity kicker")

Leveraged recapitalizations do not require any personal guarantee by you for the institutional debt.

A leveraged recapitalization does not require significant growth prospects. Your company must have only sufficient assets to attract an asset-based lender or sufficient cash flow to cover the senior debt service and other debt service until maturity.

If you cannot qualify for a senior debt recapitalization but have significant growth prospects, and you are not ready to go public, you may still be able to effect a leveraged recapitalization.

There are providers of so-called mezzanine debt who will lend your company money in exchange for debt plus an equity kicker if they can project a return of least 30 percent per annum. This does not mean that you have to pay 30 percent interest per year. It means that the potential growth in value of the equity kicker, plus the interest, must equal at least 30 percent per year.

Assume that your business has explosive growth potential, but you are not ready to go public and your current cash flow cannot support much more debt service than you already have. You should consider a private equity fund as an investor. They typically are interested only if they can expect a return of 35 percent to 45 percent per year.

The problem with any leveraged recapitalization is that you will have to provide an exit for your lenders/investors. The exit for the senior and mezzanine debt is obviously the maturity date of that debt. However, the exit for the equity must usually occur in five to seven years through any of the following:

- going public
- selling the business
- repurchasing the lender/investor equity

The primary advantages of the leveraged recapitalization are the following:

- You receive some cash from the company, thereby achieving a degree of liquidity.
- You retain control of the company, subject to the restriction imposed by the lender or institutional investors.

The primary disadvantages are the following:

- Your company is highly leveraged, and you must operate in that environment.

- The institutional lenders/investors have some equity in your business, so you have minority shareholders to contend with.

- The institutional lenders/investors will impose restrictions on the operation of your company until they exit.

If you engage in a leveraged recapitalization, consider making family gifts of stock immediately thereafter, as your stock valuation will be depressed.

A leveraged recapitalization could be followed by a public offering after an appropriate growth period.

CHAPTER TWENTY

GOING PUBLIC

Some entrepreneurs attempt to go public hoping to instead sell their business before they actually sell stock to the public. This is commonly called double tracking. The publicity surrounding the filing of your registration statement with the Securities and Exchange Commission can attract buyers. Moreover, in a hot initial public offering (IPO) market, the higher valuations proposed by the underwriter for your business can give you significant leverage in your negotiations with any buyer.

To go public, you typically need a company with significant growth prospects, at least in the short term. Going public with your company requires hard work. If you would prefer to retire, this is not a suggested alternative unless you have a top-notch management team.

The primary advantage of an IPO versus a sale is that you will either initially or ultimately receive cash and still control your company. In contrast, in a sale you lose control.

If you have an S corporation, a limited liability company, or tax flow through entity, many underwriters will permit you to withdraw your previously taxed undistributed earnings at the time of the initial public offering. Thus, even if you do not sell a single share of stock in the IPO, you may still wind up with substantial dollars in your pocket after the IPO.

Some underwriters will permit you to sell some of your shares in the IPO, especially if you are not part of the management team. However, it is usually difficult, if not impossible, to find an underwriter who will permit the management team to sell any part of their shares in the IPO. Occasionally, IPO underwriters who exercise their over-allotment options because the offering is oversubscribed may allow some of the shares to be sold by active management.

Because most underwriters expect a minimum valuation of at least $100 million for your company in order to consider you for an IPO, and because of the high costs of an IPO and maintaining public company status, it may be necessary to grow your business well before your IPO target date. There is plentiful amount of private equity available to help you grow your business sufficiently to be of interest to an IPO underwriter; however, private equity investors have their own agenda and you may not be happy with the relationship. Despite the drawbacks of accepting funds from private equity investors, a majority of the companies going public today have been funded by private equity investors.

THE ADVANTAGES

The major advantages of going public are as follows:

1. *Lower cost of capital.*   A public company has more alternatives for raising capital than a private company. A private company, once it has exhausted its bank lines, generally raises additional equity and subordinated debt capital from individual and institutional investors in so-called private placements. These investors, particularly venture capital funds, insurance companies, and others, usually require very stiff terms, including significant operational restrictions.

In contrast, a public company has the alternative of going to the public marketplace. The public marketplace typically does not demand the same stiff terms. This results in less dilution to the existing shareholders if equity capital is raised. If debt securities are publicly sold, the public market place tends to be much more liberal in imposing operational restrictions.

Two identical companies, one private and the other public, are valued quite differently by investors. Investors in the private company discount the value of its equity securities by reason of their illiquidity, that is, the inability to readily sell them for cash.

The availability of the public capital alternative also permits the public company greater leverage in its negotiations with individual

and institutional investors. Most institutional investors prefer investing in public companies because they have a built-in exit, that is, they
can sell their stock in the public market.

Suppose the market price of your company's stock never rises
above the IPO price (a so-called broken IPO). Even in this disaster
scenario, the IPO has permitted you to raise what is probably the
cheapest form of equity capital—even if you have not achieved your
other IPO objectives.

2. *Personal wealth.*   A public offering can enhance your personal net
worth. Stories abound of the many millionaires and multimillionaires
created through public offerings. Even if you don't realize immediate
profits by selling a portion of your existing stock during the initial offering, you can use publicly traded stock as collateral to secure loans.

In as little as three months after your IPO, you may be able to
have another registered underwritten public offering in which you
sell a significant percentage of your personal holdings. These secondary or follow-on offerings are only possible if your company's
earnings have grown and your market price has risen significantly
since your IPO.

These secondary or follow-on offerings permit you to diversity
your personal wealth without selling or otherwise losing control of
your company. You can have your cake and eat it too!

For approximately six months after the IPO (the lock-up period),
the underwriter will restrict you from selling your personal stock, except in a secondary or follow-on offering authorized by the underwriter. Thereafter, you can sell stock under Rule 144. Rule 144
permits you to personally sell up to 1 percent of the total outstanding
stock of the company every three months, or one week's average trading volume, whichever is higher. The sales have to be in unsolicited
brokerage transactions or transactions with brokerage firms that
make a market in your stock. You also have to publicly report these
sales. Thus, it may not be desirable for you to utilize Rule 144 too frequently for fear of giving the investment community the impression
that you are bailing out.

3. *Competitive position.*   Many businesses use the capital from the IPO
to enhance their competitive position. The additional capital resources permit greater market penetration.

Some businesses have only a short window of opportunity to make a move. For example, a technology-based company can use the IPO proceeds to achieve a dominant position in the marketplace well before its underfinanced competitors.

Customers like to deal with well-financed businesses. A strong balance sheet is a good marketing tool.

4. *Prestige.* You and your cofounders gain an enormous amount of personal prestige from being associated with a company that goes public. Such prestige can be very helpful in recruiting key employees and in marketing your products and services. For example, the publicity surrounding the Internet IPOs, such as eBay, Inc., significantly increased the visitors to their web site.

5. *Ability to take advantage of market price fluctuations.* The market price of the stock of public companies can fluctuate greatly. These fluctuations may relate to overall stock market trends and have nothing to do with your company's performance. The stock market from time to time tends to unreasonably overprice your stock or severely underprice it. So-called momentum investing, caused primarily by day-traders, can occasionally cause wild price gyrations.

During the period that your stock is severely underpriced, your company has the ability to repurchase its stock on the stock market at these depressed prices, provided you have been wise enough to retain a cash reserve. Likewise, during the period that your stock is unreasonably overpriced, you can sell stock on very favorable terms. None of these opportunities are available to a private company.

6. *Enhanced ability to grow through acquisitions.* The cash proceeds from the IPO can be used to make acquisitions to help your company grow faster. Indeed, underwriters prefer companies that can use the IPO proceeds to grow the business. A publicly traded company also may grow by using its own stock to make acquisitions. This option is generally not available to a private company that is forced to use cash or notes for acquisitions. Private company stock is not an attractive form of consideration to a seller because it lacks liquidity.

Your company's ability to use stock instead of cash as an acquisition currency will permit greater growth opportunities than are available to competing private companies.

7. *Enhanced ability to borrow; no personal guarantees.*   When your company sells stock, it increases its net worth and improves its debt-to-equity ratio. This should allow your company to borrow money on more favorable terms in the future.

The principals of private companies are often required to personally guarantee bank loans made to their companies. Once your company is public, banks and other financial institutions are less likely to require any personal guarantees.

8. *Enhanced ability to raise equity.*   If your company continues to grow, you will eventually need additional equity financing. If your stock performs well in the stock market, you will be able to sell additional stock on favorable terms.

You may be able to raise equity quickly if the volume of your company's stock trading permits it to attract equity in so-called PIPE transactions (private investment, public equity). In a PIPE transaction, your company sells equity to hedge funds and other institutional equity investors on a private placement basis at a discount below its then market price, together with investor registration rights, which permit the investor to resell the stock in the public marketplace.

However, if your stock is not heavily traded or is not followed by securities analysts because your company is too small, it is likely that the stock will fall below the IPO price and make it more difficult to raise additional equity in either PIPE or other transactions. Many smaller companies today are not followed by securities analysts and, as a result, their prices have drifted below the IPO price.

9. *Attracting and retaining key employees.*   Stock options offered by emerging public companies have much appeal and can help you to recruit or retain well-qualified executives and motivate your employee-shareholders. Although it is likely that the accounting for such options will require expensing of such options in the future, the benefit of using stock options to attract and retain key employees will remain.

10. *Liquidity and valuation.*   Once your company goes public, a market is established for your stock and you will have an effective way of valuing that stock. Subject to Rule 144, you can sell whenever the need arises.

Also, your stock prices can easily be followed. Prices are quoted daily and many newspapers print them.

11. *Estate planning.*   Many private companies have to be sold upon the death of their founder in order to pay death taxes. This may prevent you from passing the ownership of your private company to your family or to key employees. Founders of private companies sometimes fund death taxes by maintaining large life insurance policies. However, the premiums on these life insurance policies can be a significant drain on the business. These premiums are not deductible for federal income tax purposes. If your company's stock is publicly traded, your estate will have a liquid asset with which to pay death taxes.

THE DISADVANTAGES

The major disadvantages of going public are as follows:

1. *Expense.*   The cost of going public is substantial, both initially and on an ongoing basis. As for the initial costs, the underwriters' discount or commission can run as high as 10 percent or more of the total offering.

In addition, you can incur out-of-pocket expenses of $1.5 million or more for even a small offering of $50 million of your securities. If as a private company you do not have audited financial statements from a large accounting firm, your IPO accounting bill can substantially balloon to the $1.5 million figure. If the offering is complicated or there is significant corporate restructuring involved, your costs can also skyrocket. The $2.5 billion IPO of China Life Insurance Company Ltd. cost over $58 million (excluding underwriters' discounts). If your IPO is cancelled at the last minute, you will be liable for substantial costs. However, it is typical to discount professional fees and printing costs in the event of a failed IPO.

On an ongoing basis, regulatory reporting requirements, stockholders' meetings, investor relations, and other expenses of being public can run substantially more than $200,000 annually even for a small public company, and are much higher for most public companies. Included in this figure are additional auditing costs (including the evaluation of internal controls) that will undoubtedly rise when you convert from a private to a public company because of the significant additional time required to comply with SEC financial disclosure requirements and the requirements of the Public Company Accounting Oversight Board established under the Sarbanes-Oxley Act of 2002. Printing and distributing your annual and quarterly reports, proxy statements, and stock certificates can be extremely costly if you choose to use expensive glossy, colorful printing processes and first class mail. These costs are in addition to your management time, which can be considerable.

You will need independent directors (typically three) to satisfy the listing requirements for Nasdaq or The New York Stock Exchange, although you will have up to one year after your IPO to find your third director. You should expect to spend at least $100,000 per year for these three directors (collectively).

There is, in addition, a significant amount of initial time and effort required to establish and maintain disclosure controls and procedures and internal control over financial reporting sufficient to satisfy the requirements of the federal securities laws as amended by the Sarbanes-Oxley Act of 2002. The initial establishment of these disclosure and internal controls can run well over $300,000 even for a very small public company and a multiple of that figure for larger public companies, although this should be a one-time expense.

You may need to hire additional financial and accounting personnel to help prepare your company's financial disclosures. Likewise, you may be required to hire a shareholder relations employee and to upgrade the quality of existing financial and accounting employees. These are all additional hidden costs of going public.

A number of smaller public companies have developed methods of minimizing their ongoing costs of being public. These methods include the judicious use of outside professionals, sending bare-bones annual and quarterly reports to shareholders, using inexpensive techniques to reproduce and mail these shareholder reports (such as third class mail), avoiding expensive shareholders' meetings, and so forth. Minimizing such expenses can help reduce your ongoing costs (exclusive of director and officer liability insurance).

Director and officer liability insurance is a must for public companies. Enron and other corporate corruption scandals have significantly increased the cost of this insurance. A $10 million policy with a $500,000 retention can cost over $300,000 per year.

A survey of 85 companies with annual revenue under $1 billion reported that their average cost of being public was $2.86 million in 2003, with the dominant costs being $850,000 for directors and officers liability insurance, $824,000 for accounting costs, and $468,000 for legal costs. Smaller companies (i.e., $100 million or less in revenue and market capitalization) should be able to substantially reduce this overall cost of being public, with the total cost being significantly less than $1 million per year. Based on a survey of 26 public companies with annual revenues of $1 billion and over, the cost of being public was $7.4 million.

2. *Pressure to maintain growth pattern.*   You will be subject to considerable pressure to maintain the growth rate you have established, particularly from analysts who follow your company's stock. If your sales or earnings deviate from an upward trend, analysts may recommend that your stock be sold and investors may become apprehensive and sell their stock, driving down its price. These price declines can be severe as investors flee your stock en masse. You may not have the capital with which to buy back the stock at these depressed prices. As a result, you will have unhappy stockholders.

You must report operating results quarterly. People will thus evaluate the company on a quarterly, rather than on an annual, basis. This intensifies the pressure and shortens your planning and operating horizons significantly. The pressure may tempt you to make short-term decisions that could have a harmful long-term impact on the company.

3. *Orphan public companies.*   Many smaller public companies are not followed by analysts, as they prefer companies with market capitalizations above $250 million. If after the IPO your company is unable to attract the attention of analysts, it is likely that your stock price will fall below the IPO price and you will have unhappy shareholders. You may even have difficulty attracting market makers to your stock. Such public companies are sometimes called orphan companies.

If your company becomes an orphan, it would be difficult to raise additional equity or use your stock as an acquisition currency without significantly diluting your existing shareholders. Thus, although your company will enjoy the benefits of the additional equity capital from the IPO, many of the other advantages of the IPO would be lost. You may ultimately have to consider a sale of the company or taking it private in a management buyout.

4. *Disclosure of information.*   Your company's operations and financial situation are open to public scrutiny. Information concerning the company, officers, directors, and certain shareholders—information not ordinarily disclosed by privately held companies—will now be available to competitors, customers, employees, and others. Information such as your company's sales, profits, your competitive edge, material contracts with major customers, and the salaries and perquisites of the chief executive officer and certain highly paid executive officers must be disclosed not only when you initially go public, but also on a continuing basis.

The SEC staff has a procedure to authorize confidential treatment for documents you file. However, you must apply to the SEC early in the IPO registration process to avoid holding up the IPO. Very sensitive information can typically be excluded from public scrutiny.

The SEC-mandated disclosures should not be a major concern to most businesses. Your competitors may already possess a lot more information about you than you realize, which may have been revealed by customers, suppliers, and former employees. Many companies already provide some financial information to business credit agencies. Although public companies disclose much more financial information than private companies, the additional information is not necessarily a competitive disadvantage.

In general, public companies are only required to disclose information that is material to investors. Information about specific customers for your products do not have to be disclosed unless the customer's purchases are such a high percentage of your total sales as to be material to investors. Likewise, the exact profitability of specific products does not normally have to be disclosed, provided the product lines do not constitute a separate industry segment for financial reporting purposes. Management is given reasonable discretion in determining whether its business includes separately reportable industry segments. Accordingly, it is usually possible to avoid disclosure of the exact profitability of separate product lines.

5. *Loss of control.*   If a sufficiently large proportion of your shares is sold to the public, you may be threatened with the loss of control of

the company. Once your company is publicly held, the potential exists for further dilution of your control through subsequent public offerings and acquisitions. Likewise, you may be subject to a hostile tender offer.

This disadvantage can be alleviated by the careful inclusion of antitakeover provisions in your charter or by creating two classes of stock with disproportionate voting rights. Although there are few, if any, antitakeover defenses that are completely, legally foolproof, some defenses can be very effective against raiders. Defenses that deprive the raiders of voting power or that otherwise penalize the raiders are particularly effective.

Many underwriters, particularly prestigious underwriters, object to antitakeover defenses in the charter of IPO companies. Such defenses may make it more difficult to attract certain institutional investors. This may result in the IPO selling at a discount ranging from 5 percent to 20 percent, or not selling at all. The few underwriters who do not primarily sell to institutional investors are usually more relaxed about these clauses.

What is a normal antitakeover defense and what is unusual are typically matters of negotiation with the underwriter. For example, some underwriters object to the staggering of the terms of the board of directors. Others will not. In general, antitakeover provisions, which are part of state law and require special shareholder action to avoid, will usually be accepted by underwriters.

Even if antitakeover defenses cannot be inserted into your charter prior to your IPO, you can usually amend your charter after your IPO to insert these defenses, although it is likely that, in today's environment, you will face shareholder opposition. This should be accomplished before your personal stock ownership falls below 50 percent of the outstanding stock.

6. *Shareholder lawsuits.*   Public companies and their directors, officers, and controlling shareholders are susceptible to being sued by the public shareholders. Shareholder class action lawsuits typically follow a significant drop in the market price of your company's stock, caused by adverse news about your company. The theory of these lawsuits is that your company knew or should have known of the adverse news and had a duty to publicize it at an earlier date than the date the news actually became public. The lawsuit will allege that failure to publicize the information earlier constitutes "fraud on the market."

Overly optimistic or exaggerated statements contained in your company's reports to shareholders or in press releases are usually cited in these lawsuits to support the allegations. These statements are typically the result of a misguided attempt to generate interest in your company.

Public companies can prevent such lawsuits, or at least win them if brought, only by a careful program of promptly disclosing adverse news to the trading markets and by avoiding overly optimistic or exaggerated comments in shareholder and press releases. This requires that you be sensitive to the need for such disclosures.

Of course, everyone makes a mistake occasionally, so it is a good idea to obtain sufficient director and officer liability insurance to cover this risk. Some private companies already maintain this insurance, but usually at lower cost. Thus, only the extra insurance premium costs of being public should be considered the real disadvantage of an IPO.

7. *Estate tax disadvantage.*   One of the advantages of an IPO is to create sufficient liquidity to pay death taxes. However, there is a concomitant disadvantage. It is more difficult to obtain a low estate tax valuation for a publicly traded stock than for the stock of a private company. This is true because the public market tends to value stocks on a multiple of earnings basis, rather than on a book value basis.

CHAPTER TWENTY-ONE

VALUING INTERNET BUSINESS

T he year 2000 may not have been the end of the world, but don't tell that to investors in Internet-related stocks. Dot-coms peaked and then plummeted in 2000, causing momentum investors to wonder what happened, and value investors to say, "I told you so." But is it so simple? Rivers of ink—most of it cyber-ink—have been spilled in 2000 in an attempt to justify or defame the valuation of so-called New Economy, e-commerce, or dot-com stocks. This chapter will attempt to explore the issues surrounding the valuation of dot-coms.

There are dozens of different kinds of Internet-related companies, but most of them fall, however loosely, into one of three categories: business-to-consumer (B2C), business-to-business (B2B), and Internet service companies.

B2C

Business-to-consumer companies are among the most prominent and well-known Internet companies (and stocks). The initial Internet

This chapter was written by Ken Patton and Matt Crow, Mercer Capital Management, Inc. (Memphis, Tennessee); www.mercercapital.com. This chapter was originally written in 2000 and appeared in Lipman, *The Complete Guide to Valuing & Selling Your Business.*

stock mania began with B2C stocks, as online retailers rapidly built brand names and purportedly threatened traditional brick and mortar companies. Among the more noteworthy B2C stocks is Amazon, whose web site was initially considered a deathblow to traditional booksellers. When a traditional bookseller, Barnes & Noble, set up its own online retail company, the focus shifted to whether upstarts could compete against established retailers with a web presence. Amazon lost market value when barnesandnoble.com went online and its stock started trading. Since then, Amazon has continued to dominate the space (or niche), but neither stock has performed particularly well.

Several significant B2C stocks, with their 2000 relative performance, are presented in this chapter, as compared to the performance of the S&P 500.

The underperformance of this group as compared to the S&P 500 is striking, with the standout performance being that of Priceline.com. Priceline opened in 2000 at just over $47 per share, reached a high of about $95 per share in early March, and then plummeted to close the year at just over $1 per share. Bellwether B2C stock Amazon opened the year at over $70 per share and fell steadily throughout 2000, closing the year at just over $15 per share. More marginal B2C players faired worse. In 2000 eToys opened at about $26 per share, but ended the year trading at less than 25 cents per share, a 99 percent decline in value during 2000.

B2B

Internet-based business-to-business companies sell goods and services to other companies. The Internet is touted as a lower-cost method of selling and sourcing, offering real time data to buyers and sellers, auction-style pricing, inventory management, and so on. As the B2C story began wearing thin, many Internet investors sought the real value of the Internet in B2B, because companies needed to use it to respond to price pressure from an increasing deflationary marketplace. Unfortunately, the market has not emerged as rapidly as investors had initially hoped. And, in the end, the price charts for 2000 for most B2B companies did not differ much from those of the B2C companies shown earlier.

One of the most touted stocks in the B2B space was Ventro,

whose Chemdex marketplace was supposed to create a huge vertical trade community, matching buyers and sellers in the market for life science enterprises, researchers, and suppliers. But Ventro announced late in the year that it would shutter Chemdex, and its stock, which reached a high in February of over $243 per share, closed the year at less than $1.

INTERNET SERVICE COMPANIES

The miscellaneous category of the dot-com world could loosely be termed the Internet service companies. These include providers of Internet access, such as America Online (AOL); web portals such as Yahoo!; Internet development companies, or incubators, such as CMGI; and more unusual companies that provide a specific service such as Cybercash or Netcentives. Generally, these companies are more developed than B2B or B2C companies and, as a result, faired better, on average, than these other spaces.

Despite underperforming the S&P 500, AOL managed to end the year down about 50 percent, a price performance that most other dot-coms could only dream of. Why? Well, how is AOL different? For one thing, it's been around for years, not months. It has a real track record, not just a projection. It already has a large base of reasonably satisfied customers. And, most important, it has sales and net income in the billions of dollars. Today, not ten years from now. Don't take that as a tout for AOL; at the end of 2000, it was still priced at over 50 times trailing earnings. But the fact that you can affix a double-digit price/earnings (P/E) ratio to the stock undoubtedly kept it from falling as far as other dot-coms in 2000.

Now that we've reviewed the basic components of the dot-com world, let's entertain two major schools of thought: (1) dot-coms are different; and (2) dot-coms are no different.

ONE PERSPECTIVE: DOT-COMS ARE DIFFERENT

Some companies just aren't ready for a typical capitalization of earnings model. Most securities analysts are trained to examine a company's earnings stream and apply a multiplier to get an answer. Value equals earnings times a P/E ratio. Certain ranges of earnings multiples and cash flow multiples are taught as being almost universal. Example: just as everyone likes bacon and eggs for breakfast, everyone thinks 4 to 8 times EBITDA is reasonable.

Fortunately, we now have a new crop of stocks that, despite their fall from grace in the market, persist in their challenge to many traditional notions of valuation.

Don't Fight the Tape

An emerging-stage company has no earnings and merely has an idea that may be useful to a particular market segment within two or three years; a traditional analyst is likely to assign only a speculative value to the enterprise. This view, however, has been contradicted by millions of professional and private investors who have poured billions of dollars into a group of information technology stocks that, although maybe not in the emerging stage, are certainly still in the development stage. The analyst who consults his or her valuation cookbook finds no help in justifying such lofty multiples. But it would be wrong to simply dismiss the buying and selling of millions of investors with trillions of dollars of real money on the line. As the saying goes, "Money is smart," meaning that the investing public doesn't make a habit of supporting lofty valuations without a reason. Speaking more technically, we are reminded that the efficient market hypothesis generally purports that stocks are valued by the marketplace for a reason.

So, what does this mean to the valuation of New Economy stocks? If a stock is valued as an earnings stream times a multiple, we must delve into the rationale for both to understand the valuation of a New Economy stock. It may be not only that the multiples are skewed, but that the reported financial results prepared in accordance with generally accepted accounting principals (GAAP) are also skewed.

Maybe We're Missing Something

GAAP is not designed for the New Economy. Like Rene Magritte's painting *Ceci n'est pas une pomme* ("This is not an apple"—i.e., it's a picture of an apple), analysts have to be cognizant of the fact that audited financial statements are a *representation* of a company's financial results, not the results themselves. The constructs of depreciation and amortization favor Old Economy stocks, allowing asset-intensive businesses to write off the costs of bricks and mortar over their useful lives.

A start-up manufacturing concern can spend millions on highly specialized buildings and equipment. If it uses straight-line depreciation and an average useful life of fifteen years, only about 6 percent of the cost of its capital investment is deducted from earnings each year as depreciation. This asset base is supposed to provide some comfort to investors in the event of a downturn in the business. But is that reasonable? If the manufacturing concern goes out of business, its highly specialized equipment may have very little value in liquidation. And if the local economy is generally depressed, its real estate could have few buyers. Despite this, GAAP allows such a company to report a substantial asset base and to charge very little of it to quarterly and annual earnings.

New Economy stocks, on the other hand, tend to make their capital investment in systems, people, and brand image. GAAP does not favor these sorts of investments. Although you might be able to capitalize some systems development (software and hardware infrastructure), the useful life over which it would be amortized would probably be short—say, five years—and thus 20 percent of the cost (on a straight-line basis) would be deducted from earnings each year. Spending on people (compensation expense) and image building (advertising) cannot be capitalized, despite the fact that their value may extend well beyond one year.

Nothing New

If this sounds crazy, think about Coca-Cola. We don't have access to the early financial statements of the soft-drink maker, but no doubt the market value of its stock was built on a very aggressive advertising campaign. Today, its operations consist primarily of advertising and carbonated sugar water. It still takes quite a lot of advertising to maintain and refine the image of Coke, but the impact is far less than if the company were trying to establish a dominant global brand identity from scratch. Coca-Cola is not a New Economy stock, but the development of the small soft-drink maker into a global brand followed the same pattern that Amazon or Yahoo! have followed. Time will tell whether or not these New Economy stocks will have the lasting brand image of Coca-Cola; it is likely that most will not.

Now think about Ford Motor Company. Again, we don't have access to Ford's early financial statements, but the development years in which Ford aggressively built factories to launch the Model-T were likely characterized by break-even or positive GAAP earnings, because those costs could be capitalized and depreciated over many years. Its cash earnings, however, were very likely negative in the early years. Yes, Ford did at least have assets to back up its value during the developmental stage. But what would an automotive factory have been worth ninety years ago if no one had wanted to buy cars?

Fortune magazine columnist Geoffrey Colvin (*The Net's Hidden Profits*: April 17, 2000) has noted that that if Amazon could capitalize its investment in intangibles, it would have reported a profit of over $400 million in 1999 versus its reported GAAP losses of –$720 million. That's over $1 per share. As of this writing, Amazon is trading at less than $15 per share, implying a fairly modest P/E ratio.

We still think investors buy companies for their earning power, but it's important not to be too restrictive in what constitutes earning power or what a rational expectation for earning power might be. Money is indeed smart, and we will continue to be open to learning from the wisdom of millions of investors, many of whom consistently manage to stay one step ahead of professional securities analysts.

ANOTHER PERSPECTIVE: DOT-COMS ARE NO DIFFERENT

It was the best of business plans; it was the worst of business plans. With due respect to Charles Dickens, let us tell *A Tale of Two Business Plans*, one that worked, one that did not. The tale is one of two business-to-consumer retailers in the household wares space, which were founded about the same time (less than two years ago).One is now acquiring the other.

The Founders

DustCollectors.com (not the real name, obviously) was formed in early 1999 by experienced U.S.-based importers of inexpensive bathroom accessories made in Eastern Europe. A seasoned and well-connected team of highly successful investors formed DustCollectors.com. With decades of experience and major connections to production facilities throughout Eastern Europe, the investor group sought an e-commerce outlet to sell its wares. The investor group had the financial capacity to make it happen, and although the group members had no background in e-commerce specifically, such experience can be bought.

Wallpaper4You.com (again, not the real name) was also formed in early 1999 by an experienced retailer of wall covering products. Unlike DustCollectors.com, Wallpaper4You.com was not established by way of enormous capital commitments. According to the founder: "When we started, we didn't know if it was going to be a real business, so we didn't want anyone else's money."

Business Plan

DustCollectors.com planned to be a major player in household wares and accessories. The investor group paid big money to hire a large and experienced team of financial wizards, information technology jocks, and e-commerce pros. You've heard the standard rationale: "Put twenty-five brilliant people in a room and good things will happen." "You get what you pay for." "Plan for success." And so on.

In exchange for an excessively fat contract, the CEO of DustCollectors.com gave the investor group an excessively fat financial projection: $25 million in sales was projected in the first year, *ex nihilo nihil fit*. Lewis Carroll, author of *Alice's Adventures in Wonderland*, would have been proud. That's a lot of soap dishes. No doubt Cheshire cat grins all around. DustCollectors.com raised lots of venture capital from a group of sophisticated investors eager to get in on the deal.

Wallpaper4You.com planned to make money. It had to. Although its founder had had a successful career retailing wall coverings to consumers and he could afford to fund the venture, he was still spending his own money. And he expected a return.

Execution

DustCollectors.com went first class. It hired a large and expensive management team. It put up a modest web site, initially, but signed a *mid-seven-figure* contract to have a fabulous web site designed (now we know who's really making money from e-commerce). The firm leased first-class office space. More important, the importer who initially started the venture engaged in what is commonly known as "channel-stuffing." He loaded DustCollectors.com with millions of dollars in inventory. After all, $25 million in sales requires ready inventory to meet customer demands. If inventory turns, say, four times a year, this mean's that the company will need over $6 million at retail—say, $3 million at wholesale. The company inventoried hundreds of SKUs (stock keeping units) and hired an expensive team of inventory managers to watch it. To attract customers, the company sharply discounted its wares. The management team was focused on building a customer base, getting eyes to look at its web site. It's called a land grab.

Wallpaper4You.com was pay as you go. The founder and his wife acted as the entire management team. They had a user-friendly web site built for the low five figures. They sent orders to the manufacturers to drop ship to consumers so they wouldn't have to carry any inventory. They hired as few people as possible and operated out of less-than-glamorous facilities. "I'm a retailer," said the founder, "nothing unusual about that." Wallpaper4You.com was price competitive but essentially sought to charge market rates and focus on customer service. The firm splurged and hired a team of customer service reps to answer an 800 number. Even in cyberspace, building repeat and referral business requires people to provide customer service, reasoned the founder.

Outcome

DustCollectors.com did not produce revenue as expected. Average sales were less than 100 per day and about $50 per sale. Year one sales were closer to $2 million, far short of the planned $25 million. Costs were eating them alive—financing inventory, paying salaries and rent, and paying off the multimillion dollar web site (which was never turned on, by the way). By the spring of 2000, just over a year after the company started, its cash burn (the rate of use of its start-up capital) would only be extinguished by running out of fuel. Globally, investor exuberance about e-commerce, especially B2C, was gone. The company's investors wouldn't throw good money after bad. They went looking for buyers but found none. In mid-1999, the company probably would have been a successful IPO; nine months later, it was facing liquidation. The company started looking for strategic alternatives and cut staff aggressively.

Yet Wallpaper4You.com still thrives. Its retail space was already successful on a catalog basis, so the lower cost of operating a web-based business worked. Its cash burn stabilized early. The company made money in 2000. It started looking to acquire a less fortunate web-based retailer with lots of traffic to channel customers to its site.

Wallpaper4You.com considered other household products that lent themselves to its style of retailing and approached DustCollectors.com with an offer. The company agreed to assume DustCollectors.com's operating assets and liabilities in exchange for an interest in Wallpaper4You.com.

DustCollectors.com avoided bankruptcy and got a piece of a business with a future. Wallpaper4You.com got 50,000 additional unique users per month and connections to very successful importers.

The Moral of the Story

Remember, all companies have to obey the primary law of financial physics: Investors expect a return. The more they invest, they more they expect to make. Return and risk are expected to rise in concert. Web-based commerce is only an outlet. Catalog retail is generally more efficient than brick-and-mortar retail. Web retail is generally more efficient than catalog retail (or can be). Opportunity in the New Economy is about efficiency: maximizing output and minimizing input.

As securities analysts, we have to be cognizant of the value of a business plan to generate a profit. Mercer Capital has had a web site for over five years now—we were early to claim our cubic foot of cyberspace. But we know the limitations of e-commerce.

VALUING A DOT-COM: SO, WHERE ARE WE NOW?

The valuation of a dot-com requires a modest degree of perspective. The valuation of anything is the present value of all of the future benefits the asset is expected to generate. Appraisers and business owners measure that value by one of three approaches: cost, income, or market.

The cost approach is based upon the net value of invested assets. This approach has little usefulness in the valuation of a dot-com. The income approach may be a discounted future benefits method or the capitalization of a measure of cash flow. As we will see, each of these methods can be useful. The market approach encompasses methods that derive value from comparison of the subject company or business interests to actual transactions in the marketplace.

The determination of future benefits begins with an examination of historical results and the business plan. Because the typical Internet-related company has little history, the focus turns to the business plan. Markets for new entrants are created by the reaction of customers, the response of existing competitors, and the success of the new company in meeting its customers' needs. During periods of rapidly changing business conditions, the company's business plan must articulate a strategy for success that takes the company in the right direction on the right timelines. In the case of the dot-coms, the pressure to succeed converted traditional business plans into something more akin to an option in the financial markets. The potential for gain was very high; however, the risks were commensurate and the timing had to be right. It was not enough to do the right things; they had to be done at exactly the right time.

The Theme Was Speed

During 1999 and 2000, there was a massive rush to succeed under the belief that only a limited number of companies could ultimately be successful in each space. Furthermore, that belief was based upon ever-changing assessments about the size of the marketplace for any product or service. Initially, many people thought the Internet would utterly transform the business landscape in a very short period of time. Furthermore, the dot-coms would do it at the expense of the existing brick-and-mortar businesses.

Valuation in a rapidly changing environment can be traced to rational measures as well as emotion. Financial markets are never perfect; furthermore, valuation indicators from the dot-com market are generally less applicable than for more-established industries. It is always important in analyzing market value to look at valuation from two perspectives (1) relative valuation within the industry segment; and (2) absolute valuation, which is a comparison of value between the industry segment and the broader market. The valuation of a particular company within the industry may be perfectly sane and explainable in comparison to other companies in the industry, but the valuation might make no sense at all when compared to the overall market. Internet stocks have certainly experienced all of these phenomena in the past eighteen months.

From Gas to Liquid to Solid

Valuation methods for an Internet-related company will parallel the stages of the company's development: (1) development stage; (2) activity measures; (3) revenue or gross profit; and (4) profits. Spatially, we move from an idea (development stage) to execution of that idea (activity measures—hits, etc.), to the top of the income statement (revenue or gross profits) and then march down the income statement until we get to the magical net income line (profits). Or, back to the theme of financial physics, we move from gas (the idea) to liquid (the idea in motion) to solid (profits). First is the pure venture capital and development stage, where little more exists than an idea in search of financial resources to implement it. Belief in success may be grounded in confidence in management, the pizzazz of the idea, and the timing of the investment. The latter factor may be the most important, yet the most difficult to measure. Owners of many web-based businesses thought they were "first" or "alone" in their space, only to find others equally advanced in developing competitive services. Valuation at this stage is often based on a belief that the business idea somehow conveys the certainty of future cash flows, which support the value. If nothing else, there was the plan to go public, as value is in the eye of the beholder. Valuations in these circumstances can be driven by the emotions of others. Some people see value where others don't. The mechanics of such a valuation are even unhinged from the most optimistic financial projections. And financing (going public) gets confused with wealth creation. Time is always the enemy of investment returns, but it is more so with any Internet investment.

The second phase of company valuation is related to activity measures. At this point, the business is generating some type of customer activity, which presumably will ultimately generate profitability. Examples include "hits," "visits," and "page views" to the web site; conversion of visits to orders; or other traffic measures. In all cases the exposure of the potential customer to the web site seemed to be the paramount driver of value. Whether or not the Internet company was organized to handle the order flow was secondary (this was the fatal flaw of many e-tailers during Christmas 1999). The use of activity measures can be very helpful in establishing the relative value of a dot-com. It does little to assess absolute value, however. Relative value measures are good when a transaction is imminent, but they can become virtually useless if it will be months or years before a liquidity event. Evaluations during this stage require an in-depth analysis of the cash burn rate as well. Does the company have the financial staying power to reach profitability?

The third phase of valuation occurs when the business is generating revenue but not to the level of accounting profits or positive cash flow. At this stage, total capital to revenue (total equity and total debt divided by revenue) and total capital to gross profits are two very common measures of value. Companies at this stage have a greater probability of earnings and are most likely able to validate the business model. The cash burn rate requires attention here as well, however.

The final stage of valuation occurs when the business generates positive cash flow. At this point, more traditional measures are in order. Price/cash flow, price/earnings ratio, and discounted cash flow models (with more reasonable assumptions) can and will be used to determine value.

ASSUMING THE FUTURE

The great pitfall in the valuation of Internet businesses is the need to ultimately rely on some sort of discounted cash flow analysis to arrive at the financial value of the business. Because few dot-coms have made it to the point that they can be valued using a single period capitalization model, almost all valuations of Internet companies will involve some projection into a very cloudy future. Unlike mature companies, or at least start-ups in mature industries, most Internet businesses are being founded on a vision of a future for which we have no precedent. It may not be unreasonable to project rapid growth in revenues and, ultimately, earnings for an Internet company, but to value such a projection requires a similarly high discount rate to account for the risk inherent in achieving such expectations. If expectations are not realistic, the variability of returns to the investor can be dramatic, especially with a dot-com. Why? Because most Internet companies do not project profitability until far into the future. If profitability is less than expected, the time value of money will rapidly destroy returns (and value). For example, consider the three possible scenarios for the projection of cash flow for a dot-com in Table 21.1:

1. Our subject company, ACMEwidgets.com, presents us with three possible scenarios. In Scenario 1, the company breaks even in year three and makes $125 in year 10, which the market is expected to reward with a terminal multiple of 10 times cash flow. Cumulatively, the investors receive interim cash flows totaling $385 and a terminal value of $1,250. Using a discount rate of 30 percent and mid-year discounting convention, this results in a total value of $146.

2. In Scenario 2, the discount rate is the same, but the company breaks even one year later, in year four, and profitability builds more slowly. As a result, the market rewards the company with a *lower* multiple on the year ten cash flow (because the company is showing lower growth prospects) and the total value is $82, almost 45 percent less than the concluded value in Scenario 1.

3. Scenario 3 is less optimistic, and results in a total value of $31 or almost 80 percent less than the concluded value in Scenario 1. Note that the difference in conclusions of value results largely from timing. The deferred profitability of Scenarios 2 and 3 results in the time value of money (our discount rate of 30 percent) taking a bigger bite out of those future profits. And slower growth in profits prompts the market to reward Scenarios 2 and 3 with lower multiples on year ten cash flows, resulting in lower terminal values.

This certainly explains some of the volatility in pricing of these stocks in 2000. Investors who thought their dot-com was a Scenario 1 stock would react negatively to any lowering of expectations. A small change in the timing of profit growth has a huge impact on value when such profits are already far off. So, if investors priced a stock like it had Scenario 1 cash flows (at $146) and then came to believe that Scenario 3 was more likely, the 80 percent decrease in value to $31 would only be expected. The performance of many public dot-coms in 2000 bore witness to this.

Some analysts advocate valuation of these types of scenarios using

TABLE 21.1 ACMEWIDGETS.COM VALUATION OF THREE CASH FLOW PROJECTIONS*

Period	1	2	3	4	5	6	7	8	9	10	Total Interim CF	Terminal CF Multiple	Terminal Value	Total Value
Scenario 1														
Cash Flow	($10)	($5)	$0	$5	$15	$30	$50	$75	$100	$125	$385	10.0	$1,250	
Present Value	*($9)*	*($3)*	*$0*	*$2*	*$5*	*$7*	*$9*	*$10*	*$11*	*$10*			*$103*	*$146*
Scenario 2														
Cash Flow	($15)	($10)	($5)	$0	$10	$15	$25	$35	$50	$100	$205	9.0	$900	
Present Value	*($13)*	*($7)*	*($3)*	*$0*	*$3*	*$4*	*$5*	*$5*	*$5*	*$8*			*$74*	*$82*
Scenario 3														
Cash Flow	($25)	($15)	($10)	($5)	$0	$10	$15	$25	$50	$75	$120	8.0	$600	
Present Value	*($22)*	*($10)*	*($5)*	*($2)*	*$0*	*$2*	*$3*	*$3*	*$5*	*$6*			*$50*	*$31*

*Discount rate of 30% assumed for present value using mid-year convention.

a probability weighted average to reach a conclusion of value. In other words, if there is reason to think that there is a 30 percent chance of Scenario 1 being correct, a 50 percent chance of Scenario 2 being correct, and a 20 percent chance of Scenario 3 being correct, then the conclusion of value would be about $91 ((30% × $146) + (50% × $82) + (20% × $31) = $91). This can be helpful if there is a reason to assign such weights. Otherwise, it's just a way to hide uncertainty behind a veil of equations.

Another way to look at valuation is to assess the sensitivity of the rate of return to the ultimate concluded value. See Table 21.2.

For example, if an investor ultimately believes Scenario 2 and pays $82 for an interest in ACMEwidgets.com, and the Scenario 2 cash flows are achieved as expected, the internal rate of return to the investor will be equivalent to the discount rate, or 30 percent. However, if the higher cash flows of Scenario 1 are achieved, the investor who paid $82 will enjoy a higher rate of return on the order of 38 percent. If returns are lower, as projected in Scenario 3, the rate of return will be 22 percent. Such analysis can be helpful for stress testing the sensitivity of assumptions. In the end, no matter how elegant the assumptions, when the future becomes fact, all that matters to investors is that the assumptions were predictive.

Going Forward

We have seen only the first round of Internet start-ups. The future will continue to evolve at a rapid pace, which means that even existing Internet companies will have to change dramatically to assure

TABLE 21.2   ACMEwidgets.com

Scenario 2			
Total Value	$82	Rate of Return if Scenario 1 Cash Flows Achieved	38%
		Rate of Return if Scenario 2 Cash Flows Achieved	30%
		Rate of Return if Scenario 3 Cash Flows Achieved	22%

their survival. Valuation in today's environment must begin and end with a thorough analysis of the company's business plan. The Old Economy questions of "Who will I serve?" (customers); "How will I do it?" (internal organization); and "Will I make a profit?" (creation of value) have not been superseded by the New Economy. The Internet is a new medium for transacting business, but it must ultimately conform to fundamental rules of economics.

EPILOGUE

This chapter was originally written in late 2000. As we update it in August of 2004, we can make several new observations. E-commerce is not dead, but it has come to recognize that the fundamentals of economics and finance still apply, just as we predicted. In the short run, Internet-based companies can still be outliers to the market with regard to common valuation metrics, but in the long run the relationship between performance and price will be pulled together by the same gravity that has ruled the market since valuation became a topic of human inquiry.

As we draft this epilogue, the potentially momentous public offering of Google is supposedly weeks away. The implied valuation multiples for Google are reminiscent, maybe even nostalgic, of the market's assessment of similar companies in the late 1990s. But like retro clothing and classic rock stations, the repetition of this historical style of thinking has come with a difference: People are considerably more conscious of the relative pricing of electronic commerce companies and are quick to put them in context.

Web-based companies are now institutionalized; they are a fixture in the business community and their impact on the marketplace can now be historically characterized:

- The notion that businesses can persistently grow earnings by improving transactional efficiency both internally and externally was derived from the disruptive creativity of Internet commerce.
- The continued popularity of option-based compensation owes its genesis to web startups from the 1990s.
- The death of the suit as the default garment of business can be

attributed to the challenge made on the traditional office environment by Internet pioneers.

But with the ecstasy has come some correlative agony:

- The ultimate relationship between value and cash flow has not been rewritten. This has resulted in the closure of thousands of e-commerce companies and the loss of billions of investment dollars.

- The Financial Accounting Standards Board and the investment community are on the warpath to charge companies' income statements for the expense of equity-based compensation.

- The number of trampolines, pinball machines, and espresso bars in offices of e-commerce companies has not increased as appreciably as the number of these same items inventoried for business liquidations.

The number of active business-to-business (B2B) companies has fallen by 90 percent in the past four years. Service providers discovered that businesses wanted something more than just a lower price or allegedly more efficiency in the order process. Has this realization of a key business issue killed the B2B concept? Of course not. It just means that successful companies will focus on more than technology. The question of how the customer is served is more important than ever. B2B companies must find ways that incorporate the speed and efficiency of the Internet with the required level of customization expected by commercial customers. As the delusion of the late 1990s is replaced by the creativity of this decade, new business models will emerge that are likely to be very competitive with the old ways of doing business.

Growth in the consumer sector (B2C) has been more sustained and visible. Consumer transactions are a small but growing segment of all consumer transactions. Furthermore, the Internet has transformed some industries such as music and travel. Some service providers have become household words (eBay for example) as well as a permanent part of the landscape.

The pricing metrics, the price/earnings ratio for example, of successful B2C companies are currently high in comparison to the stock market in general. However, it is important to note that they are more in line with realistic growth prospects of the company rather than being wildly speculative as we observed in 1999 and 2000. Additionally, stock prices are moving in response to actual performance. As the fundamentals of e-commerce continue to improve, the outlook for successful companies will be good.

In closing, the business questions posed in the preceding section remain valid. Innovation will continue unabated, but recent history has clearly demonstrated that the fundamentals of business and economics remain unchanged.

PART VI

APPENDIXES

APPENDIX 1

SELECTED SALES OF BUSINESSES WITH SALE PRICES FROM $10 MILLION TO $3 BILLION

INTRODUCTION

This appendix contains valuation information on acquisition transactions in 49 different industries, for which both a purchase price and the seller's net earnings were available and whose sale prices were between $10 million and $3 billion. The appendix is not intended to be exhaustive, but merely to provide the reader with examples of recent transactions, many of which involve publicly-held entities. The information was taken from *Mergerstat Review 2004* and the reader is invited to visit www.mergerstat.com for the most recent merger and acquisition activity.

The following information is provided for each transaction:

1. The date of announcement is supplied along with the completion date, unless the deal was pending as of January 13, 2004.

2. The names of the buyer and seller are provided, along with a brief description.

3. Where a transaction involved the sale of a division or subsidiary, the unit sold is identified and appears in parentheses under the seller's name.

4. For sellers in the Banking & Finance Industry, total assets are indicated rather than annual revenues.

Reprinted with permission by FactSet Mergerstat, LLC.

5. The total price offered is listed in millions of dollars along with the method of payment.

6. The price to earnings ratio is offered.

7. The premium offered over the public market price of the seller, if any, is provided. (N/A in this column would typically mean that the seller was private.)

8. The price to book value is supplied.

9. "REM" after the seller's name represents the remaining equity percent being sought. These generally represent the final stage in a multistage acquisition. A percentage alone after the seller's name indicates the percent being sought.

10. "UMIN" after the seller's name represents an unspecified minority interest being sought.

11. "UMAJ" after the seller's name represents an unspecified majority interest being sought.

TRANSACTION ROSTER 2003

Announce Date / Close Date	Buyer Name / Seller Name (Unit Sold) / Business	Seller's Annual Revenues (Millions)	Price Offered (Millions)	Method of Payment	P/E Offered	Percent Premium Offered	Price to Book
1. AGRICULTURAL PRODUCTION							
11/17/03	Snyder Associated Cos. Inc. / Sylvan Inc. / Produces mushroom spawn and distributes other products used by mushroom growers	N/A	63.2	Cash	17.6	21.6	1.6
2. FOOD PROCESSING							
9/3/03	Ferrari Investments / Zapata Corp. / (Omega Protein Corp - REM 96%) / Manufactures fish oils, fish meals, and fish oil	118.7	220.8	Cash	19.9	58.6	1.6
3. BEVERAGES							
1/16/03 / 4/9/03	Constellation Brands Inc. / BRL Hardy Ltd. / Manufactures wine	488.6	1,050.8	Cash	25.8	41.9	2.8
4. APPAREL							
2/4/03 / 6/19/03	Perry Ellis International Corp. / Salant Corp. / Designs, manufactures, and imports menswear	232.9	84.9	Combo	19.0	130.3	0.9
5. TEXTILES							
9/16/03 / 12/16/03	WL Ross & Co LLC / Cone Mills Corp. / Produces denim fabrics and prints home furnishing fabrics	412.5	90.0	Cash	13.5	N/A	1.0

(continues)

Announce Date / Close Date	Buyer Name / Seller Name / (Unit Sold) / Business	Seller's Annual Revenues (Millions)	Price Offered (Millions)	Method of Payment	P/E Offered	Percent Premium Offered	Price to Book
6. TIMBER AND FOREST PRODUCTS							
3/5/03 7/1/03	Alcan Inc. Baltek Corp. Manufactures balsa wood products and operates a shrimp farming business	N/A	35.3	Cash	22.2	75.0	1.0
9. FURNITURE							
8/13/03 10/2/03	Flexsteel Industries Inc. DMI Furniture Inc. Manufactures, imports, and sells household and commercial office furniture	N/A	14.2	Cash	6.8	36.9	0.8
10. BUILDING PRODUCTS							
11/25/03 3/31/03	Berkshire Hathaway Inc. Oakwood Homes Corp Produces, sells, finances, and insures manufactured housing	926.6	373.0	Cash	NEG	N/A	N/A
11. HOUSEHOLD GOODS							
6/3/03 7/16/03	Audiovox Corp. ReCoton Corp. Develops, manufactures, and markets home and mobile audio products and accessories	N/A	40.0	Cash	53.1	N/A	N/A
12. PRINTING AND PUBLISHING							
3/3/03 4/10/03	Kinkos Inc. ImageX Inc. Provides technology for on-line management of branded communication materials	36.3	16.0	Cash	NEG	170.9	0.5
13. CHEMICALS, PAINTS, AND COATINGS							
4/7/03 12/9/03	CYAN Investments LLC Pacer Technology - REM 74.3% Manufactures advanced technology adhesives and sealants	25.9	15.1	Cash	19.6	71.6	1.7

14. DRUGS, MEDICAL SUPPLIES, AND EQUIPMENT

3/18/03	Integra LifeSciences Corp.	30.9	44.5	Cash	5.8	N/A	6.7
3/18/03	JARIT Surgical Instruments Inc.						
	Manufactures surgical instruments and medical equipment						

15. TOILETRIES AND COSMETICS

1/21/03	Energizer Holdings Inc.	651.7	930.0	Cash	24.3	N/A	3.3
3/28/03	Pfizer Inc.						
	(Schick-Wilkinson Sword)						
	Manufactures and markets shaving products						

16. PLASTICS AND RUBBER

3/10/03	PW Eagle Inc.	89.5	28.0	N/A	38.3	N/A	6.0
3/14/03	Uponor Oyj						
	(Uponor ETI Co.)						
	Manufactures plastic water and sewer pipe systems						

17. STONE, CLAY, AND GLASS

10/31/03	Private Group	N/A	40.3	Cash	NEG	80.2	0.9
1/31/04	Media Arts Group Inc. - 76.1%						
	Designs, manufactures, and retails products based on the works of Thomas Kinkade						

18. PRIMARY METAL PROCESSING

6/11/03	Reliance Steel & Aluminum Co.	121.8	220.0	Cash	6.6	N/A	1.6
7/2/03	Precision Strip Inc.						
	Provides premier metals processing services						

19. FABRICATED METAL PRODUCTS

10/13/03	Euramax International Ltd.	44.1	20.6	Cash	32.6	23.4	10.8
11/18/03	Berger Holdings Ltd.						
	Makes and sells roof drainage products						

(continues)

Announce Date Close Date	Buyer Name Seller Name (Unit Sold) Business	Seller's Annual Revenues (Millions)	Price Offered (Millions)	Method of Payment	P/E Offered	Percent Premium Offered	Price to Book
20. INDUSTRIAL AND FARM EQUIPMENT AND MACHINERY							
11/13/03 1/5/04	Gardner Denver Inc. Syltone PLC Designs, manufactures, and distributes equipment for the petroleum industry	124.1	80.1	Cash	15.6	28.9	2.7
21. CONSTRUCTION, MINING, AND OIL EQUIPMENT AND MACHINERY							
7/17/03 8/28/03	The Carlyle Group Inc. Kito Corp. - 91% Manufactures and markets hoists, cranes, and automated systems	175.6	44.6	Cash	15.9	28.5	0.4
23. AUTOS AND TRUCKS							
7/23/03 12/10/03	Armor Holdings Inc. Simula Inc. Designs and manufactures crash restraint and energy absorption technologies for motor vehicles	N/A	110.5	Combo	NEG	55.8	NEG
24. AUTOMOTIVE PRODUCTS AND ACCESSORIES							
5/6/03 7/31/03	Ripplewood Holdings LLC Asahi Tec Corp. - 51% Manufactures transmission cases and alloy wheels	365.0	37.4	N/A	NEG	10.7	0.5
25. ELECTRICAL EQUIPMENT							
12/18/03	The Stanley Works Blick PLC Designs, installs, and maintains security, communication, and time management solutions	109.6	161.1	Cash	23.5	3.6	5.3
26. OFFICE EQUIPMENT AND COMPUTER HARDWARE							
9/3/03 11/3/03	Electronics For Imaging Inc. T/R Systems Inc. Manufactures and sells printing machinery and electronic equipment	15.3	19.6	Cash	NEG	67.0	2.4

27. ELECTRONICS

6/9/03	ESS Technology Inc.					
6/9/03	Pictos Technologies Inc.	N/A	27.0	Cash	NEG	N/A	NEG
	Manufactures and markets digital imaging semiconductor products					

29. INSTRUMENTS AND PHOTOGRAPHIC EQUIPMENT

7/14/03	USA Technologies Inc.						
7/14/03	Bayview Technology Group LLC	5.8	9.8	Combo	19.7	N/A	5.1
	Develops and provides intelligent power control systems for vending machines						

30. TOYS AND RECREATIONAL PRODUCTS

11/26/03	K2 Inc.						
1/31/04	Fotoball USA Inc.	32.6	15.8	Stock	37.9	13.9	1.4
	Manufactures souvenirs and promotional products						

32. OIL AND GAS

7/1/03	Unit Corp.						
	PetroCorp. Inc.	31.3	182.0	Cash	21.0	N/A	1.3
	Explores and develops oil and gas properties						

33. MINING AND MINERALS

1/9/03	Ameralia Inc.						
2/21/03	IMC Global Inc.	14.8	20.7	Cash	NEG	N/A	0.9
	(White River NahColite Minerals LC)						
	Mines sodium bicarbonate						

34. TRANSPORTATION

3/25/03	Deutsche Post World Net AG						
8/15/03	Airborne Inc.	3,343.7	1,029.5	Cash	69.4	38.0	1.2
	Provides shipping and delivery services						

(continues)

Announce Date / Close Date	Buyer Name / Seller Name / (Unit Sold) / Business	Seller's Annual Revenues (Millions)	Price Offered (Millions)	Method of Payment	P/E Offered	Percent Premium Offered	Price to Book
35. COMMUNICATIONS							
7/31/03 7/31/03	National Auto Credit Inc. The Campus Group Inc. Provides satellite video-conferencing and corporate meeting services	12.6	15.5	Combo	4.7	N/A	33.3
36. BROADCASTING							
8/6/03 8/11/03	Private Group KirchHolding GmbH & Co. KG (ProSiebenSat 1 Media AG - 72%) Provides television broadcasting services	1,867.5	590.8	Cash	59.3	6.7	1.4
37. ELECTRIC, GAS, WATER, AND SANITARY SERVICES							
3/25/03 3/28/03	MarkWest Hydrocarbon Inc. Energy Spectrum Partners LP (Pinnacle Natural Gas Co.) Transmits and distributes natural gas	43.7	23.4	Cash	14.2	N/A	3.6
38. WHOLESALE AND DISTRIBUTION							
5/8/03 6/11/03	HT Hackney Co. Spartan Stores Inc. (L&L/Jiroch Co. / JF Walker Co.) Provides grocery distribution services	720.0	40.8	Cash	21.2	N/A	N/A
39. RETAIL							
3/18/03 4/15/03	American Co. in Merchandising Inc. Folz Vending Co. Owns and operates vending machines	54.2	22.0	Cash	35.8	N/A	3.2

40. BANKING AND FINANCE

Date	Company						
6/9/03	Community Bank System Inc.	N/A	69.5	Combo	18.1	9.0	2.7
11/24/03	Grange National Banc Corp.						
	National Commercial Bank						

41. INSURANCE

10/27/03	UnitedHealth Group Inc.	2,540.1	3,016.0	Combo	22.6	14.2	6.9
3/31/04	Mid Atlantic Medical Services Inc.						
	Provides health care plans and network services						

42. REAL ESTATE

11/3/03	General Electric Co.	260.4	1,730.5	Cash	13.8	6.2	1.7
	Sophia SA						
	Provides property management services						

43. BROKERAGE INVESTMENT AND MANAGEMENT CONSULTING

12/8/03	ProxyMed Inc.	32.7	23.6	Stock	5.5	NEG	NEG
	Plan Vista Corp.						
	Administers health and other benefit plans for large, self-funded companies						

44. COMPUTER SOFTWARE, SUPPLIES, AND SERVICES

1/21/03	SunGard Data Systems Inc.	83.3	151.0	Cash	NEG	252.9	2.8
4/8/03	Caminus Corp.						
	Develops energy industry software and provides IT consulting services						
2/13/03	Symantec Corp.	7.8	17.8	Cash	40.3	96.9	NEG
5/14/03	Nexland Inc.						
	Designs, develops, and markets Internet security appliances						

45. CONSTRUCTION CONTRACTORS AND ENGINEERING SERVICES

1/7/03	Lone Star Funds	281.4	209.1	N/A	21.4	N/A	1.9
	Kukdong Engineering & Construction Co.						
	Constructs roadways, bridges, water supply, and sewage treatment systems						

(continues)

Announce Date / Close Date	Buyer Name / Seller Name / (Unit Sold) / Business	Seller's Annual Revenues (Millions)	Price Offered (Millions)	Method of Payment	P/E Offered	Percent Premium Offered	Price to Book
46. ENERGY SERVICES							
10/3/03 10/3/03	Goldman Sachs Group Inc. El Paso Corp. (GulfTerra Energy Partners LP) Explores for, transports, and distributes oil and gas	1,036.3	88.0	Cash	5.1	N/A	0.8
47. HEALTH SERVICES							
6/23/03 8/4/03	InSight Health Services Corp. CDL Medical Technologies Inc. (Mobile Imaging Ops) Provides diagnostic imaging services	21.9	48.5	Cash	17.0	N/A	16.3
48. LEISURE AND ENTERTAINMENT							
9/30/03	Fairmont Capital Inc. Garden Fresh Restaurant Corp. Owns and operates salad buffet style restaurants	217.5	95.2	Cash	20.0	54.8	1.2
49. MISCELLANEOUS SERVICES							
3/7/03 4/1/03	Weight Watchers International Inc. The WW Group Inc. (Nine Weight Watchers Franchises) Operates weight Control centers	99.5	181.5	Cash	8.7	N/A	55.0

APPENDIX 2

SELECTED SALES OF BUSINESSES WITH SALE PRICES FROM $1 MILLION TO $10 MILLION

DATABASE REPORT KEY

SIC #	=	Standard Industrial Classification Number
BUS TYPE	=	Best Description of Subject Business
ASK PRICE	=	Asking Price (000's) (In this study, inventory is included in asking price.)
ANN GROSS	=	Annual Gross Sales (Normally Net of Sales Tax)
SDCF	=	Seller's Discretionary Cash Flow (000s) (Net Profit Before Taxes and ANY COMPENSATION TO OWNER plus Amortization, Depreciation, Other Non-Cash Expense, and Non-Business-Related Expense) (Normally to One Working Owner)
SALE DATE	=	Actual Date of Sale
SALE PR	=	Actual Sale Price (in 000's) (In this study, inventory is included in sale price.)
% DOWN	=	Down Payment as a Percent of Sale Price
TERMS	=	Terms of New or Assumed Encumbrance
INV AMT	=	Inventory at the Time of Sale (in 000's) (is included in both asking and sale price)
FF&E	=	Estimate of Value of Furniture, Fixtures, and Equipment
RENT/SALES	=	Rent as a Percentage of Sales
AREA	=	Region of Geographical Location of Business
#ERR	=	Information Unavailable

Sic #	Bus Type	Asking PR (000) W/INV.	Ann Sales (000)	SDE (000)	SDE/ Gross Sales	Sale Date	Sale PR (000) W/INV.	% Down
3272	Pre-Stress Concrete	1400	1,621	244	0.15	6/30/95	1000	69%
7371	Developer-Jail Software	1000	1,469	0	0.00	10/28/99	1000	100%
3354	Mfg-Interior Fixtures	1100	2,400	270	0.11	8/2/02	1000	N/A
7371	Computer Software	1200	656	393	0.60	7/3/00	1000	50%
7361	Employment Agency	1395	3,300	400	0.12	7/31/00	1000	12.5%
5211	Distr-Building Materials	1000	1,800	280	0.16	11/30/98	1000	25% SBA
5085	Distr-Industrial Supplies	1046	2,000	150	0.08	9/30/94	1000	15%
7372	Computer Software	1200	2,000	270	0.14	6/30/98	1000	100%
0782	Lawn Maintenance	1005	1,226	277	0.23	3/31/01	1000	80%
3599	Mfg-Machine Shop	1000	1,220	572	0.47	6/25/02	1000	50%
0782	Lawn Maintenance	1000	1,349	389	0.29	7/10/00	1000	88% SBA
4212	Contract Postal Delivery	1000	1,875	(14)	-0.01	11/21/03	1000	100%
3444	Mfg-Precision Sheet Metal	1500	4,775	589	0.12	1/12/03	1000	100%
3444	Mfg-Metal Fabrication	1000	2,036	700	0.34	2/8/00	1000	100%
3842	Mfg-Prosthetic Devices	1313	898	473	0.53	5/31/97	1013	17%
1752	Contr-Comm Flooring	1275	2,101	400	0.19	7/13/00	1017	SBA
2752	Printer-Commercial	1212	1,299	373	0.29	11/5/99	1022	70%
7389	Fund Raising Services	1075	1,443	381	0.26	8/21/01	1025	90% SBA
0782	Lawn Maintenance	850	2,473	712	0.29	11/13/02	1025	100%
3672	Mfg-Electro Assembly	1500	2,000	396	0.20	11/30/00	1030	44%
5047	Distr-Hearing Aids	1280	2,700	320	0.12	12/31/01	1030	20% SBA
5047	Distr-Medical Supplies	1120	636	179	0.28	1/2/02	1039	53%
3732	Mfg-Marine Products	1250	2,432	258	0.11	1/27/03	1040	50%
5047	Distr-Medical Equipment	1300	1,091	362	0.33	7/30/99	1046	64%
2394	Mfg-Spa Covers	1250	1,100	367	0.33	2/28/98	1050	20% SBA
2499	Mfg-Wood Products	1080	1,655	398	0.24	3/29/02	1050	25%

Terms	Sale/ Sales	Sale/ SDE	Invq AMT	FF&E (000)	Rent/ Sales	Days on Mkt	Area
15 Yrs @ 9%	0.62	4.1	84	420	N/A		Western Montana
N/A	0.68	#ERR	0	51	3.4%	720	Northwest
N/A	0.42	3.7	22	N/A	N/A	196	Santa Clara, CA
5 Yrs @ 9%	1.52	2.5	100	0	N/A	238	Central Florida
N/A	0.30	2.5	0	N/A	0.5%	35	Torrance, CA
10 Yrs @ 10%	0.56	3.6	300	200	6%	150	Texas
15 Yrs @ 9%	0.50	6.7	750	250	N/A		Western Montana
N/A	0.50	3.7	250	90	N/A		Rocky Mountains
N/A	0.82	3.6	0	N/A	N/A	135	Florida
5 Yrs @ 8%	0.82	1.7	20	150	2.5%	180	Florida
15 Yrs @ 12%	0.74	2.6	100	207	N/A	156	Southeast Florida
N/A	0.53	-71.4	30	4	N/A	434	Southeast
N/A	0.21	1.7	0	N/A	3.3%	150	San Diego, CA
N/A	0.49	1.4	0	100	N/A	332	N Central Georgia
15 Yrs @ 11%	1.13	2.1	13	54	3%		Central Florida
10 Yrs @ 11.5%	0.48	2.5	100	25	2%	360	Southeast
2 Yrs @ 0%	0.79	2.7	12	600	3%	311	Eastern Washington
10 Yrs @ PR+2	0.71	2.7	225	50	0.5%	60	Florida
N/A	0.41	1.4	0	454	0.4%	50	Florida
8 Yrs @ 8%	0.51	2.6	0	N/A	6.6%	270	Sunnyvale, CA
5 Yrs	0.38	3.2		450	N/A	95	Oklahoma
2 Yrs @ 10%	1.63	5.8	289	300	N/A	272	Florida
5 Yrs @ 10%	0.43	4.0	150	450	N/A	616	Florida
N/A	0.96	2.9	25	425	3.2%	217	West Central Florida
10 Yr @ PR+2.5	0.95	2.9	30	85	0.3%	60	West Central Florida
10 Yrs @ 9%	0.63	2.6	15	450	3.1%	130	Florida

Sic #	Bus Type	Asking PR (000) W/INV.	Ann Sales (000)	SDE (000)	SDE/ Gross Sales	Sale Date	Sale PR (000) W/INV.	% Down
5113	Distr-Packaging Products	1050	2,688	665	0.25	10/15/01	1050	100%
3949	Mfg-Recreational Equipt	1250	1,081	354	0.33	2/27/98	1050	100%
3721	Mfg-Trailers	1200	2,000	200	0.10	6/30/99	1050	80%
8071	Clinical Monitoring	1050	1,871	410	0.22	8/31/98	1050	70%
5039	Distr-Steel	1230	1,832	278	0.15	8/31/95	1051	69%
2752	Printing Shop	1215	2,939	395	0.13	8/31/01	1053	61%
5099	Distr-Fire Equipment	1340	1,863	266	0.14	5/30/03	1055	100%
7359	Equipment Rental	1365	347	270	0.78	9/4/03	1065	100%
2752	Printer-Laminating	1575	2,136	267	0.12	10/19/99	1077	80%
2311	Mfg-Clothing	1100	2,200	415	0.19	11/30/98	1083	91%
3281	Mfg-Marble Products	1635	1,982	164	0.08	1/1/03	1085	100%
5714	Mfg-Window Coverings	1250	2,173	414	0.19	4/28/00	1086	100%
2741	Publisher-Directory	1500	3,703	N/A	#ERR	9/30/99	1091	100%
1711	Contr-Fire Sprinklers	1200	2,425	408	0.17	6/1/00	1100	20%
5074	Whsle-HVAC Products	1330	4,392	316	0.07	1/2/03	1100	100%
3699	Mfg-Power Plant Products	1500	750	350	0.47	3/31/01	1100	65%
7363	Temporary Personnel	1200	6,000	400	0.07	12/21/94	1100	70%
7379	Internet Service Provider	1750	2,400	300	0.12	4/1/03	1100	100%
4213	Long Distance Trucking	1200	4,880	388	0.08	3/31/96	1100	36%
7372	Vertical Mkt Software	1000	1,000	300	0.30	10/31/01	1100	68%
3993	Sign Manufacturer	1300	1,800	398	0.22	11/21/00	1102	10% SBA
5074	Distr & Service Boilers	1325	2,268	298	0.13	4/30/96	1105	37%
3993	Sign Manufacturer	1160	1,019	400	0.39	6/30/01	1110	77%
8721	CPA Practice	1115	1,025	277	0.27	2/13/02	1115	100%
3679	Mfg-Signal Processing Equip	1200	2,600	300	0.12	4/30/96	1125	100%
3421	Mfg-Archery Products	1125	1,500	321	0.21	3/12/01	1125	95%
3444	Mfg-Metal Fabrication	1580	1,138	295	0.26	9/13/01	1130	100%
2591	Mfg-Window Coverings	1140	1,600	245	0.15	6/30/99	1140	83%
2899	Mfg-Roll Shutters	1147	1,463	296	0.20	9/30/01	1147	77%

Terms	Sale/ Sales	Sale/ SDE	Invq AMT	FF&E (000)	Rent/ Sales	Days on Mkt	Area
N/A	0.39	1.6	250	N/A	3.7%	75	Georgia
N/A	0.97	3.0	40	84	5%	90	West Central Florida
3 Yrs @ PR+1	0.52	5.2	100	N/A	N/A	150	Oklahoma
7 Yrs @ 8%	0.56	2.6	0	64	N/A	125	Southeastern US
4 Yr @ 10%	0.57	3.8	400	50	N/A		South Florida
N/A	0.36	2.7	25	800	1.9%	798	Florida
N/A	0.57	4.0	90	175	2.9%	146	Florida
N/A	3.07	3.9	0	755	N/A	270	Los Angeles, CA
5 Yrs @ 10%	0.50	4.0	75	675	N/A	90	Central Kentucky
3 Yrs @ 8%	0.49	2.6	0	N/A	0.7%	120	Arleta, CA
N/A	0.55	6.6	135	425	4.3%	184	Florida
N/A	0.50	2.6	150	100	N/A	131	Central Florida
N/A	0.29	#ERR	371	29	N/A	499	N Central Georgia
5 Yrs @ 10%	0.45	2.7	15	228	N/A	30	N Central Georgia
N/A	0.25	3.5	125	51	1%	160	Florida
5 Yrs @ 8.5%	1.47	3.1	350	400	N/A	210	Southwest
5 Yrs @ 8%	0.18	2.8		150	6%		Austin, TX
N/A	0.46	3.7	0	183	N/A	180	Cresent City, CA
7 Yrs @ 9%	0.23	2.8	0	665	1%		Midwest
5 Yrs @ 8%	1.10	3.7	0	70	1%	999	Colorado
10 Yrs @ 11.5%	0.61	2.8	85	250	N/A	550	Denver, CO
7 Yrs @ PR+2	0.49	3.7	340	180	1%		Wichita, KS
N/A	1.09	2.8	10	150	N/A	N/A	Phoenix, AZ
N/A	1.09	4.0	0	12	N/A	78	Florida
N/A	0.43	3.8		250	6%		Austin, Texas
15 Yrs @ 7%	0.75	3.5	48	1.1M	N/A	132	NW Florida
N/A	0.99	3.8	30	75	N/A	67	Florida
N/A	0.71	4.7	140	37	N/A	N/A	Phoenix, AZ
N/A	0.78	3.9	147	128	N/A	N/A	Phoenix, AZ

Sic #	Bus Type	Asking PR (000) W/INV.	Ann Sales (000)	SDE (000)	SDE/ Gross Sales	Sale Date	Sale PR (000) W/INV.	% Down
5063	Distr-Electric Motors	2000	3,005	463	0.15	4/30/98	1175	100%
2439	Mfg-Trusses & Docks	1225	1,787	470	0.26	1/29/03	1179	33%
2299	Mfg-Pet Bedding	1400	1,735	N/A	#ERR	5/1/01	1200	100%
3079	Mfg-Injection Molding	1700	7,000	950	0.14	12/31/94	1200	33%
4832	Radio Broadcasting Station	1309	208	21	0.10	10/2/01	1200	40%
7363	Temporary Personnel	1200	2,500	315	0.13	5/31/98	1200	87%
8099	Medical Testing	1200	893	436	0.49	11/15/02	1200	22%
3552	Mfg-Textile Equipment	1200	4,000	552	0.14	7/31/00	1200	30%
7359	Equipment Rental	2300	1,200	400	0.33	10/1/02	1200	100%
7359	Equipment Rental	1200	1,872	551	0.29	3/10/99	1200	33%
2752	Printer-Commercial	1210	1,940	425	0.22	4/16/01	1210	100%
3599	Mfg-Machine Shop	1420	1,474	378	0.26	10/30/98	1220	29% SBA
3585	Mfg-Refrigeration Equipment	1245	1,184	N/A	#ERR	5/16/02	1222	N/A
3993	Sign Manufacturer	1300	1,300	450	0.35	2/1/01	1235	95%
3713	Mfg-Utility Truck Beds	1239	2,850	296	0.10	9/12/97	1239	25%
5084	Distr-Hydraulic Equipment	1400	3,250	208	0.06	12/31/00	1250	15%
2098	Mfg-Bulk Pasta	1500	1,283	462	0.36	4/30/02	1250	100%
3531	Mfg-Concrete Vibrators	1250	1,075	272	0.25	1/2/01	1250	15% SBA
2521	Mfg-Office Furniture	1500	3,000	350	0.12	6/30/93	1252	83%
1761	Contr-Roofing	1704	3,676	796	0.22	7/30/00	1254	90%
3599	Mfg-Machine Shop	1600	2,100	278	0.13	2/28/93	1260	22%
1711	Contr-Heating & AC	1260	2,600	431	0.17	10/31/97	1260	100%
4953	Waste Management	1475	765	168	0.22	6/30/02	1270	50%
5085	Distr-Industrial Bearings	1300	3,500	350	0.10	2/28/97	1270	38%
3079	Mfg-Plastic Products	1288	6,600	198	0.03	4/30/97	1288	41%
2679	Mfg/Distr-Die-cut Gift Bags	1300	890	204	0.23	8/1/00	1300	100%
2675	Print/Glue/Fold Cardboard	1750	1,861	450	0.24	4/30/99	1300	20% SBA
1623	Contr-Utility Pipeline	1300	1,935	712	0.37	7/19/00	1300	11%
5113	Distr-Pharm Packaging	1300	2,400	414	0.17	3/31/99	1300	59%

Terms	Sale/ Sales	Sale/ SDE	Invq AMT	FF&E (000)	Rent/ Sales	Days on Mkt	Area
N/A	0.39	2.5	300	106	1.7%	587	Altamonte Springs, FL
N/A	0.66	2.5	100	500	N/A	232	Oklahoma
N/A	0.69	#ERR	75	107	N/A	365	South Carolina
5 Yrs @ 8%	0.17	1.3		N/A	1.3%		Los Angeles, CA
10 Yrs @ 8%	5.77	57.1	0	321	N/A	380	North Carolina
6 Mos. @ 8.75%	0.48	3.8	0	60	8%	240	Midwest
10 Yrs @ 7%	1.34	2.8	18	35	2%	116	Florida
7 Yrs @ PR	0.30	2.2	200	150	1%	365	Southeast
N/A	1.00	3.0	0	1.8M	6%	300	Atlanta, GA
5 Yrs @ 9%	0.64	2.2	450	345	3%	660	Central Florida
N/A	0.62	2.8	10	250	5%	55	Colorado
N/A	0.83	3.2	20	N/A	2.3%	360	San Diego County
N/A	1.03	#ERR	550	50	N/A	59	Minnesota
5 Yrs @ 7%	0.95	2.7	20	50	N/A	90	San Diego, CA
8 Yrs @ 9%	0.43	4.2	339	N/A	3%	142	LA County, CA
7 Yrs @ PR+1	0.38	6.0	320	50	6%	180	Southeast
N/A	0.97	2.7	0	N/A	N/A	N/A	Denver, CO
10 Yrs @ 11.5%	1.16	4.6	415	350	5%	365	Denver, CO
7 Yrs @ 8%	0.42	3.6	180	800	2%		Central Florida
5 Yrs @ 10.5%	0.34	1.6	219	232	N/A	275	N Central Georgia
7 Yrs @ 9%	0.60	4.5	127	851	1.7%		Orange, CA
N/A	0.48	2.9	0	600	1.4%	80	Denver, CO
N/A	1.66	7.6	0	495	N/A	N/A	Payson, AZ
5 Yrs	0.36	3.6	800	N/A	10%	360	North Rocky Mtns.
4 Yrs @ 11%	0.20	6.5	98	950	N/A	69	Wyoming
N/A	1.46	6.4	100	2	3%	112	North California
N/A	0.70	2.9	15	417	2.7%	401	Sierra Foothills, CA
10 Yrs @ 11%	0.67	1.8	0	40	N/A	360	Brighton, CO
6 Yrs @ 8%	0.54	3.1	128	32	7%	156	Midwest

Sic #	Bus Type	Asking PR (000) W/INV.	Ann Sales (000)	SDE (000)	SDE/ Gross Sales	Sale Date	Sale PR (000) W/INV.	% Down
3949	Mfg-Sporting Goods	1300	1,818	425	0.23	5/31/02	1300	63%
3599	Mfg-Machine Shop	1300	1,000	250	0.25	6/30/99	1300	92%
5113	Distr-Packaging Prod	1300	2,900	400	0.14	12/8/99	1300	100%
5013	Distr-Automotive Parts	1350	2,399	351	0.15	8/23/02	1300	100%
3671	Mfg-Security Systems	1200	1,500	300	0.20	9/30/93	1300	38%
3079	Mfg-Plastic Products	1730	2,000	553	0.28	9/1/00	1303	100%
4832	Radio Broadcasting Station	1313	443	164	0.37	10/18/01	1313	N/A
1731	Contr-Tele Communication	1410	1,570	282	0.18	9/30/96	1320	17%
1731	Contr-Electrical	1300	2,750	700	0.25	6/16/98	1329	N/A
1541	Contr-General Building	1615	6,441	532	0.08	3/5/03	1335	45%
3672	Mfg-PC Circuit Boards	1650	2,370	391	0.16	6/30/94	1340	22%
3599	Mfg-Machine Shop	1550	1,900	560	0.29	6/30/02	1350	54%
1731	Contr-Cable & Wire Install	1450	1,158	385	0.33	8/25/00	1350	80%
2499	Mfg-Wood Products	1350	2,345	286	0.12	12/12/95	1350	N/A
4212	Express Del. Franchise	1500	1,545	414	0.27	2/28/02	1350	100%
1741	Contr-Masonry	1495	1,838	360	0.20	2/4/03	1350	20%
8712	Architectural Design	1300	2,530	847	0.33	4/3/01	1352	58%
2741	Publisher HiTech Directory	1800	1,500	495	0.33	8/2/96	1365	90%
5013	Distr-Automotive Parts	1450	8,640	741	0.09	2/28/97	1370	55%
3599	Mfg-Machinery	1550	1,800	450	0.25	8/17/01	1375	71%
3274	Mfg-Agricultural Product	1380	2,438	455	0.19	7/24/00	1380	36%
2499	Mfg-Wood Products	1400	1,250	390	0.31	9/29/00	1400	N/A
3444	Mfg-Fabricated Metal	1425	1,062	574	0.54	7/17/03	1400	85%
5087	Distr-Cleaning & Pool Supplies	1401	3,464	238	0.07	6/19/98	1401	64%
2519	Mfg/Retail Furniture	1445	3,400	222	0.07	10/30/96	1445	76%
7361	Employment Agency	1450	1,750	850	0.49	5/10/01	1450	14%
2819	Mfg-Chemicals	1860	1,899	348	0.18	8/28/01	1460	10%

Terms	Sale/ Sales	Sale/ SDE	Invq AMT	FF&E (000)	Rent/ Sales	Days on Mkt	Area
N/A	0.72	3.1	450	40	1.2%	120	Florida
N/A	1.30	5.2	50	1.0 M	N/A	N/A	Phoenix, AZ
N/A	0.45	3.2	60	110	0.6%	178	West Central Florida
N/A	0.54	3.7	650	150	2.3%	160	Florida
5 Yrs @ 7%	0.87	4.3	200	139	5%		Austin, TX
N/A	0.65	2.4	130	925	5.4%	0	Central Florida
N/A	2.96	8.0	0	209	N/A	450	South Carolina
N/A	0.84	4.7	20	100	N/A	185	Scottsdale, AZ
5 Yrs @ 9%	0.48	1.9	13	119	N/A		Altamonte Springs, FL
N/A	0.21	2.5	15	19	0.2%	462	Florida
10 Yrs @ 10.5%	0.57	3.4	104	312	2%		Ventura County, CA
N/A	0.71	2.4	50	800	N/A	N/A	Tucson, AZ
7 Yrs @ 10%	1.17	3.5	103	89	0.8%	128	Southeast Florida
N/A	0.58	4.7	150	400	N/A	82	Minnesota
N/A	0.87	3.3	0	15	N/A	60	South Florida
10 Yrs @ 7.5%	0.73	3.8	50	90	1.6%	812	Florida
5 Yrs @ 7.5%	0.53	1.6	0	200	N/A	180	Florida
1 Yr @ 0%	0.91	2.8	0	25	3%		Northern California
4 Yrs @ PR+1	0.16	1.8	740	62	1%	68	Rocky Mtns, CO
10 Yrs @ 9%	0.76	3.1	290	200	0.2%	0	Florida
10 Yrs @ 9%	0.57	3.0	255	475	N/A	110	N Central Georgia
N/A	1.12	3.6	40	150	N/A	60	N Central Georgia
5 Yrs @ 6%	1.32	2.4	10	600	N/A	180	Los Angeles, CA
12 Mo Earnout	0.40	5.9	251	660	2%	450	Southwest
10 Yrs @ 8%	0.43	6.5	200	268	N/A		North Rocky Mtns.
N/A	0.83	1.7	0	20	3.4%	130	Georgia
5 Yrs @ 11%	0.77	4.2	110	215	1.5%	385	Florida

Sic #	Bus Type	Asking PR (000) W/INV.	Ann Sales (000)	SDE (000)	SDE/ Gross Sales	Sale Date	Sale PR (000) W/INV.	% Down
5013	Distr-Auto Parts	1530	1,760	140	0.08	9/30/96	1470	9%
3449	Mfg-Iron Products	1475	3,000	360	0.12	7/15/00	1475	34%
5149	Distr-Fruit Juices	1500	3,250	337	0.10	2/28/98	1480	100%
2834	Water Purification	1600	4,267	476	0.11	4/14/02	1495	67%
5046	Distr-Scales	1500	2,391	409	0.17	8/1/99	1500	33%
5092	Distr-Craft Supplies	1700	2,500	404	0.16	4/25/97	1500	50%
3625	Mfg-Electronics	1500	2,000	320	0.16	1/31/98	1500	50%
2431	Mfg-Windows	1500	4,313	494	0.11	10/21/01	1500	54%
3325	Steel Processing	1750	1,826	154	0.08	3/31/99	1500	100%
7336	Art & Graphic Design	1500	2,400	507	0.21	7/31/96	1500	33%
3599	Precision Machine Shop	2500	2,600	354	0.14	1/7/02	1504	25%
7377	Comm Computer Rental	1520	1,167	664	0.57	8/15/01	1520	95%
5085	Sales/Service Material Handling	2080	3,237	606	0.19	6/30/97	1548	100%
2521	Mfg-Office Furniture	1975	3,781	400	0.11	2/18/03	1550	25%
2752	Printer-Commercial	1765	1,800	456	0.25	6/30/00	1565	90%
0782	Sales/Install Trees	1570	2,654	487	0.18	10/31/98	1570	80% SBA
3661	Mfg/Distr-Phone Cords	2400	8,474	259	0.03	1/4/01	1574	54%
2752	Printer-Commercial	1600	3,500	750	0.21	1/31/98	1600	75%
4813	Trucking Brokerage	1700	4,734	557	0.12	11/30/01	1600	63%
5083	Distr-Golf Turf Equip	1950	18,355	993	0.05	1/31/02	1600	100%
3842	Disposable Med Prod	2000	850	300	0.35	6/30/00	1600	50%
2541	Mfg-Store Fixtures	1400	5,600	400	0.07	10/5/00	1600	20%
2951	Mfg-Concrete Recycling	1300	1,200	180	0.15	1/23/98	1610	N/A
7389	Building Inspections	1615	904	690	0.76	4/30/99	1615	16% SBA
5110	Distr-Advert Specialties	1600	2,559	427	0.17	11/27/00	1648	88%
5031	Distr-Commercial Doors	2950	2,400	4640	1.93	9/30/01	1650	83%
7359	Medical Equipment Leasing	1686	1,527	594	0.39	3/31/03	1686	100%

Terms	Sale/ Sales	Sale/ SDE	Invq AMT	FF&E (000)	Rent/ Sales	Days on Mkt	Area
10 Yrs @ 10%	0.84	10.5	300	1.1M	N/A	152	Phoenix, AZ
10 Yrs @ 8%	0.49	4.1	0	N/A	N/A	195	N Central Georgia
N/A	0.46	4.4	170	200	3%	95	Cincinnati, OH
10 Yrs @ 10%	0.35	3.1	200	35	1.1%	435	Florida
10 Yrs @ 9%	0.63	3.7	150	30	2%	168	Colorado
10 Yrs @ 10.5%	0.60	3.7	300	450	1%		Altamonte Springs, FL
3 Yrs @ 9.75%	0.75	4.7	270	30	8%	84	Midwest
15 Yrs @ 10%	0.35	3.0	500	1.5M	4.5%	293	Florida
N/A	0.82	9.7	230	800	N/A	118	Texas
10 Yrs @ 8.3%	0.62	3.0	0	1.0M	1.5%	15	Southeastern US
10 Yrs @ 8%	0.58	4.2	150	1.5M	4%	270	Texas
10 Yrs @ 9%	1.30	2.3	700	700	2%	371	Colorado
N/A	0.48	2.6	591	950	N/A		North Carolina
3 Yrs @ 7%	0.41	3.9	200	450	N/A	480	Los Angeles, CA
N/A	0.87	3.4	15	900	N/A	239	Mesa, AZ
2 Yrs @ 9.5%	0.59	3.2	70	550	3.6%	305	Rocky Mountains, CO
N/A	0.19	6.1	1108	92	N/A	300	Boise, ID
3 Yrs @ 10%	0.46	2.1	75	1 M	N/A	270	Texas
5 Yrs @ 9%	0.34	2.9	0	284	0.7%	91	Georgia
N/A	0.09	1.6	660	250	7%	510	Texas
5 Yrs	1.88	5.3	130	25	2%	100	Rocky Mountains
15 Yrs @ 10%	0.29	4.0	1000	238	N/A	630	Central Texas
Earnout	1.34	8.9	500	650	6.7%		Altamonte Springs, FL
N/A	1.79	2.3	15	40	1.5%	270	Fort Collins, CO
5 Yrs @ 10%	0.64	3.9	633	50	4.7%	239	˙ Boulder, CO
N/A	0.69	0.4	450	280	N/A	N/A	Phoenix, AZ
N/A	1.10	2.8	5	750	2.9%	335	Florida

Sic #	Bus Type	Asking PR (000) W/INV.	Ann Sales (000)	SDE (000)	SDE/ Gross Sales	Sale Date	Sale PR (000) W/INV.	% Down
3714	Mfg-CV Joints & Axels	2200	5,400	480	0.09	9/30/96	1695	70%
2819	Mfg-Chemicals	2400	1,665	425	0.26	9/30/02	1700	100%
2671	Mfg-Paper Products	1900	3,411	617	0.18	6/30/98	1706	N/A
4119	Charter Buses	1750	886	51	0.06	4/5/01	1750	25%
6159	Factoring Company	2500	1,358	758	0.56	4/12/00	1750	43%
2511	Mfg-Furniture	1850	3,702	485	0.13	10/31/97	1750	65%
5031	Distr-Kitchen Cabinets	1750	7,500	400	0.05	1/31/99	750	85%
2992	Mfg/Distr-Drilling Fluids	2815	2,632	1,029	0.39	3/1/00	1751	24%
3079	Mfg-Injection Molding	1755	2,116	615	0.29	5/23/97	1755	90%
3931	Mfg-Instrument Accessory	1420	1,752	441	0.25	8/16/02	1770	33%
5084	Forklift Sales/ Service	1795	3,937	315	0.08	6/20/00	1795	100%
5719	Distr-Fireplace Equip	1800	4,700	275	0.06	8/31/97	1800	90%
3713	Mfg-Truck Bodies	1800	4,028	300	0.07	10/31/99	1800	60%
3625	Mfg-Electronics	2000	4,886	618	0.13	2/28/96	1800	33%
3699	Mfg-Power Plant Products	2000	6,000	600	0.10	9/30/01	1800	100%
3444	Mfg-Metal Fabrication	2298	1,950	484	0.25	3/6/01	1800	100%
5148	Whsle-Produce	2200	8,502	476	0.06	10/11/02	1800	27%
3993	Mfg-Golf Signs	2079	1,698	493	0.29	6/30/01	1804	85%
3061	Mfg-Custom Rubber Products	2783	2,500	N/A	#ERR	6/10/99	1836	N/A
5087	Distr-Car Wash Equipment	1850	3,252	258	0.08	2/28/97	1850	100%
2032	Mfg-Mexican Sauces	2100	2,200	600	0.27	2/28/98	1850	55%
0782	Contr-Landscaping	1850	1,983	356	0.18	6/30/99	1850	90%
1721	Contr-Painting	2500	2,353	1,050	0.45	11/1/00	1875	53%
5047	Distr-Safety Supplies	2000	4,458	395	0.09	2/15/00	1882	81%
5199	Distr-Gifts/Glassware	2199	2,100	480	0.23	1/31/98	1899	52%
3451	Mfg-Screw Machine	2200	3,330	425	0.13	2/15/93	1900	55%
7699	Medical Equipment Repair	2400	1,450	507	0.35	1/15/00	1900	16%
3993	Sign Manufacturer	2510	3,000	200	0.07	3/31/98	1910	50%
3993	Sign Manufacturer	2000	5,237	1,425	0.27	4/2/02	1917	16%

Terms	Sale/ Sales	Sale/ SDE	Invq AMT	FF&E (000)	Rent/ Sales	Days on Mkt	Area
8 Yrs @ 7%	0.31	3.5	763	438	1%	350	Florida
N/A	1.02	4.0	175	85	8%	200	South Florida
3 Yrs @ 8%	0.50	2.8	230	367	N/A		Altamonte Springs, FL
10 Yrs	1.98	34.3	100	50	N/A	462	Southeast
N/A	1.29	2.3	0	0	N/A	282	Central Florida
4 Yrs @ 8%	0.47	3.6	425	300	N/A	210	Southeast
1 Year	0.23	4.4	800	250	6%	N/A	Southeastern US
10 Yrs @ 7%	0.67	1.7	15	70	0.7%	630	Greeley, CO
2 Yrs @ 8%	0.83	2.9	356	700	N/A		Cincinnati, OH
5 Yrs @ 9%	1.01	4.0	100	212	4.1%	14	North Texas
N/A	0.46	5.7	761	N/A	3.8%	396	Los Angeles, CA
90 Days	0.38	6.5	675	155	1.5%	110	Southeast
5 Yr Earnout	0.45	6.0	680	280	N/A	553	North Rocky Mtns.
7 Yrs @ 9%	0.37	2.9	250	400	3%		Texas
N/A	0.30	3.0		250	N/A	180	Southwest
N/A	0.92	3.7	208	N/A	N/A	207	Florida
15 Mos @ 7%	0.21	3.8	0	625	N/A	793	Central Florida
N/A	1.06	3.7	79	68	N/A	N/A	Tempe, AZ
N/A	0.73	#ERR	283	100	N/A	523	Minnesota
N/A	0.57	7.2	790	114	N/A		Midwest
N/A	0.84	3.1	90	500	N/A	125	Central Texas
2 Yrs @ 10%	0.93	5.2	0	81	N/A	150	Western US
N/A	0.80	1.8	300	N/A	1.7%	195	Sun Valley, CA
4 Yrs @ 10%	0.42	4.8	475	150	0.5%	117	Central Florida
N/A	0.90	4.0	999	N/A	4.6%	330	San Francisco, CA
7 Yrs @ 8%	0.57	4.5	800	N/A	N/A		Michigan
5 Yrs @ 8%	1.31	3.7	300	65	1.6%	165	Western Florida
7 Yrs @ 8.5%	0.64	9.6	10	250	4%	160	Minneapolis, MN
N/A	0.37	1.3	14	245	1.2%	143	Florida

Sic #	Bus Type	Asking PR (000) W/INV.	Ann Sales (000)	SDE (000)	SDE/ Gross Sales	Sale Date	Sale PR (000) W/INV.	% Down
5082	Sale/Serv-Air Compr	2198	1,923	16	0.01	8/30/02	1948	38%
1761	Contr-Roofing	2410	3,677	796	0.22	7/30/99	1960	92%
5065	Whsle-Value-add Electr	1995	6,894	646	0.09	10/8/03	1995	43%
1795	Concrete Core Drilling	1500	1,748	770	0.44	4/14/97	1999	50%
2499	Mfg-Wood Products	2000	3,300	420	0.13	11/30/95	2000	60%
3728	Mfg-Aerospace	2000	2,000	0	0.00	2/28/03	2000	10%
6163	Mortgage Brokers	2000	7,241	749	0.10	12/3/03	2000	100%
2752	Printer-Commercial	2000	3,700	550	0.15	5/31/96	2000	40%
1799	Contr-Earth Drilling	1505	1,748	418	0.24	6/13/97	2000	50%
3398	Metal Heat Treating	2500	3,000	500	0.17	12/31/97	2010	100%
3231	Mfg-Glass products	2800	3,000	700	0.23	9/27/02	2020	22%
5063	Distr-Electric Gate Operators	3450	4,450	262	0.06	5/5/98	2037	56%
5172	Distr-Propane	2374	914	184	0.20	1/2/01	2043	27%
7832	Inst-Fire Alarm Systems	2500	2,169	661	0.30	9/17/99	2080	100%
3499	Mfg-Gokart Clutches	3500	3,377	696	0.21	12/10/01	2100	17%
7389	Fulfillment Company	2270	2,000	500	0.25	9/30/00	2120	90%
3444	Mfg-Metal Fabrication	2577	3,400	400	0.12	5/11/01	2127	100%
2499	Mfg-Wood Products	2100	8,520	974	0.11	12/2/02	2140	19%
5211	Whsle-Lumber Yard	2965	11,000	1,000	0.10	2/28/95	2165	50%
5063	Distr-Electronics	2400	18,156	202	0.01	4/30/97	2200	37%
5085	Distr-Welding Supplies	1400	3,730	461	0.12	12/31/93	2200	79%
7361	Employment Agency	2000	6,400	800	0.12	6/30/96	2200	100%
5031	Whsle-Wood Frames	2500	2,185	640	0.29	2/5/03	2200	30%
3451	Mfg-Screw Machining	2201	1,521	706	0.46	7/31/00	2201	20% SBA
7363	Temp Medical Placement	2235	2,900	460	0.16	11/30/96	2235	100%
5110	Dist-Advert. Promotions	1610	2,600	427	0.16	11/30/00	2248	88%
4222	Cold Storage	3950	2,300	1,200	0.52	4/1/95	2250	60%
2511	Mf/Retail-Furniture	2282	2,500	210	0.08	3/31/97	2282	N/A
1761	Contr-Sheet Metal	2300	4,094	741	0.18	6/27/97	2300	50%
2752	Printer-Commercial	2600	3,000	924	0.31	1/31/98	2330	90%

Terms	Sale/ Sales	Sale/ SDE	Invq AMT	FF&E (000)	Rent/ Sales	Days on Mkt	Area
10 Yrs @6.5%	1.01	121.8	98	36	N/A	140	Southeast
5 Yrs @ 10.5%	0.53	2.5	219	672	2%	283	Atlanta, GA
N/A	0.29	3.1	950	30	1.5%	999	Northern California
5 Yrs @ 4.25%	1.14	2.6	14	550	0.7%	27	Texas
17 Yrs @ Pr+2	0.61	4.8	150	N/A	N/A		Southern Minnesota
3 Yr Earnout	1.00	#ERR	1500	100	N/A	90	Los Angeles, CA
N/A	0.28	2.7	0	259	3.8%	523	Colorado
5 Yrs @ 8%	0.54	3.6		500	2%		Seattle, WA
10 Yrs © 8.5%	1.14	4.8	5	550	0.7%	27	Texas
N/A	0.67	4.0	10	1.3M	7%	140	Southeastern US
10 Yrs @ 8%	0.67	2.9	200	250	2%	258	San Diego, CA
3 Yrs @ 8.5%	0.46	7.8	720	160	1.5%	314	Aurora, CO
10 Yrs @8.5%	2.24	11.1	92	560	2.6%	281	Pennsylvania
N/A	0.96	3.1	50	31	0.9%	690	Portland, OR
10 Yrs @7%	0.62	3.0	540	800	3%	490	San Diego, CA
N/A	1.06	4.2	20	150	N/A	244	Mesa, AZ
N/A	0.63	5.3	327	1.2M	NA	161	Central Florida
15 Yrs @6.3%	0.25	2.2	287	993	2.4%	350	Georgia
5 Yrs. @9%	0.20	2.0	518	475	N/A		Minneapolis, MN
5 Yrs @8%	0.12	10.9	1840	84	0.7%	412	California
5 Yrs @9.5%	0.59	4.8	1400	184	1%		Los Angeles, CA
N/A	0.34	2.8	0	150	1%		Iowa
5 Yrs @8%	1.01	3.4	800	60	N/A	90	
PR+1.5	1.45	3.1	137	800	N/A	300	Oakdale, CA
N/A	0.77	4.9		100	0.3%		West Coast
5 Yrs @10%	0.86	5.3	633	50	4.7%	239	Denver, CO
3 Yrs. @9%	0.98	1.9	0	N/A	N/A		Western WA
N/A	0.91	10.9	177	200	N/A	434	Minnesota
14 Yrs. @11%	0.56	3.1	50	1600	N/A		Altamonte Springs,
5 Yrs @0%	0.78	2.5	150	1M	N/A	210	Temple, TX

Sic #	Bus Type	Asking PR (000) W/INV.	Ann Sales (000)	SDE (000)	SDE/ Gross Sales	Sale Date	Sale PR (000) W/INV.	% Down
3079	Plastic Injection Molding	3000	2,994	510	0.17	6/30/98	2350	100%
	START							
8741	Construction Management	2500	14,000	1,164	0.08	7/15/99	2350	21%
3444	Mfg-Metal Stamping	2350	3,341	763	0.23	7/1/00	2350	100%
2448	Mfg-Pallets/Skids	3088	2,609	710	0.27	3/10/98	2388	44%
3545	Mfg-Fastening Tools	2600	3,275	830	0.25	6/30/95	2400	92%
3599	Mfg-Machine Shop	2300	1,768	727	0.41	9/30/01	2400	83%
7389	Telemarketing Service	2450	4,300	1,750	0.41	8/31/02	2450	40%
5171	Distr-Heating Oil/ Propane	2985	2,144	447	0.21	9/10/01	2479	38%
1731	Contr-Electrical	2500	6,929	428	0.06	4/30/95	2500	N/A
2311	Mfg-Label Garments	2645	2,100	600	0.29	1/5/00	2517	90%
8732	Hi-Tech Sales Consultants	2000	1,900	384	0.20	3/24/98	2585	90%
1623	TeleCom Cabling	2520	1,000	1,000	1.00	1/4/00	2585	100%
5023	Distr-Home Accessones	3000	3,586	1,040	0.29	917/01	2600	69%
4213	Moving & Storage	2750	3,099	831	0.27	1/30104	2614	35%
5172	Distr-Petroleum Products	3500	14,468	893	0.06	7/7/00	2632	50%
5141	Distr-Dry Food Products	3845	10,500	830	0.08	4/30/01	2645	100%
5047	Distr-Medical Equipment	2700	6,400	805	0.13	10/31/98	2700	70%
8243	Computer Training	2735	1,800	570	0.32	6/15/00	2735	83%
3086	Mfg-Packaging	2600	6,545	741	0.11	6/30/97	2750	35%
5172	Fuel Distributor	3300	5,800	720	0.12	7/31/99	2775	20%
6411	Insurance Consulting	2900	1,426	816	0.57	7/21/00	2800	14%
3569	Mfg-Vibrating Screens	2580	2,900	610	0.21	12/31/97	2804	14%
2819	Mfg-Chemicals	3000	7,400	551	0.07	11/28/01	2970	74%
7371	Mfg-Computer Software	3000	7,530	847	0.11	11/30/95	3000	33%
2395	Embroidery Service	3000	6,300	884	0.14	1/4/00	3100	24%
3545	Mfg-Precision Mach Shop	2705	2,500	900	0.36	6/30/97	3105	85%
3079	Mfg-Irrigation Products	3520	10,000	1,550	0.16	5/31/94	3120	78%

Terms	Sale/ Sales	Sale/ SDE	Invq AMT	FF&E (000)	Rent/ Sales	Days on Mkt	Area
N/A	0.78	4.6	0	N/A	N/A		Denver, CO
10 Yrs @ 8%	0.17	2.0	0	100	0.3%	67	Texas
N/A	0.70	3.1	148	1.8M	7.7%	253	Colorado
10 Yrs @ 10%	0.92	3.4	100	450	1%	240	Massachusetts
7 Yrs @ 9%	0.73	2.9	600	380	2.7%		Central Florida
N/A	1.36	3.3		N/A	N/A	N/A	Denver, CO
7 Yrs @ 5%	0.57	1.4	20	120	N/A	96	Phoenix, AZ
5 Years	1.16	5.5	63	814	N/A	171	Western New York
N/A	0.36	5.8	70	100	0.3%		Eastern WA
N/A	1.20	4.2	0	N/A	1.4%	342	Los Angeles, CA
N/A	1.36	6.7	0	37	3.2%	270	Boston, MA
N/A	2.59	2.6	0	N/A	N/A	150	Oregon
4 Yrs @ 10.5%	0.73	2.5	675	1.5M	4%	270	Georgia
3 Yrs @ 7%	0.84	3.1	0	1.2 M	0.4%	370	South Florida
N/A	0.18	2.9	100	900	N/A	217	N Central Georgia
N/A	0.25	3.2	500	970	N/A	184	Florida
24 Mos @ 10%	0.42	3.4	420	N/A	1%	312	Midwest
3 Yrs	1.52	4.8	68	149	5.6%	165	Midwest
4 Yrs @ 10%	0.42	3.7	312	274	1.7%	165	Rocky Mtns, CO
3 Yr @ 6%	0.48	3.9	320	750	3%	200	Southeast
5 Yrs @9%	1.96	3.4	0	282	N/A	855	N Central Georgia
2 Yrs @ 7%	0.97	4.6	275	380	N/A	180	Oklahoma
5 Yrs @ 9%	0.40	5.4	860	740	2.2%	205	Georgia
10 Yrs @ 9%	0.40	3.5	25	150	1%		Texas
N/A	0.49	3.5	300	N/A	3%	220	Los Angeles, CA
7 Yrs @ 10%	1.24	3.5	41	845	N/A	480	Fredericksburg, TX
5 Yrs @ 7%	0.31	2.0		N/A	3%		Riverside, CA

Sic #	Bus Type	Asking PR (000) W/INV.	Ann Sales (000)	SDE (000)	SDE/ Gross Sales	Sale Date	Sale PR (000) W/INV.	% Down
5039	Distr-Metal Fastners	3123	5,719	656	0.11	7/31/00	3123	94%
5171	Distr-Heating Oil	3027	6,161	497	0.08	10/15/01	3145	96%
3721	Mfg-Truck Trailers	3800	5,500	1,050	0.19	12/31/99	3150	25%
3625	Mfg-Electronics	3200	3,000	1,200	0.40	10/31/99	3200	62%
1711	Contr-Heating & AC	3600	2,770	424	0.15	7/31/99	3200	N/A
3079	Plastic Fabrication	3500	2,000	1,000	0.50	11/12/98	3250	46%
3829	Mfg-Appliance Controls	3700	3,000	725	0.24	8/15/00	3300	28%
7382	Bank Security Systems	3500	5,400	1,420	0.26	10/31/99	3400	41%
3599	Mfg-Machine Shop	6000	4,000	N/A	#ERR	11/21/00	3500	14%
3728	Mfg-Aircraft HVAC	5000	3,400	1,055	0.31	9/30/97	3500	100%
4812	Reseller of Cellular Serv	4005	3,500	767	0.22	6/30/95	3505	60%
5084	Distr-Bonng Tooling	3600	9,200	965	0.10	12/10/00	3600	66%
3674	Mfg-Custom Electronics	3400	3,200	633	0.20	11/15/96	3650	27.4%
1541	Contr-Commercial	4900	10,484	1,425	0.14	10/8/99	3814	64%
5082	Sale/Serv-Air Compr	3397	6,272	111	0.02	4/10/02	3922	100%
1541	Contr-Commercial	3950	5,195	1,310	0.25	2/4/00	3950	25%
4213	Moving & Storage	4250	5,247	882	0.17	10/31/99	4000	90%
2741	Magazine Publisher	4200	2,451	416	0.17	10/15/99	4200	N/A
3441	Mfg-Structural Steel	4500	9,000	900	0.10	2/28/99	4200	80%
3999	Mfg-Modular Storage	4200	3,300	1,500	0.45	1/8/97	4200	100%
2037	Frozen Fruit Processor	4297	5,200	1,283	0.25	4/30/99	4205	100%
3559	Mfg-Semi-Conduct Equip	5000	9,600	950	0.10	7/31/98	4275	88%
5172	Distr-Propane	4300	2,358	424	0.18	10/15/99	4300	89%
2752	Litho Printing Shop	4500	6,900	1,087	0.16	2/28/93	4500	30%
5085	Distr-Industrial Products	4700	7,879	977	0.12	11/3/01	4700	100%
5065	Distr-Electronic Equipt	4900	7,084	3101	0.44	3/29/02	4775	100%
5047	Distr-Optical Instruments	5000	8,634	1,154	0.13	4/27/00	4827	66%
2499	Rernfg-Wood Products	5300	18,000	1,250	0.07	3/31/94	5000	100%
5122	Institutional Pharmacy	4000	11,343	452	0.04	11/9/00	5200	100%

Terms	Sale/ Sales	Sale/ SDE	Invq AMT	FF&E (000)	Rent/ Sales	Days on Mkt	Area
3 Yrs @10%	0.55	4.8	1301	308	2.9%	240	Denver, CO
N/A	0.51	6.3	82	310	N/A	161	Pennsylvania
7 Yrs @ PR	0.57	3.0	700	1 M	N/A	365	Southeast
4 Yrs @ 6.5%	1.07	2.7	260	N/A	1.6%	216	Midwest
N/A	1.16	7.5	0	1.1M	N/A	240	South Florida
15 Yrs @ 9%	1.62	3.2	6	430	1.5%	515	Southwest
10 Yrs @ 8%	1.10	4.6	100	N/A	1.6%	30	Orange County, CA
10 Yrs @ 9%	0.63	2.4	350	675	0.8%	112	Texas
N/A	0.88	#ERR	275	N/A	6.6%	47	Garden Grove, CA
N/A	1.03	3.3	402	32	N/A	720	Oklahoma
Earnout	1.00	4.6	5	25	1%		Washington
1 Year	0.39	3.7	800	150	2%	60	Southeastern US
6 Yrs @ 10%	1.14	5.8	445	720	1.3%		Midwest
7 Yrs @ 9%	0.36	2.7	0	4 M	N/A	35	West Central Flonda
10 Yrs @6.5%	0.63	35.3	597	417	N/A	315	Southeast
10 Yrs @10%	0.76	3.0	0	2.3M	1%	783	Central Florida
3 Years	0.76	4.5	0	497	10%	125	Midwest
N/A	1.71	10.1		44	4%	365	Northern California
5 Yrs @ PR+1	0.47	4.7	900	N/A	N/A	180	Tulsa, OK
N/A	1.27	2.8	0	400	2.5%	180	Phoenix, AZ
N/A	0.81	3.3	2100	2.6M	N/A	420	West Coast
3 Yrs @ 7.5%	0.45	4.5	0	N/A	0.6%	120	Santa Barbara, CA
5 Yrs @ 0%	1.82	10.1	35	2.0M	N/A	210	Indiana
7 Yr @ PR+1	0.65	4.1	100	1 .8M	1.5%		Dallas, TX
N/A	0.60	4.8	2300	400	N/A	927	Georgia
N/A	0.67	1.5	1000	109	0.9%	287	Florida
5 Years	0.56	4.2	1895	150	1%	450	Central Ohio
N/A	0.28	4.0		2.3M	1.2%		East Washington
N/A	0.46	11.5	667	133	0.9%	450	Norhtwest

Sic #	Bus Type	Asking PR (000) W/INV.	Ann Sales (000)	SDE (000)	SDE/ Gross Sales	Sale Date	Sale PR (000) W/INV.	% Down
7371	Computer Consulting	5450	4,100	335	0.08	2/10/97	5450	100%
1623	Contr-Fiber Optic Cables	5500	10,200	1,200	0.12	6/1/01	5500	0%
3599	Mfg-Precision Machine	5500	1,560	0	0.00	11/30/01	5500	27%
6163	2nd Mortgage Processing	9000	3,567	2,867	0.80	4/3/98	5500	100%
5043	Distr-Electronics	6000	24,000	2,000	0.08	2/2/01	6000	88%
3599	Mfg-Machine Shop	6000	5,200	1,000	0.19	1/31/99	6000	78%
3731	Ship Repair/Dry Dock	6000	4,325	1248	0.29	2/28/96	6000	33%
7363	Temporary Personnel	6250	10,543	645	0.06	2/28/96	6250	33%
7389	Employment Screening	7000	3,761	1,300	0.35	5/31/01	6250	84%
1771	Concrete Contractor	6750	18,000	1,630	0.09	8/31/99	6500	100%
5211	Whsle-Masonry Supply	6748	11,354	1,035	0.09	9/30/02	6748	69%
1794	Contr-Excavation	8000	11,200	1,300	0.12	9/30/99	7000	10%
3585	Mfg-Refrigeration Equipt	7000	6,966	1,418	0.20	3/31/01	7000	100%
3699	Mfg-Flight Simulators	7800	6,500	1,500	0.23	10/31/01	7200	65%
5035	Mfg/Distr-Steel	8400	26,451	1,403	0.05	12/31/96	8000	50%
1623	Contr-Utilities	9511	15,750	N/A	#ERR	3/7/02	8111	84%
3949	Mfg-Outdoor Products	9300	13,000	1,550	0.12	12/31/97	9300	100%
7374	Data Processing Services	9400	3,294	982	0.30	1/7/00	9400	64%
3444	Mfg-Metal Fabrication	10001	4,120	1,531	0.37	6/28/98	10001	100%

Terms	Sale/ Sales	Sale/ SDE	Invq AMT	FF&E (000)	Rent/ Sales	Days on Mkt	Area
N/A	1.33	16.3	0	219	1.4%	270	Portland, OR
6 Mos @ 0%	0.54	4.6	0	2 M	1%	90	North Carolina
5 Yr Eamout	3.53	#ERR	100	N/A	7.3%	999	Fremont, CA
N/A	1.54	1.9	0	126	2.5%	515	Southwest
5 Yrs @ 9%	0.25	3.0	2000	500	0.6%	215	Florida
Earnout	1.15	6.0	350	1.6M	N/A	144	Midwest
10 Yrs @ 9%	1.39	4.8		3.0M	3%		Louisiana
4 Yrs © 5%	0.59	9.7		83	2.1%		Illinois
1 Yr @0%	1.66	4.8	0	48	1.7%	356	Florida
N/A	0.36	4.0	0	250	0.2%	67	Texas
N/A	0.59	6.5	1284	1.8 M	N/A	N/A	Phoenix, AZ
10 Yrs @ 9.5%	0.62	5.4	150	3.7M	N/A	700	Southwest Florida
N/A	1.00	4.9	1250	135	N/A	180	West Coast
5 Yrs @ PR+1	1.11	4.8		1.5M	N/A	450	Southwest
4 Yrs @ PR+2	0.30	5.7	4654	1.6M	0.3%	201	Rocky Mtns, CO
7 Yrs @ 6.5%	0.51	#ERR	1	2.9M	N/A	30	Central Florida
N/A	0.72	6.0	400	1.7M	4%		Rocky Mountains
6 Yrs @ 8%	2.85	9.6	0	337	1.7%	381	Colorado
N/A	2.43	6.5	26	1.7M	N/A	270	Oklahoma

SELECTED RECENT SALES OF BUSINESSES WITH SALE PRICES FROM $500,000 TO $1 MILLION

DATABASE REPORT KEY

SIC #	=	Standard Industrial Classification Number
BUS TYPE	=	Best Description of Subject Business
ASK PRICE	=	Asking Price (000's) (In this study, inventory is included in the asking price.)
ANN GROSS	=	Annual Gross Sales (Normally Net of Sales Tax)
SDCF	=	Seller's Discretionary Cash Flow (Net Profit Before Taxes and ANY COMPENSATION TO OWNER plus Amortization, Depreciation, Other Non-Cash Expense and Non-Business-Related Expense) (Normally to One Working Owner)
SALE DATE	=	Actual Date of Sale
SALE PR	=	Actual Sale Price (in 000's) (In this study, inventory is included in the sale price.)
% DOWN	=	Down Payment as a Percent of Sale Price
TERMS	=	Terms of New or Assumed Encumbrance
INV amt	=	Inventory at the Time of Sale (in 000's) (included in both asking and sale price)
FF&E	=	Estimate of Value of Furniture, Fixtures, and Equipment
RENT/SALES	=	Rent as a Percent of Sales
AREA	=	Region of Geographical Location of Business
#ERR	=	Information Unavailable

Sic #	Bus Type	Asking PR (000) W/INV.	Ann Sales (000)	SDE (000)	SDE/ Gross Sales	Sale Date	Sale PR (000) W/INV.	% Down
1781	Well Drilling Service	715	1,200	301	0.25	10/6/97	500	50%
2741	Publisher-Directory	550	703	170	0.24	11/22/00	500	50%
1711	Contr-Heating & AC	550	981	177	0.18	6/15/01	500	35%
5141	Distr-Prepared Meals	650	2,444	187	0.08	3/23/00	500	100%
5085	Distr-Industrial Products	680	1,622	182	0.11	6/11/01	500	33%
2395	Embroidery Service	750	1,639	149	0.09	5/23/02	500	54%
3479	Mfg/Distr-Indust Coatings	600	450	100	0.22	5/31/99	500	100%
2098	Mfg-Gourmet Pasta	425	839	127	0.15	4/30/02	500	55%
2752	Printing Shop	600	605	179	0.30	7/27/00	500	20%
3993	Mfg-Custom Signs	690	897	195	0.22	9/30/96	500	100%
3713	Mfg-Truck Sleepers	500	985	227	0.23	10/1/97	500	50%
1711	Contr-Heating & AC	1000	2,500	150	0.06	7/30/99	500	0%
6531	Property Management	510	417	220	0.53	10/31/01	500	40%
8711	Engineering Services	500	1,779	112	0.06	12/14/00	500	20%
7629	Elect-Breakers Repair	550	1,200	150	0.12	7/31/93	500	40%
2675	Mfg-Die Cutting	435	446	187	0.42	10/1/99	500	100%
8721	Accounting Practice	600	500	160	0.32	9/30/98	500	25%
7349	Cleaning Restr Equipment	590	1,079	189	0.18	12/16/02	500	100%
7349	Janitorial Service	800	2,016	292	0.14	8/14/02	500	15% SBA
7311	Advertising Agency	705	5,400	310	0.06	9/30/03	501	50%
3541	Mfg-Tool & Die	750	1,300	200	0.15	10/18/02	502	47%
7379	Internet Marketing Co	500	N/A	162	#ERR	2/11/98	502	N/A
0782	Lawn Maintenance	452	521	146	0.28	12/31/98	502	35%
7381	Detective Services	605	688	103	0.15	3/15/02	505	N/A
7349	Janitorial Services	508	1,105	440	0.40	6/30/00	508	100%
7699	Boiler Repair Service	538	354	136	0.38	4/21/00	509	100%
1791	Steel Fabrication	810	2,680	365	0.14	11/1/01	510	100%
5084	Distr-CD Recording Equip	680	760	250	0.33	10/13/99	510	20% SBA
7389	Mail Box Rental	551	844	163	0.19	6/19/98	511	20% SBA
2875	Mfg-Composted Humus	565	444	200	0.45	9/30/95	511	59%
3444	Mfg-Metal Fabrication	618	1,513	280	0.19	8/10/01	514	19%

Terms	Sale/ Sales	Sale/ SDE	Invq AMT	FF&E (000)	Rent/ Sales	Days on Mkt	Area
7 Yrs @ 8%	0.42	1.7	25	190	1.5%	45	Venice, FL
7 Yrs @11%	0.71	2.9	0	410	5.5%	25	Southwest Florida
3 Yrs @ 8%	0.51	2.8	18	150	N/A	180	Texas
N/A	0.20	2.7	100	232	2.3%	55	Southeast Florida
5 Yrs @10%	0.31	2.7	250	N/A	3.2%	241	Florida
N/A	0.31	3.4	40	250	2.9%	89	Florida
N/A	1.11	5.0	150	100	N/A	270	Southwest
N/A	0.60	3.9	0	N/A	N/A	N/A	Denver, CO
N/A	0.83	2.8	0	100	2.2%	189	Central Florida
N/A	0.56	2.6	25	120	2.5%		Denver, CO
6 Yrs @ 10%	0.51	2.2	220	130	2.85%	753	North Texas
N/A	0.20	3.3	100	98	1%	540	Southeast
6 Yrs @ 7.5%	1.20	2.3	0	25	4%	90	Colorado
3 Yrs @ 5.8%	0.28	4.5	0	147	2%	89	Wisconsin
7 Yrs @ 8%	0.42	3.3	120	110	2%		Southwest Florida
N/A	1.12	2.7	200	175	4%	138	Colorado
5 Yr Earnout	1.00	3.1	0	100	5%	70	Texas
N/A	0.46	2.6	6	118	N/A	380	Georgia
5yrs @ 8%	0.25	1.7	0	N/A	1.5%	53	Inland Empire, CA
5 Yrs @ 6%	0.09	1.6	0	135	N/A	513	Boise, ID
10 Yrs @ 6%	0.39	2.5	75	100	6%	350	South Florida
N/A	#ERR	3.1	92	220	N/A	150	Boise, ID
5 Yrs @ 9.25%	0.96	3.4	2	115	3%	64	Texas
N/A	0.73	4.9	5	30	N/A	312	Minnesota
N/A	0.46	1.2	8	45	N/A	50	Phoenix, AZ
N/A	1.44	3.7	261	60	N/A	114	Kansas
N/A	0.19	1.4	10	100	N/A	210	Colorado
N/A	0.67	2.0	30	10	3.2%	452	Lake Forest, CA
10 Yrs @ 11%	0.61	3.1	8	50	4.4%	20	San FrancisCo Area
10 Yrs @ 8%	1.15	2.6	30	N/A	N/A		Iowa
12 Yrs @ 7%	0.34	1.8	50	255	2.4%	153	Spokane, WA

Sic #	Bus Type	Asking PR (000) W/INV.	Ann Sales (000)	SDE (000)	SDE/ Gross Sales	Sale Date	Sale PR (000) W/INV.	% Down
1731	Conservation Lighting	515	1,000	150	0.15	2/13/96	515	39%
5074	Whsle-Plumbing Products	575	1,817	174	0.10	4/30/03	515	52%
1721	Contr-Painting	590	2,266	568	0.25	9/30/01	515	51%
2741	Specialty Publication	650	610	52	0.09	5/31/95	515	79%
3999	Mfg-Aftermarket Products	550	493	207	0.42	9/28/01	516	23%
5149	Coffee Service Route	501	846	232	0.27	6/11/01	520	69%
3423	Mfg-Fiberglass Handles	650	1,000	179	0.18	7/1/98	520	100%
5047	Distr-Medical Supplies	725	772	149	0.19	9/17/01	520	100%
7319	FSBO Advertising	567	787	208	0.26	6/30/03	522	73%
3599	Mfg-Machine Shop	525	500	150	0.30	1/31/01	525	100%
7363	Temporary Personnel	550	2,741	204	0.07	10/1/01	525	25%
8711	Engineering Services	595	876	265	0.30	12/13/01	525	93%
0782	Lawn Maintenance	575	1,107	254	0.23	8/30/02	525	10%
0782	Lawn Maintenance	550	775	280	0.36	10/26/99	530	52%
5112	Distr-Filing Systems	800	1,200	160	0.13	1/31/95	530	25%
5087	Distr-Chemicals	580	487	247	0.51	6/30/99	530	100%
7371	Mfg-Software	530	1,300	153	0.12	1/21/01	530	N/A
0782	Landscape Maintenance	555	1,400	290	0.21	9/30/96	530	48%
3599	Mfg-Machine Shop	613	771	206	0.27	3/16/98	533	100%
5148	Whsle-Produce	535	2,271	158	0.07	9/5/01	535	38%
1711	Contr-Mechanical	795	900	145	0.16	12/31/98	535	60%
5111	Distr-Writing Paper	850	1,831	328	0.18	9/15/99	535	12% SBA
3089	Plastics Polishing	600	600	180	0.30	3/31/98	540	90%
2519	Mfg-Home/Office Furniture	785	1,063	57	0.05	9/8/97	540	11%
5085	Distr-Mat. Handling Equipment	685	965	207	0.21	9/30/95	540	85%
5087	Whsle-Chemicals	625	475	138	0.29	9/30/02	540	100%
5031	Distr-Kitchen/ Bath Cabinets	541	2,302	376	0.16	3/22/00	541	95%
2752	Printing Shop	650	823	219	0.27	4/11/01	542	90%
6531	Property Management	578	960	225	0.23	12/20/01	543	100%
0782	Landscape Maintenance	450	1,227	284	0.23	9/2/97	548	72%

Terms	Sale/ Sales	Sale/ SDE	Invq AMT	FF&E (000)	Rent/ Sales	Days on Mkt	Area
10 Yr @ 9%	0.51	3.4	150	143	N/A		Maine
5 Yrs @ 7%	0.28	3.0	210	55	3.5%	156	Florida
N/A	0.23	0.9	0	145	N/A	N/A	Glendale, AZ
5 Yrs @ 9%	0.84	9.9	0	23	4.6%		Central Florida
4 Yrs @ 7%	1.05	2.5	200	145	N/A	565	Arizona
6 Yrs @ 10%	0.61	2.2	20	436	N/A	382	Florida
N/A	0.52	2.9	78	216	N/A	240	Oklahoma
N/A	0.67	3.5	136	100	9%	122	San Diego, CA
6 Yrs @ 7%	0.66	2.5	2	89	2.4%	220	North Carolina
N/A	1.05	3.5	75	350	4%	360	Midwest
7 Yrs @ 8%	0.19	2.6	0	3	1%	178	North Carolina
10 Yrs	0.60	2.0	0	71	4%	119	NW Florida
10 Yrs @ 7.5%	0.47	2.1	3	71	1.7%	395	Florida
3 Yrs @ 10%	0.68	1.9	0	138	3.3%	131	Central Florida
7 Yrs @ 9%	0.44	3.3	78	15	5%		Minneapolis, MN
N/A	1.09	2.1	5	20	N/A	N/A	Phoenix, AZ
N/A	0.41	3.5	0	N/A	N/A	450	Eastern Oregon
N/A	0.38	1.8	5	250	N/A	667	Phoenix, AZ
N/A	0.69	2.6	10	340	5%	270	Massachusetts
5 Yrs @ 8%	0.24	3.4	60	75	1.0%	30	Florida
5 Yrs @9%	0.59	3.7	20	170	5%	130	Southeastern US
N/A	0.29	1.6	0	535	N/A	170	Salt Lake City, UT
5 Yrs @10%	0.90	3.0	82	N/A	4.8%	150	Campbell, CA
15 Yrs @ 8%	0.51	9.5	75	357	2.5%	174	Knoxville, TN
3 Yrs @ 11%	0.56	2.6	200	84	12%		Denver, CO
N/A	1.14	3.9	0	N/A	N/A	N/A	Phoenix, AZ
1 Yr @ 0%	0.24	1.4	46	154	1.6%	146	Central Florida
N/A	0.66	2.5	10	100	3.6%	663	Georgia
N/A	0.57	2.4	3	N/A	5.3%	155	Santa Cruz, CA
5 Yrs @ 9.5%	0.45	1.9	0	240	3.4%	150	Colorado

Sic #	Bus Type	Asking PR (000) W/INV.	Ann Sales (000)	SDE (000)	SDE/ Gross Sales	Sale Date	Sale PR (000) W/INV.	% Down
7363	IT Employee Staffing	950	2,904	282	0.10	6/25/00	550	55%
5044	Sales/Serv-Office Equipt	550	1,781	254	0.14	8/7/98	550	100%
5013	Distr-Remfg Engine	550	1,680	147	0.09	7/31/96	550	91%
4213	AutoTransport	600	687	106	0.15	3/6/98	550	9%
3281	Mfg-Marble Products	580	1,109	266	0.24	7/27/00	550	100%
3479	Mfg-Auto After-market	650	637	192	0.30	6/5/02	550	90%
5169	Mfg/Distr-Concrete Products	750	1,300	230	0.18	2/28/96	550	100%
3272	Mfg-Concrete Products	600	900	140	0.16	2/28/96	550	20%
3566	Mfg-Gears	550	500	N/A	#ERR	3/31/93	550	100%
1731	Contr-Electrical	580	719	N/A	#ERR	5/24/00	554	10%
5046	Distr-Ice/Juice Machines	555	564	240	0.43	7/31/97	555	100%
4213	Moving & Storage	571	1,400	200	0.14	4/30/96	558	80%
4212	Blanket Wrap Freight	575	580	217	0.37	7/3/03	560	23%
5074	Whsle-Plumbing Supply	770	770	151	0.20	4/28/00	560	93%
7331	Direct Mail Service	695	2,005	197	0.10	1/18/02	560	100%
5064	Distr-Trash Compactors	565	1,106	166	0.15	3/31/98	565	47%
7334	Blueprint Service	566	1,090	210	0.19	2/28/00	566	29% SBA
7349	Janitorial Service	517	882	251	0.28	11/30/00	567	100%
7699	Locksmith	599	541	247	0.46	10/31/02	569	17%
4212	Trucking-Rollup Dumpsters	685	792	N/A	#ERR	7/1/02	570	100%
1731	Contr-Electrical	619	979	227	0.23	3/31/03	570	36%
3585	Mfg-Ice Machines	570	280	130	0.46	3/31/98	570	20% SBA
2752	Printing Shop	480	707	194	0.27	4/1/99	572	100%
3444	Mfg-Metal Fabrication	720	633	241	0.38	7/2/03	575	100%
5087	Distr-Janitorial Supplies	650	759	175	0.23	1/2/98	575	N/A
5084	Equipment Sales/ Service	350	1,017	164	0.16	11/20/01	575	79%
3993	Sign Manufacturer	650	950	215	0.23	10/30/98	575	30%
1799	Fencing Contractor	700	1,300	110	0.08	9/26/01	575	100%
1799	Contr-Specialty	580	1,936	185	0.10	7/22/02	580	100%

Terms	Sale/ Sales	Sale/ SDE	Invq AMT	FF&E (000)	Rent/ Sales	Days on Mkt	Area
2 Mos @ 0%	0.19	2.0	0	N/A	1.3%	55	San Jose, CA
N/A	0.31	2.2	71	96	0.9%	562	Southeast Florida
5 Yrs Int Only	0.33	3.7	200	60	1.6%	340	Kentucky
10 Yrs @ 9%	0.80	5.2	0	450	N/A	160	Spokane, WA
N/A	0.50	2.1	20	205	3.1%	146	Central Florida
3 Yrs @ 10%	0.86	2.9	28	188	N/A	62	Caldwell, ID
N/A	0.42	2.4	100	22	3%		Houston, Texas
10 Yrs @ 9%	0.61	3.9	100	60	2%		Houston, TX
N/A	1.10	#ERR	100	550	N/A		Dallas, TX
10 Yrs @ 10%	0.77	#ERR	28	359	N/A	94	Boise, ID
N/A	0.98	2.3	30	200	4%		Altamonte Springs, Florida
5 Yrs @ 9%	0.40	2.8	0	106	N/A		Texas
6 Yrs @ 6%	0.97	2.6	0	60	8%	360	South Florida
3 Yrs @ 8.8%	0.73	3.7	70	4	4.3%	87	NW Florida
N/A	0.28	2.8	0	224	4%	375	Florida
8 Yrs @ 10%	0.51	3.4	25	65	1%		Danville, CA
N/A	0.52	2.7	0	N/A	N/A		Houston, TX
N/A	0.64	2.3	2	29	0.7%	124	Central Florida
10 Yrs @ 8%	1.05	2.3	8	100	6.4%	240	Florida
N/A	0.72	#ERR	0	350	N/A	213	Minnesota
10 Yrs @ 8%	0.58	2.5	20	N/A	3.9%	71	Florida
15 Yrs @ 10%	2.04	4.4	2	262	N/A	166	Eastern Florida
N/A	0.81	2.9	0	78	5.7%		Madison, WI
N/A	0.91	2.4	62	56	N/A	210	Los Angeles, CA
5 Yrs @ 11%	0.76	3.3	70	20	3.3%		Altamonte Springs, Florida
8 Yrs @ 8.5%	0.57	3.5	100	50	N/A	586	Florida
N/A	0.61	2.7	0	150	4%	297	Southeast Florida
N/A	0.44	5.2	100	200	N/A	229	Colorado
N/A	0.30	3.1	64	300	N/A	52	Georgia

Sic #	Bus Type	Asking PR (000) W/INV.	Ann Sales (000)	SDE (000)	SDE/ Gross Sales	Sale Date	Sale PR (000) W/INV.	% Down
3354	Mfg-Outdoor Light Fixtures	615	870	185	0.21	2/28/99	580	29%
6531	Property Management	650	805	209	0.26	3/30/01	580	100%
5013	Auto Parts/Service	875	1,100	160	0.15	11/4/02	589	62%
1711	Contr-Heating & AC	439	1,366	157	0.11	3/29/01	589	39%
5087	Distr-Janitorial Supplies	665	759	175	0.23	1/2/98	590	11%
2752	Printing Shop	681	766	83	0.11	5/30/01	591	32%
1731	Contr-Cablel/Wire Install	800	2,400	210	0.09	9/11/98	591	100%
5091	Distr-Pool/Spa Equipment	595	944	265	0.28	3/24/03	595	19%
5088	Golf Cart Sales & Service	597	2,340	202	0.09	4/1/98	597	100%
5171	Distr-Heating Oil	744	1,176	115	0.10	11/2/99	597	100%
2752	Printing Shop	598	792	203	0.26	9/11/01	599	90%
1799	Contr-Sprayon Fireproof	600	1,151	423	0.37	1/31/00	599	100%
3443	Mfg-ASME Vessels	1250	2,500	200	0.08	11/30/01	600	50%
8721	Tax Preparation	700	1,250	276	0.22	10/25/99	600	40%
7371	Computer Service	600	877	253	0.29	12/15/99	600	33%
1795	Concrete Sawing	900	755	226	0.30	5/25/01	600	83%
7338	Medical Billing Serv	600	784	172	0.22	2/1/01	600	80%
5072	Distr-Hardware	650	2,160	97	0.04	8/31/97	600	40%
8721	Accounting Practice	600	600	150	0.25	3/31/96	600	25%
7381	Guard Service	700	1,377	242	0.18	9/12/02	600	50%
5087	Distr-Cleaning Supplies	650	1,125	246	0.22	11/21/02	600	100%
5088	Distr/Brkr-Aircraft Parts	1200	791	400	0.51	1/15/01	600	86%
5093	Metal Recycling	860	1,241	371	0.30	10/31/95	600	100%
7381	Guard Service	700	770	41	0.05	9/12/02	600	50%
2051	Whsle-Bread Bakery	649	850	245	0.29	10/3/03	600	100%
2499	Mfg-Wood Products	700	3,000	400	0.13	9/6/02	600	100%
0782	Lawn Maintenance	625	1,283	185	0.14	2/1/02	600	100%
1711	Contr-Heating & AC	600	1,503	150	0.10	9/30/96	600	33%
2851	Mfg-Paint Products	575	451	194	0.43	4/10/98	600	50%
8921	Tax Consulting	700	1,247	276	0.22	10/31/99	600	42%
2396	Silk Screen Printing	495	620	111	0.18	3/8/99	600	100%

Terms	Sale/ Sales	Sale/ SDE	Invq AMT	FF&E (000)	Rent/ Sales	Days on Mkt	Area
5Yrs @ 9.5%	0.67	3.1	15	180	N/A	142	Downey, CA
N/A	0.72	2.8	0	35	N/A	135	Central Florida
10 Yrs @ 8.5%	0.54	3.7	220	102	N/A	600	Vale, Oregon
5 Yrs @12%	0.43	3.8	39	50	1.0%	241	Florida
4 Yrs @ 9%	0.78	3.4	15	N/A	1.9%	74	West North Carolina
N/A	0.77	7.1	6	465	4.5%	360	Georgia
N/A	0.25	2.8	12	72	1.8%	143	West Central Florida
7 Yrs @ 7%	0.63	2.2	25	50	4.7%	374	Florida
N/A	0.26	3.0	335	200	1.7%	51	Louisville, KY
N/A	0.51	5.2	60	107	N/A	92	Pennsylvania
N/A	0.76	3.0	3	328	6.9%	75	Florida
N/A	0.52	1.4	15	80	0.1%	90	Southeast Florida
5 Yrs @ 8.5%	0.24	3.0	50	250	N/A	270	Southwest
5 Yrs @ 10%	0.48	2.2	0	40	N/A	130	Austin, TX
5 Yrs @ 10%	0.68	2.4	0	45	1%	47	Texas
6 Yrs @ 9%	0.79	2.7	10	200	2.5%	368	Colorado
5 Yrs @ 8%	0.77	3.5	5	40	5%	142	San Diego, CA
5 Yrs @ 12%	0.28	6.2	264	26	3%	184	Rocky Mtns, CO
5 Yrs @ 9%	1.00	4.0	0	20	6%		Oklahoma
5 Yrs @ 8%	0.44	2.5	0	10	0.7%	84	Florida
N/A	0.53	2.4	120	100	4%	99	Colorado
10 Yr Earnout	0.76	1.5	250	10	N/A	222	Florida
N/A	0.48	1.6	10	475	N/A		DesMoines, IA
5 Yrs @ 5%	0.78	14.6	0	12	0.5%	98	South Florida
N/A	0.71	2.4	4	350	N/A	90	South Florida
N/A	0.20	1.5	70	337	N/A	306	Georgia
N/A	0.47	3.2	0	100	1.4%	350	Florida
10 Yrs @ 9%	0.40	4.0	0	141	2%		Englewood, CO
5 Yrs @ 10%	1.33	3.1	37	37	5.3%	217	Florida
6 Yrs @10%	0.48	2.2	0	40	3%	120	Texas
N/A	0.97	5.4	45	285	6.2%	340	West Central Florida

Sic #	Bus Type	Asking PR (000) W/INV.	Ann Sales (000)	SDE (000)	SDE/ Gross Sales	Sale Date	Sale PR (000) W/INV.	% Down
6361	Title Insurance	795	1,437	317	0.22	9/18/01	600	100%
1521	Contr-Fire Restoration	600	1,500	250	0.17	9/30/96	600	25%
3086	Mfg/Distr-Foam Products	600	1,400	151	0.11	7/9/02	600	80%
7361	Skilled Staff Recruiting	734	2,406	91	0.04	4/9/01	600	33%
7363	Temporary Personnel	800	2,800	110	0.04	9/30/96	600	33%
7379	Internet Serv Provider	801	362	234	0.65	6/30/99	601	90%
7334	Blueprint Reproduction	695	468	225	0.48	9/29/03	604	100%
1799	Fencing Contractor	615	984	282	0.29	8/21/01	605	100%
5085	Distr-Industrial Supplies	750	1,300	147	0.11	2/28/97	610	43%
2396	Silk Screen Printing	600	644	208	0.32	12/27/02	610	64%
2819	Mfg-Chemicals	658	961	310	0.32	7/31/99	611	41%
2519	Mfg-Home Improve Products	358	651	165	0.25	8/16/01	613	100%
3446	Mfg-Metal Canopies	750	2,100	250	0.12	8/1/96	615	40%
7381	Security Systems	560	1,248	217	0.17	12/4/01	620	21%
1711	Contr-Heating & AC	613	1,510	220	0.15	1/2/97	622	10% SBA
1761	Constr-Comm Roofing	650	850	166	0.20	7/31/99	623	100%
5714	Mfg-Window Coverings	650	1,717	215	0.13	8/18/99	625	90%
7331	Direct Mail/ Advertising	625	2,950	275	0.09	1/31/96	625	72%
3993	Sign Manufacturer	790	1,272	237	0.19	11/19/02	625	100% SBA
0782	Lawn Maintenance	675	1,230	195	0.16	7/25/96	625	44%
1731	Contr-Electrical	599	634	247	0.39	5/19/00	630	100%
7699	Pumping Equipt Repair	600	851	202	0.24	9/27/00	630	100%
8742	Human Resources Consulting	630	1,001	242	0.24	8/18/99	630	31%
6531	Property Management	650	458	164	0.36	6/30/02	635	63%
5211	Sales/Serv-O/H Doors	625	1,397	341	0.24	10/31/00	635	20%
1731	Install-Alarm/TelCo Cabling	720	1,063	259	0.24	4/4/00	646	16%

Terms	Sale/ Sales	Sale/ SDE	Invq AMT	FF&E (000)	Rent/ Sales	Days on Mkt	Area
N/A	0.42	1.9	0	38	1.2%	166	Florida
N/A	0.40	2.4	0	150	N/A	5	Phoenix, AZ
5 Yr @ PR+1	0.43	4.0	65	230	5.1%	30	Ft Worth, Texas
4 Yrs. @ PR+1	0.25	6/6	0	9	1.5%	194	Wisconsin
N/A	0.21	5.5	0	25	N/A	202	Phoenix, AZ
N/A	1.66	2.6	1	225	N/A	N/A	Tempe, AZ
N/A	1.29	2.7	10	95	4%	230	Colorado
N/A	0.61	2.1	25	275	N/A	706	Florida
5 Yrs @ 0%	0.47	4.1	230	141	3%	100	Oxford, MA
2.5 Yrs @ 8%	0.95	2.9	20	151	7.2%	164	Colorado
3 Yrs @ 0%	0.64	2.0	14	64	5.4%	364	Denver, CO
NA	0.94	3.7	13	100	N/a	72	Florida
10 Yrs @ 9%	0.29	2.5	115	175	3%	120	New Mexico
6 Yrs @ 8.8%	0.50	2.9	60	143	N/A	117	Florida
10 Yrs @ PR+2.8	0.41	2.8	13	200	2.7%	113	San Jose, CA
N/A	0.73	3.8	10	47	2%	160	Texas
N/A	0.36	2.9	47	170	3%	153	West Central Florida
7 Yrs @ 0%	0.21	2.3	5	50	1%		Cincinnati, OH
N/A	0.49	2.6	300	305	2.8%	550	NW Florida
5 Yrs @ 10%	0.51	3.2	0	135	2%	270	Grapevine, TX
N/A	0.99	2.6	10	16	0.1%	133	Southeast Florida
N/A	0.74	3.1	205	174	N/A	800	Oklahoma
10 Yrs @ 8.5%	0.63	2.6	0	41	10.4%	320	Atlanta, GA
N/A	1.39	3.9	0	25	N/A	N/A	Phoenix, AZ
8 Yrs @ 10%	0.45	1.9	34	168	4%	111	Austin, TX
N/A	0.61	2.5	130	N/A	1.9%	45	Lomita, CA

Sic #	Bus Type	Asking PR (000) W/INV.	Ann Sales (000)	SDE (000)	SDE/ Gross Sales	Sale Date	Sale PR (000) W/INV.	% Down
5087	Distr-Cleaning Supplies	650	1,900	178	0.09	6/30/96	647	100%
5047	Sales/Rental Medical Equip	650	688	180	0.26	6/28/96	650	38% SBA
1791	Steel Fabrication	775	2,166	210	0.10	9/30/02	650	15.$%
4213	Moving & Storage	695	1,131	222	0.20	12/2/02	650	23%
7359	Medical Equip Leasing	731	636	178	0.28	1/4/02	650	30% SBA
8721	Accounting Practice	675	604	268	0.44	12/1/98	650	96%
1731	Contr-Elect Lighting	650	635	247	0.39	5/19/00	650	100%
5113	Distr-Packaging	740	2,549	186	0.07	2/28/97	650	32%
2741	Publ-Rental Guide	800	600	150	0.25	5/31/99	650	20%
8999	Calibration Services	750	450	253	0.56	10/23/03	650	80%
2621	Mfg-Paper Products	700	774	264	0.34	7/1/02	650	100%
3499	Mfg-Specialty Equipment	650	1,020	175	0.17	8/31/00	650	22%
3585	Mfg/Distr-A/C Products	775	2,000	165	0.08	6/30/99	650	30%
5099	Distr-Saddles/Tack	650	650	235	0.36	5/14/02	650	25%
7641	Upholstery Repair	750	655	276	0.42	3/31/96	655	15.3%
5099	Distr-Misc Supplies	811	1,075	214	0.20	1/16/97	656	28%
5148	Whsle-Fresh Produce	750	4,100	195	0.05	1/15/01	660	100%
1541	Contr-Steel Buildings	617	1,600	208	0.13	3/14/02	660	N/A
7336	Mfg-Pre-Press	664	538	176	0.33	9/17/99	664	50%
2752	Printing Shop	725	595	181	0.30	2/11/00	664	94%
4959	Parking Lot Sweeping	700	686	290	0.42	7/14/00	665	45%
3534	Mfg-Elevator Product	725	596	211	0.35	12/3/99	665	20% SBA
7361	Employment Agency	749	2,413	159	0.07	10/18/02	669	100%
5199	Distr-Balloons	1000	5,100	466	0.09	3/31/00	670	34%
5171	Distr-Heating Oil	733	3,890	85	0.02	11/25/02	672	100%
7641	Furniture Restoration	725	1,686	183	0.11	1/4/99	673	67%
1521	Contr-Home Improvement	875	1,500	374	0.25	12/3/99	675	15%
7349	Window Cleaning	729	831	246	0.30	7/31/99	675	100% SBA
2752	Printing Shop	724	2,150	102	0.05	7/31/98	675	N/A
2752	Printer-Commercial	695	1,377	281	0.20	12/16/02	678	100%
3599	Machined Parts/ Stampings	865	959	325	0.34	11/30/01	682	21%
4953	Waste Management	775	627	188	0.30	6/30/02	685	70%

Terms	Sale/ Sales	Sale/ SDE	Invq AMT	FF&E (000)	Rent/ Sales	Days on Mkt	Area
N/A	0.34	3.6	266	27	2.4%	312	Rocky Mtns, CO
10 Yrs at _____%	0.94	3.6	390	40	4.6%	104	San Francisco Area
10 Yrs @ 7.5%	0.30	3.1	100	296	1.8%	105	Florida
10 Yrs @ 7%	0.57	2.9	5	142	7%	90	Georgia
10 Yrs @ 9%	1.02	3.7	289	300	N/A	270	Florida
5 Yrs @ 8%	1.08	2.4	0	10	3.9%		Central Florida
N/A	1.02	2.6	10	16	1.4%	134	Central Florida
5 Yrs @ 8%	0.26	3.5	345	63	2.4%	48	Rocky Mtns, CO
5 Yrs @ 8%	1.08	4.3	10	50	3%	250	Southeast
N/A	1.44	2.6	0	285	2%	30	Massachusetts
N/A	0.84	2.5	20	175	2.0%	212	Florida
N/A	0.64	3.7	150	N/a	6.6%	71	Orange, CA
7 Yrs @ 9.5%	0.32	3.9	50	250	1%	180	Oklahoma
10 Yrs @ 7.5%	1.00	2.8	225	20	11%	180	Colorado
7 Yrs @ 8%	1.00	2.4	55	120	1.6%		Maine
10 Yrs @ 10%	0.61	3.1	136	35	N/A	120	Salt Lake City, UT
N/A	0.16	3.4	223	157	6.5%	210	Orange County, CA
N/A	0.41	3.2	42	100	N/A	298	Minnesota
4 Yrs @ 9.5%	1.23	3.8	4	210	1%	150	Central Iowa
2 Yrs @ 8.5%	1.12	3.7	0	210	N/A	114	NW Florida
6 Yrs @ 9%	0.97	2.3	0	228	N/A	N/A	Salt Lake City, UT
10 Yrs @10%	1.12	3.2	5	175	4.8%	70	Southeast Florida
N/A	0.28	4.2	0	43	N/A	267	Central Florida
3 Yrs @ 8%	0.13	1.4	80	125	0.1%	450	Texas
N/A	0.17	7.9	73	159	N/A	191	Pennsylvania
5 Yrs @ 10.3%	0.40	3.7	30	105	2.2%	187	Central Florida
N/A	0.45	1.8	0	6	N/A	172	Central Florida
N/A	0.81	2.7	0	75	1.7%	120	Rocky Mountains
5 Yrs @ 8.5%	0.31	6.6	5	113	6%	127	Altamonte Springs, Florida
N/A	0.49	2.4	19	451	4.5%	378	Colorado
20 Yrs @ 7.2%	0.71	2.1	20	353	2.8%	415	Ohio
N/A	1.09	3.6	0	475	N/A	N/A	Tempe, AZ

Sic #	Bus Type	Asking PR (000) W/INV.	Ann Sales (000)	SDE (000)	SDE/ Gross Sales	Sale Date	Sale PR (000) W/INV.	% Down
5047	Distr-Medical Equipment	775	1,118	206	0.18	9/30/93	685	47%
4812	Distr-Communications	825	1,579	373	0.24	4/30/02	685	100%SBA
2499	Mfg-Wood Products	800	2,437	248	0.10	10/14/98	690	38%
3086	Mfg-Styrofoam Products	790	1,103	209	0.19	11/13/01	690	100%
1711	Contr-Refrigeration	675	862	280	0.32	5/1/01	690	69%
3599	Mfg-Machine Shop	700	787	214	0.27	11/2/98	693	90%
1791	Steel Fabrication	695	1,800	265	0.15	10/1/98	695	60%
3441	Mfg-Structural Steel	808	1,555	259	0.17	5/21/98	698	40%
3625	Mfg-Cust Automation Equip	525	1,339	99	0.07	4/30/99	700	19%
7349	Janitorial Service	750	954	269	0.28	7/30/99	700	89%
7349	Cleaning & Restoration	775	1,411	553	0.39	9/2/03	700	100%
3471	Metal Plating Company	750	1,060	298	0.28	6/30/93	700	29%
1799	Fencing Contractors	750	1,299	397	0.31	6/3/98	700	43%
2519	Mfg-Home Accessories	750	1,300	170	0.13	11/30/96	700	80%
5087	Distr—Janitorial Supplies	750	2,235	263	0.12	8/31/99	700	43%
7363	Temporary Personnel	770	725	310	0.43	11/1/97	700	60%
1761	Contr-Roofing	1000	8,000	166	0.02	11/1/01	700	20%
5044	Retail-Copy Machines	735	2,522	282	0.11	8/31/96	700	100%
1721	Contr-Painting	750	1,502	241	0.16	10/17/01	700	61%
4812	Wireless Communication	1000	1,681	302	0.18	9/25/02	700	100%
5013	Mfg-Aftermarket Accessories	700	1,200	197	0.16	10/31/97	700	30%
3999	Mfg-Fiberglass Products	879	1,321	336	0.25	5/1/03	704	60%
7334	Commercial Copy Center	745	1,000	280	0.28	11/30/01	705	43%
5044	Distr-Office Supplies	900	2,430	340	0.14	8/1/00	707	100%
3355	Mfg-Aluminum Fabrication	640	387	234	0.60	7/20/99	710	73% SBA
2499	Mfg/Distr-Weed Products	790	1,300	162	0.12	6/2/00	714	79%
1541	Mfg-Custom Skylights	715	2,400	195	0.08	12/31/02	715	42%

Terms	Sale/ Sales	Sale/ SDE	Invq AMT	FF&E (000)	Rent/ Sales	Days on Mkt	Area
7 Yrs @ 10%	0.61	3.3	50	260	3%		Carlsbad, CA
N/A	0.43	1.8	50	110	2.7%	109	Tampa Bay, FL
8 Yrs @ 10%	0.28	2.8	110	10	N/A	277	West Central Florida
N/A	0.63	3.3	40	212	6%	326	Florida
4 Yrs @ 9%	0.80	2.5	40	135	N/A	210	Georgia
N/A	0.88	3.2	0	430	5%		Denver, CO
5 Yrs	0.39	2.6	195	400	3.4%	100	Southwest Florida
3 Yrs @ 10%	0.45	2.7	48	239	3.4%	350	Ohio
5 Yrs @ 0%	0.52	7.1	10	150	2.7%	410	Denver, CO
3 Yrs @ 10%	0.73	2.6	50	224	N/A	90	Central Kentucky
N/A	0.50	1.3	0	100	1.6%	810	North Carolina
15 Yrs @ 10%	0.66	2.3		250	4.5%		Dallas, TX
10 Yrs @ 8%	0.54	1.8	75	120	1.6%	220	Colorado
2 Yrs	0.54	4.1	350	125	5%	80	Southeastern US
5 Yrs @ 9%	0.31	2.7	450	30	2%	86	Texas
5 Yrs @ 7%	0.97	2.3	0	40	5%	90	Minneapolis, MN
10 Yrs	0.09	4.2	25	125	2%	300	South Florida
N/A	0.28	2.5	350	150	N/A		Midwest
5 Yrs @ 8%	0.47	2.9	25	120	1%	500	Colorado
N/A	0.42	2.3	0	25	N/A	714	Minnesota
5 Yrs @ 9%	0.58	3.6	125	54	N/A		Orange County, CA
4 Yrs @ 7%	0.53	2.1	4	78	3.5%	304	Florida
10 Yrs @ 9%	0.70	2.5	10	240	5%	165	San Diego, CA
N/A	0.29	2.1	0	25	N/A	190	N Central Georgia
10 Yrs @ 9.5%	1.83	3.0	85	573	1.2%	667	Phoenix, AZ
7 Yrs @ 9%	0.55	4.4	120	150	N/A	300	Houston, TX
5 Yrs @ 10%	0.30	3.7	115	200	3%	330	Irvine, CA

Sic #	Bus Type	Asking PR (000) W/INV.	Ann Sales (000)	SDE (000)	SDE/ Gross Sales	Sale Date	Sale PR (000) W/INV.	% Down
1711	Contr-Plumbing	995	4,659	575	0.12	3/5/01	720	42%
1731	Contr-Electrical	725	1,403	427	0.30	3/19/02	725	31%
2499	Mfg-Wood Products	725	2,295	249	0.11	2/21/00	725	100%
4213	Freight Broker	850	2,000	280	0.14	6/30/02	725	50%
2396	Silk Screen Printing	745	850	220	0.26	5/1/01	725	100%
2099	Mfg-Health Food	775	444	146	0.33	4/17/02	725	100%
8734	Research Management	725	711	315	0.44	3/31/00	725	20%
2752	Printing Shop	975	1,195	354	0.30	9/30/02	730	86%
7342	Pest Control	856	593	283	0.48	4/11/03	732	15%
5063	Distr-Control Parts	900	2,895	194	0.07	12/1/97	735	100%
7361	Management Recruiting	750	1,150	329	0.29	1/8/99	735	100%
2499	Mfg-Wood Products	1020	1,483	245	0.17	5/15/03	740	25%
3273	Ready-Mixed Concrete	845	2,250	250	0.11	1/1/00	740	35%
7359	Equipment Rental(3)	940	872	287	0.33	9/4/98	740	20% SBA
7319	Advertising Sales	700	821	123	0.15	1/31/96	740	25%
5072	Distr-Durable Goods	725	2,016	98	0.05	1/15/99	743	N/A
5099	Import/Export Housewares	754	6,000	412	0.07	3/24/98	744	30%
7389	Check Verification	750	677	287	0.42	10/30/97	750	80%
5141	Distr-Food Products	750	1.500	257	0.17	1/2/03	750	80%
2752	Printing Shop	750	1,350	282	0.21	8/27/99	750	90%
5211	Distr-Building Materials	800	2,062	369	0.18	8/10/01	750	20% SBA
7371	Software Design	750	1,356	230	0.17	2/02/00	750	33%
2741	Publ-Cards/ Calendars	800	803	419	0.52	1/19/00	750	50%
7361	Employment Agency	795	1,212	258	0.21	9/7/01	750	100%
3599	Mfg-Machine Shop	985	724	225	0.31	6/30/00	751	100%
2752	Printer-Commercial	779	731	177	0.24	8/31/99	754	35%
2741	Newspaper Publisher	875	1,500	335	0.22	10/1/01	755	50%
0782	Lawn Maintenance	1005	1,223	239	0.20	12/18/02	755	50%
1611	Paving Contractor	1005	4,783	352	0.07	11/8/01	755	13%
1799	Fencing Contractor	1200	1,288	272	0.21	7/6/98	765	26%
3829	Mfg-Wind Measure Device	721	875	297	0.34	5/24/01	767	32%
4212	Freight Trucking	786	1,007	211	0.21	12/31/00	773	80%

Terms	Sale/ Sales	Sale/ SDE	Invq AMT	FF&E (000)	Rent/ Sales	Days on Mkt	Area
4 Yrs @ 8%	0.15	1.3	0	220	0.6%	245	Georgia
10 Yrs @ 10%	0.52	1.7	0	11	0.6%	193	Florida
N/A	0.32	2.9	110	198	N/A	142	Central Florida
N/A	0.36	2.6	0	65	N/A	240	Chicago, IL
N/A	0.85	3.3	250	100	12%	114	Georgia
N/A	1.63	5.0	75	75	2%	472	Pacific Northwest
10 Yrs @ PR+1.2	1.02	2.3	34	281	7.6%	206	Colorado
N/A	0.61	2.1	0	340	N/A	N/A	Phoenix, AZ
12 Yrs @ 8%	1.23	2.6	1	10	1.8%	380	Florida
N/A	0.25	3.8	400	85	3.6%	150	Santa Clara, CA
N/A	0.64	2.2	0	116	4%	110	Eastern US
N/A	0.50	3.0	20	138	3.2%	533	Florida
9 Yrs @ 8%	0.33	3.0	20	400	2.8%	283	San Diego, CA
N/A	0.85	2.6	10	446	5.5%	384	Southwest
5 Yrs @ 9.2%	0.90	6.0	150	55	4%		Worcestor, MA
N/A	0.37	7.6	300	40	N/A	67	Minnesota
10 Yrs @ PR+2	0.12	1.8	69	65	1%	300	West Central Florida
10 Yrs @ 6%	1.11	2.6	0	112	N/A	240	Northwest Florida
10 Yrs @ 6.5%	0.50	2.9	40	2	5%	540	Colorado
10 Yrs @ 10%	0.56	2.7	10	200	1.6%	88	Atlanta, GA
10 Yrs @ PR+2	0.36	2.0	150	60	1.9%	120	Florida
5 Yrs	0.55	3.3	0	50	7%	147	Texas
N/A	0.93	1.8	100	4	N/A	150	SF Bay Area, CA
N/A	0.62	2.9	0	60	2.6%	216	Florida
N/A	1.04	3.3	0	444	N/A	180	N Central Georgia
5 Yrs @ 9.5%	1.03	4.3	4	480	2.5%	165	Rocky Mountains, CO
20 Yrs @ 8%	0.50	2.3	100	400	N/A	97	Boise, ID
5 Yrs @ 8%	0.62	3.2	5	185	3.3%	18	Georgia
5 Yrs @ 10%	0.16	2.1	5	140	1.1%	216	Florida
12 Yrs @ 7.5%	0.59	2.8	80	80	3%	123	Knoxville, TN
N/A	0.88	2.6	196	136	3.7%	189	Colorado
5 Yrs @ 9%	0.77	3.7	3	388	N/A	144	Southwest

Sic #	Bus Type	Asking PR (000) W/INV.	Ann Sales (000)	SDE (000)	SDE/ Gross Sales	Sale Date	Sale PR (000) W/INV.	% Down
5148	Distr-Fresh Herbs	775	1,800	345	0.19	9/30/97	775	52%
2047	Mfg-Pet Food	775	600	150	0.25	7/15/00	775	90%
5191	Distr-Feed & Additives	900	4,553	252	0.06	1/31/02	775	100%
5142	Distr-Frozen Food	800	819	293	0.36	8/27/02	781	51%
1623	TeleCom Cabling	474	1,200	244	0.20	12/31/99	784	15%
2448	Mfg-Wood Pallets	850	890	276	0.31	6/30/00	795	100%
2396	Silk Screen Printing	800	1,420	119	0.08	3/29/01	800	50%
7371	Software Integrator	815	1,200	390	0.32	2/29/04	800	26% SBA
5014	Distr-Industrial Tires	800	2,400	200	0.08	8/31/98	800	100%
2741	Newsletter Publisher	800	720	261	0.36	4/30/97	800	41%
2396	Silk Screen Printing	800	1,515	347	0.23	1/30/98	800	91%
8732	Marketing Consultant	1200	2,780	620	0.22	7/30/01	800	25%
5169	Distr-Sealants	1000	1,500	190	0.13	2/28/93	800	38%
2499	Mfg-Wood Serving Boards	800	1,600	204	0.13	6/30/95	800	31%
0782	Landscaping w/ Nursery	1525	2,127	446	0.21	5/31/96	800	100%
4212	Const Office Towing	901	790	335	0.42	5/22/98	801	38%
0782	Lawn Maintenance	850	1,138	333	0.29	5/8/02	804	22%
1761	Contr-Roofing	924	1,983	371	0.19	5/31/02	810	100%
3479	Mfg-Name Plates	900	2,300	275	0.12	5/12/96	810	69%
2519	Mfg-Home Accessories	855	1,483	324	0.22	3/31/99	810	100%
7359	Plant Maintenance	895	1,200	420	0.35	2/28/00	815	20% SBA
1793	Contr-Windows & Doors	850	1,000	400	0.40	1/06/00	825	20%
5112	Distr-Office Products	720	1,100	199	0.18	12/31/97	825	66%
1731	Contr-Electrical	1396	8,500	505	0.06	2/15/02	825	100%
3999	Mfg-Wax Candles	1500	767	316	0.41	6/1/99	825	100%
5047	Distr-Medical Supplies	825	2,932	204	0.07	3/1/02	825	100%
5085	Distr-Industrial Supplies	75	1,050	180	0.17	5/30/01	830	17%
3599	Mfg-Machine Shop	842	560	201	0.36	1/05/98	832	33%
2752	Printer-Commercial	960	1,958	340	0.17	9/30/02	835	12%
1799	Contr-Specialty	850	1,173	190	0.16	8/8/02	835	13%
3564	Mfg-Exhaust Systems	1350	1,501	195	0.13	8/28/00	840	77%
3441	Mfg-Steel Fabrication	950	1,200	343	0.29	11/28/01	840	74%

Terms	Sale/ Sales	Sale/ SDE	Invq AMT	FF&E (000)	Rent/ Sales	Days on Mkt	Area
7 Yrs @ 9.5%	0.43	2.2	0	45	3.6%	35	San Diego, CA
2 Yrs @ 9%	1.29	5.2	10	100	N/A	165	N Central Georgia
N/A	0.17	3.1	225	75	4.9%	21	Florida
5 Yrs @ 8%	0.95	2.7	50	500	1.6%	191	Florida
4 Yrs @ 0%	0.65	3.2	124	N/A	1.2%	N/A	Northwest
N/A	0.89	2.9	36	233	0.4%	70	Southeast Florida
10 Yrs @ 8.5%	0.56	6.7	402	500	400	155	Southeast
N/A	0.67	2.1	0	195	5%	355	Orange Cty, CA
N/A	0.33	4.0	150	100	8%	180	Texas
10 Yrs @ 9%	1.11	3.1	0	60	4%	60	Southeast Florida
3 Yrs @ 8%	0.53	2.3	53	55	2.7%	180	Orange County, CA
N/A	0.29	1.3	0	135	5%	530	Middlesex County, NJ
7 Yrs @ 8%	0.53	4.2	170	13	N/A		New England
10 Yrs @ 11%	0.50	3.9	400	325	2.7%		Vermont
N/A	0.38	1.8	395	225	N/A	284	Rocky Mtns, CO
10 Yrs @ 9%	1.01	2.4	1	205	N/A	366	Portland, OR
12 Yrs @ 8%	0.71	2.4	0	215	N/A	250	Florida
N/A	0.41	2.2	0	36	N/A	351	Southeast
7 Yrs @ 7%	0.35	2.9	250	235	N/A		Michigan
N/A	0.55	2.5	92	320	N/A	130	Central Florida
N/A	0.68	1.9	110	N/A	5.5%	90	San Jose, CA
3 Yrs @ 10%	0.82	2.1	10	20	1.1%	90	West Central Florida
8 Yrs @ 9%	0.75	4.1	142	100	N/A	300	Rocky Mtns, CO
N/A	0.10	1.6	25	240	0.3%	560	Georgia
N/A	1.08	2.6	30	164	2%	60	Worcester, MA
N/A	0.28	4.0	375	100	2.5%	182	Florida
N/A	0.79	4.6	75	50	1.7%	95	Florida
% Yrs @ 8.5%	1.49	4.1	92	300	4.8%	365	Colorado
N/A	0.43	2.5	10	500	N/A	N/A	Phoenix, AZ
10 Yrs @ 9%	0.71	4.4	70	80	2.6%	150	Florida
N/A	0.56	4.3	100	N/A	11%	301	Los Angeles, CA
10 Yrs @ 6.3%	0.70	2.4	63	95	3.7%	302	Colorado

Sic #	Bus Type	Asking PR (000) W/INV.	Ann Sales (000)	SDE (000)	SDE/ Gross Sales	Sale Date	Sale PR (000) W/INV.	% Down
5211	Distr-Building Products	1115	2,528	434	0.17	11/21/01	840	40%
5045	Distr-Computer Equipt	1100	2,273	361	0.16	8/31/98	845	60%
1731	Contr-Electrical	998	3,100	192	0.06	10/13/00	848	100%
5043	Distr-LCD Projectors	850	2500	360	0.14	1/15/97	848	17%
3444	Mfg-Metal Fabrication	950	3,000	220	0.07	5/31/99	850	30%
3444	Mfg-Metal Fabrication	850	1,900	364	0.19	12/31/98	850	78%
1623	Utilities Contractor	1020	1,384	461	0.33	10/15/99	850	70%
1761	Contr-Roofing	950	1,900	500	0.26	12/8/03	850	76%
3443	Mfg-Pressure Vessels	950	3,000	275	0.09	1/31/99	850	80%
6361	Title Insurance	850	1,275	317	0.25	11/15/99	850	35%
1791	Struct Street Erection	895	1,000	400	0.40	4/21/00	850	100%
3079	Mfg-Plastic Products	895	1,345	446	0.33	8/31/94	850	70%
1791	Steel Erection	980	1,257	452	0.36	4/24/00	850	100%
5047	Distr-Medical Supplies	900	1,900	285	0.15	3/3/98	850	50%
2499	Mfg-Wood Products	950	2,036	329	0.16	11/19/02	850	72%
3823	Mfg-Indust Process Equipment	720	650	205	0.32	9/6/00	860	50%
2395	Mfg-Embroidery	895	787	294	0.37	12/2/92	860	N/A
5141	Distr-Food Products	875	6,500	337	0.05	5/31/97	865	40%
1799	Fencing Contractor	600	1,400	485	0.35	1/16/99	875	90%
3357	Mfg-Medical Products	875	1,800	N/A	#ERR	1/28/03	875	N/A
5211	Lumber Yard/ Planning Mill	999	2,097	309	0.15	1/31/96	875	35%
2752	Printing Shop	1262	1,355	172	0.13	5/14/99	877	100%
5251	Whsle/Retail-Light Fixtures	878	1,869	221	0.12	1/1/00	878	98%
7359	Equipment Rental	1105	927	225	0.24	1/31/94	880	34%
5085	Dist-Const Materials	892	4,309	274	0.06	7/14/00	892	75%
2519	Mfg-Closet Systems	950	1,331	264	0.20	8/22/00	895	100%
1711	Contr-Heating & AC	900	4,300	938	0.22	8/31/98	900	100%
3544	Mfg-Extrusion Tools	1100	1,000	160	0.16	1/31/99	900	60%
2519	Mfg-Home Furniture	900	970	230	0.24	4/7/00	900	38%
4813	TelCo InterConnect	1000	3,460	215	0.06	11/20/99	900	17%
5251	Hardware/Bldg Supply	900	830	175	0.21	11/16/98	900	87% SBA

Terms	Sale/ Sales	Sale/ SDE	Invq AMT	FF&E (000)	Rent/ Sales	Days on Mkt	Area
5 Yrs @ 8%	0.33	1.9	40	320	3.5%	165	Florida
10 Yrs @ 9%	0.37	2.3	518	132	1.2%	126	Atlanta, GA
N/A	0.27	4.4	20	172	N/A	90	Tampa Bay, FL
SBA Loan	0.34	2.4	248	240	1%	90	New Mexico
10 Yrs @ 9%	0.28	3.9	50	200	2%	150	Oklahoma
10 Yrs @ 9%	0.45	2.3	35	350	N/A	169	Atlanta, GA
N/A	0.61	1.8		N/A	N/A		Grand Junction, CO
5 Yrs @ 7%	0.45	1.7	5	50	N/A	270	Los Angeles, CA
5 Yrs @ PR+1	0.28	3.1	100	N/A	N/A	270	Oklahoma
5 Yrs @ 9%	0.67	2.7	0	75	2.7%	233	West Central Florida
N/A	0.85	2.1	0	125	N/A	30	Northeast Florida
10 Yrs @ 7.5%	0.63	1.9	22	300	3%		Rocky Mountain
N/A	0.68	1.9	0	N/A	N/A	84	Central Florida
7 Yrs @ 8%	0.45	3.0	250	350	8%	93	Southwest Florida
10 Yrs @ 7%	0.42	2.6	189	208	3.1%	455	Florida
5 Yrs @ 10%	1.32	4.2	80	25	N/A	66	Atlanta, Georgia
N/A	1.09	2.9	0	100	N/A	54	Minnesota
7 Yrs @ 9%	0.13	2.6	250	100	N/A		Inland Empire, CA
N/A	0.62	1.8	5	150	4%	20	Denver, CO
N/A	0.49	#ERR	125	100	N/A	264	Minnesota
5 Yrs @ 8%	0.42	2.8	300	450	15%		Colorado
N/A	0.65	5.1	155	1.5M	1.9%	135	Macon, GA
6 Mos @ 0%	0.47	4.0	512	50	N/A	905	Colorado
15 Yr Note	0.95	3.9	5	N/A	15%		North Rocky Mtns
5 Yrs @ 5%	0.21	3.3	492	300	1.4%	400	Colorado
N/A	0.67	3.4	35	350	0.2%	60	Southeast Florida
N/A	0.21	1.0	0	910	N/A	30	Southeastern US
9 Yr Royalty	0.90	5.6	400	450	N/A	270	Texas
6 Yrs @ 8%	0.93	3.9	261	176	N/A	64	Atlanta, Georgia
10 Yrs @ 9%	0.26	4.2	300	210	2%	314	Central Oregon
5 Yrs @ 10%	1.08	5.1	406	180	N/A	107	Louisville, KY

Sic #	Bus Type	Asking PR (000) W/INV.	Ann Sales (000)	SDE (000)	SDE/ Gross Sales	Sale Date	Sale PR (000) W/INV.	% Down
5031	Distr-Doors & Windows	1200	3,100	400	0.13	2/28/93	900	20%
5065	Distr-Electronics	900	4,387	298	0.07	2/28/96	900	33%
5191	Mfg/Distr-Chemical Seed	900	820	276	0.34	3/30/01	900	33%
2394	Mfg-Canvas Products	1825	695	245	0.35	7/3/01	925	20%
1711	Contr-Mechanical	925	6,500	375	0.06	3/18/02	925	30%
2732	Contr-Electrical Maint	1000	1,200	250	0.21	6/30/99	925	17%
5191	Distr-Landscaping Supplies	1005	2,323	311	0.13	5/15/98	930	100%
1793	Vinyl Doors/ Windows	935	1,742	318	0.18	6/30/01	936	66%
5023	Distr-Home Furnishings	990	1,400	250	0.18	12/31/02	939	100%
4212	Moving Company	940	1,636	325	0.20	9/30/02	940	100%
5063	Whsle-Electrical Supplies	1000	2000	250	0.12	1/31/97	947	100%
7349	Janitorial Services	950	1,500	480	0.32	12/31/96	950	20%
7338	Executive Suites	1100	1,244	359	0.29	7/7/00	950	100%
8734	Envir. Testing-Asbestos	1270	2,193	364	0.17	6/30/96	950	89%
1711	Contr-Heating & AC	825	2,025	343	0.17	10/11/98	950	20%
2394	Mfg-Canvas Awnings	950	915	524	0.57	8/28/03	950	100%
4783	Industrial Packaging	995	1,451	332	0.23	4/1/00	950	100%
3599	Machine Shop-Auto Parts	1100	825	305	0.37	12/31/99	950	17% SBA
4812	Wireless Communications	1250	3,813	500	0.13	4/28/99	950	100%
3479	Powder Coating	1100	761	331	0.43	7/30/99	950	68%
7311	Advertising Agency	950	906	N/A	#ERR	2/13/04	950	50%
6531	Escrow Company	952	829	430	0.52	8/31/03	952	50%
7338	Executive Suites	1100	1,240	208	0.17	7/7/00	960	100%
7331	Mailing Service	1050	1,759	416	0.24	7/31/02	970	100%
3993	Sign Manufacturer	1308	1,300	340	0.26	12/5/01	970	38%
7389	Answering Service	975	2,000	441	0.22	1/31/01	975	37%
7361	Executive Recruiter	975	2,258	469	0.21	1/17/03	975	21%
3444	Precision Sheet Metal	1628	1,690	269	0.16	7/31/98	978	3% SBA
2511	Mfg/Sales-Futon Beds	990	3,113	481	0.15	11/3/98	990	N/A
2519	Mfg-Closet Systems	1150	1,433	301	0.21	2/28/03	990	15%

Terms	Sale/ Sales	Sale/ SDE	Invq AMT	FF&E (000)	Rent/ Sales	Days on Mkt	Area
10 Yrs @ 10%	0.29	2.2	70	39	N/A		New England
5 Yrs @ 9%	0.21	3.0	450	45	2%		Louisiana
5 Yrs	1.10	3.3	155	13	N/A	540	Boise, ID
N/A	1.33	3.8	30	228	N/A	345	Wyoming
12 Yrs @ 8%	0.14	2.5	75	321	0.6%	48	Georgia
N/A	0.77	3.7	50	300	N/A	N/A	Mesa, AZ
N/A	0.40	3.0	80	750	N/A	101	Glendale, AZ
7 Yrs @ 9%	0.54	2.9	370	41	4%	475	North Carolina
N/A	0.67	3.8	339	15	N/A	N/A	Texas
N/A	0.57	2.9	0	190	N/A	N/A	Phoenix, AZ
N/A	0.47	3.8	250	200	2%	150	Marble Falls, TX
SBA @ PR+2	0.63	2.0	0	N/A	1.2%		Orange Cty, CA
N/A	0.76	2.6	0	140	40%	90	Texas
N/A	0.43	2.6	0	N/A	1.5%		Orange Cty, CA
N/A	0.47	2.8	98	255	1%	180	Denver, CO
N/A	1.04	1.8	200	118	N/A	156	Southeast
N/A	0.65	2.9	85	85	2.7%	92	Colorado
10 Yrs @ 9.5%	1.15	3.1	0	374	N/A	180	W. Central Florida
N/A	0.25	1.9	0	80	N/A		Denver, CO
N/A	1.25	2.9	0	N/A	N/A	N/A	Denver, CO
4 Yrs @ 7%	1.05	#ERR	0	50	N/A	138	South Florida
10 Yrs @ 6%	1.15	2.2	2	40	N/A	150	Los Angeles, CA
N/A	0.77	4.6	0	140	40%	90	Austin, TX
N/A	0.55	2.3	684	N/A	5.4%	30	Midwest
N/A	0.75	2.9	8	491	4.2%	109	Georgia
N/A	0.49	2.2	0	N/A	1.2%	139	Plains States
5 Yrs	0.43	2.1	0	134	18%	120	South Florida
N/A	0.58	3.6	28	N/A	5.7%	120	San Jose, CA
14 Yrs @ 10%	0.32	2.1	339	160	2.3%	232	Altamonte Springs
10 Yrs @ 7%	0.69	3.3	20	146	3.2%	234	Florida

Appendix 4

Sample Confidentiality Agreement

S Corporation
200 Main Square
Anywhere, USA
Attn: Mr. John Doe
President

RE: *Confidentiality Agreement*

Dear Gentlemen:

In connection with our possible interest in purchasing S Corporation and/or its subsidiary, Sub. Inc. (individually and collectively the "Company"), you are furnishing us with certain information that is either nonpublic, confidential, or proprietary in nature. The information furnished to us, together with analyses, compilations, studies, or other documents prepared by us, or by our partners, directors, officers, employees, representatives, attorneys, accountants, financial advisors, and other agents (individually and collectively the "Representatives"), which contain or otherwise reflect, such information or our review of, or interest in, the Company, are hereinafter referred to individually and collectively as the "Information." In consideration of the Company furnishing us with the Information, we agree that:

1. The Information shall be kept confidential and shall not, without the prior written consent of the Company, be disclosed by us, or by our Representatives. Moreover, we agree to reveal the information only to our Representatives who need to know the Information for the purpose of evaluating the transaction described above, who are informed by us of the confidential nature of the Information and who shall agree in writing to be bound by the terms and conditions of this Agreement. The Company shall be named as a

third-party beneficiary of the Agreement with our Representatives. We will be responsible for any breach of this Agreement by our Representatives.

2. Without the Company's prior written consent, we and our Representatives will not disclose to any individual or entity the Information, the fact that the Information has been made available, that discussions or negotiations are taking place concerning a possible transaction involving us and the Company, or any of the terms, conditions or other facts with respect to any such possible transaction (including the status thereof).

3. We shall keep a record of the Information furnished to us and of the location of such Information. The Information, except for that portion of the Information which consists of analyses, compilations, studies, or other documents prepared by us or by our Representatives, will be returned to the Company immediately upon the Company's request, together with all copies thereof. That portion of the Information which consists of analyses, compilations, studies, or other documents prepared by us or by our Representatives will be held by us and kept confidential and subject to the provisions of this Agreement, or destroyed by us upon the request of the Company. Such destruction shall be confirmed by us in writing.

4. This Agreement shall not apply to such portions of the Information which (a) are already or become generally available to the public through no fault or action by us or by our Representatives, or (b) become available to us on a nonconfidential basis from a source, other than the Company or its Representatives, which is not prohibited from disclosing such portions to us by a contractual, legal, or fiduciary obligation to the Company or its Representatives.

5. Without the Company's prior written consent, neither we nor any of our Affiliates (as hereafter defined) will for a period of one year from the date hereof either (i) directly or indirectly solicit for employment any person who is now employed by the Company or any of its subsidiaries or (ii) employ any such person whether or not we or our Affiliates solicited such employment. The term "Affiliates" as used herein includes any individual or entity directly or indirectly, through one or more intermediaries, controlling us or controlled by or under common control with us.

6. For a period of one year from the date of this Agreement neither we nor any of our Affiliates will use any of the Information that is nonpublic in any business that is competitive to the business of the Company.

7. We understand that the Company has endeavored to include in the Information those materials that it believes to be reliable and relevant for the purpose of our evaluation, but we acknowledge that neither the Company nor its Representatives make any representation or warranty as to the accuracy or completeness of the Information. The only representations or warranties for which the Company is responsible are those set forth in any definitive acquisition that the Company may execute.

8. If we are requested or directed in a judicial, administrative, or governmental proceeding to disclose any Proprietary Information, we will notify the Company as promptly as practicable so that the Company may either (a)

seek an appropriate protective order or other relief or (b) waive the provisions of this Agreement.

9. In the event of a breach of any of the provisions of this Agreement or of any written agreement referred to in paragraph 1 hereof, the actual damages incurred by the Company will be difficult, if not impossible, to ascertain. Such damages will include (but not be limited to) (a) a loss of goodwill (including damage to the reputation of the Company and its shareholders, subsidiaries and other affiliates) and a loss of morale among employees of each of these entities; and (b) a competitive injury to the Company and its shareholders, subsidiaries, and other affiliates. The parties hereto have agreed that in the event of a breach by us of any of the provisions of this Agreement or of any written agreement referred to in paragraph 1 hereof, the Company shall be entitled, in compensation for the Company's loss of goodwill, to receive from us the sum of $_____ as fixed and agreed liquidated damages, it being understood and agreed that such liquidated damages will not compensate for other damages or prejudice the Company's right to equitable relief as recited in paragraph 10 hereof.

10. We acknowledge that each of the provisions of this Agreement or of any written agreement referred to in paragraph 1 hereof is necessary to preserve the confidentiality of the Information provided pursuant to this Agreement and that a breach of any such provision will result in irreparable damage to the Company and its shareholders, subsidiaries, and other affiliates, in an amount now impossible to calculate (except to the extent of the liquidated damages provided in paragraph 9 hereof). Therefore, in the event of any breach of any provision of this Agreement or of any written agreement referred to in paragraph 1 hereof, the Company shall be entitled (in addition to any other rights and remedies it may have at law or in equity) to have an injunction issued by any competent court of equity enjoining us and any other person from continuing such breach.

11. No failure or delay by the Company in exercising any right, power, or privilege hereunder shall operate as a waiver thereof, nor shall any single or partial exercise thereof preclude any other or further exercise thereof or the exercise of any right, power, or privilege hereunder.

12. This Agreement constitutes our entire agreement with respect to its subject matter, may not be amended, supplemented, waived or terminated except by a written instrument executed by the parties, and shall be governed by the internal laws of the State of _____. Each counterpart of this Agreement shall constitute an original against any party signing it.

Very truly yours,

B CORPORATION

BY: _____
　　　　　Name

TITLE: _____

Date: _____
                 Accepted

S CORPORATION

BY: _____
                 Name

TITLE: _____

Date: _____

Sample Standstill Agreements

PRO-SELLER STANDSTILL

Until March 31, 2004 or the earlier signing of the definitive agreements, the Seller shall not, directly or indirectly, through any officer or director, solicit, initiate, or engage in any discussions or negotiations with any entity, person, or group of persons relating to any acquisition of Seller, whether by asset or stock sale, merger, consolidation, share exchange, or otherwise (a "Competing Transaction"). The Seller shall not be liable for a violation of this restriction by an officer or director (other than Seller's executive officers) if Seller has used reasonable efforts to prevent such violation.

PRO-BUYER STANDSTILL

In consideration of the efforts and resources to be devoted by Buyer to the Proposed Transaction, Seller agrees to the following restrictions, which will remain applicable until June 30, 2004, or such earlier date on which the negotiations with respect to the Proposed Transaction are terminated. Seller will not (and will not permit any director, officer, employee, affiliate, agent, or other person acting on its behalf to) discuss a possible alternative transaction with any other party; nor will Buyer provide any nonpublic information to any other party (other than information that is traditionally provided in the ordinary course of Seller's business to third parties when Seller has no reason to believe that such information may be utilized by a third party to evaluate a possible alternative transaction to the Proposed Transaction.)   Seller agrees to promptly notify Buyer if Seller receives any inquiries from any other person suggesting an interest in or proposing an alternative transaction.

APPENDIX 6

SAMPLE LETTER OF INTENT

Dear S Corporation:

This letter[1] is intended to summarize the discussions between S Corporation and B Corporation and to constitute a nonlegally binding Letter of Intent.[2] The discussions expressed in this Letter of Intent are intended to be embodied into a legally binding definitive agreement ("Definitive Agreement") to be signed by parties and which is subject to the approval of the respective boards of directors of the parties. Our discussions were as follows:

Purchase Price

Pursuant to the Definitive Agreement, S Corporation will sell all of its assets to B Corporation for $25,000,000.

Conditions to Closing

The consummation of the sale shall be subject to the satisfaction of the following conditions:

(a) the parties shall have executed on or prior to _____, 2001 a Definitive Agreement containing mutually acceptable provisions relating to, among other things, representations, warranties, conditions, covenants, and indemnification; and

(b) the boards of directors of both shall have approved the Definitive Agreement; and

(c) the majority of the shareholders of S Corporation shall have voted in favor of the Definitive Agreement; and

(d) the parties shall have received all required approvals and consents from governmental authorities and agencies and third parties.

---

[1]Substitute "document" for "letter" if the Letter of Intent is not expressed as a letter.
[2]You may use the words "Agreement in Principle" instead of "Letter of Intent."

General

Neither of the parties to this letter shall disclose to the public or to any third party the existence of this letter or the proposed sale described herein other than with the express prior written consent of the other party, except as may be required by law.

From and after the date hereof, upon reasonable prior notice and during normal business hours, S Corporation will grant to B Corporation and its agents, employees, and designees full and complete access to the books and records and personnel of S Corporation. Except as may be required by law or court order, all information so obtained, not otherwise already public, will be held in confidence.

This Letter of Intent reflects certain major business terms that are intended to be embodied into the Definitive Agreement; it is understood that the Definitive Agreement will contain many of the other terms and conditions that will have to be negotiated and agreed to before the Definitive Agreement can be finalized. Until the Definitive Agreement is finalized, approved by the respective Boards of Directors (which approval shall be in the sole subjective discretion of the respective Boards of Directors), and properly executed, neither party shall have any legally binding obligation to the other (whether under this Letter of Intent or otherwise), including, but not limited to, a legal duty to continue negotiations to reach such a Definitive Agreement, and either party may discontinue negotiations at any time for any reason whatsoever.[3, 4]

If the enclosed correctly expresses our understanding, please execute this letter where indicated below.

Very truly yours,

B CORPORATION

---

[3]Consider adding the following in appropriate situations: "In the event that either party brings suit to enforce any alleged legal obligations arising from this Letter of Intent, the other party shall be entitled) to summary judgment and to be reimbursed for its attorney's fees and expenses."

[4]In certain cases, the Letter of Intent may contain clauses, such as confidentiality provisions, that are intended to be legally binding. In such cases, add the following: "Notwithstanding anything to the contrary contained herein, the provisions set forth in [identify place in Letter of Intent where provisions appear e.g., 'the third paragraph of page 2'] are intended to be legally binding upon the parties."

APPENDIX 7

SAMPLE AGREEMENT TO SELL ASSETS FOR CASH

THIS AGREEMENT made as of the 1st day of May, 1994 by and among Albertson Medical Specialists, P.C., a Pennsylvania professional corporation ("AS"), Albertson Physical Therapy, P.C., a Pennsylvania professional corporation ("APT"), Jenkins-Michael Associates, a Pennsylvania general partnership ("J-R"; AS, APT and J-R are hereinafter referred to collectively as the "Companies"), Sara Ann Rubin, M.D. ("Sara"), Michael Daniel Rubin, M.D. ("Michael"), Kimberly Lageman, M.D. ("Kim") and Andrew Mortenson, M.D. ("Andrew"); Sara, Michael, Kim and Andrew are hereinafter referred to collectively as the "Shareholders", and ClinCare Corporation, a Delaware corporation (the "Purchaser").

WITNESSETH:

WHEREAS, AS is engaged in the businesses of (i) providing orthopedic medical services and owning and operating an orthopedic medical practice and related activities in the Commonwealth of Pennsylvania and (ii) providing physical therapy services and owning and operating rehabilitation facilities and related activities in the Commonwealth of Pennsylvania (such activities set forth in clause (ii) hereof being hereinafter referred to as the "AS Business");

WHEREAS, APT is engaged in the business of providing physical therapy services and owning and operating a rehabilitation facility and related activities in the Commonwealth of Pennsylvania (such activities being hereinafter referred to as the "APT Business"; and together with the AS Business, the "Business");

WHEREAS, the Shareholders are holders of all of the common stock (the "AS Common Stock"), of AS, which shares constitute all of the issued and outstanding shares of capital stock of AS (all such shares of AS Common Stock held by the Shareholders being hereinafter referred to as the "AS Shares");

271

WHEREAS, the Shareholders are holders of all of the common stock (the "APT Common Stock"), of APT, which shares constitute all of the issued and outstanding shares of capital stock of APT (all such shares of APT Common Stock held by the Shareholders being hereinafter referred to as the "APT Shares");

WHEREAS, the Shareholders are the holders of all of the outstanding partnership interests (the "Partnership Interests") of J-R (the "Partnership");

WHEREAS, the Purchaser desires to acquire certain assets of the Companies relating to the Business as described in Section I(C)(i) hereof (the "Assets") and to assume certain liabilities and contractual obligations of the Companies relating to the Business as described in Section I(C)(ii) hereof (the "Assumed Liabilities"), and the Companies desire to sell or assign the Assets and to assign the Assumed Liabilities to the Purchaser, on the terms and subject to the conditions hereinafter set forth; and

WHEREAS, to induce the Purchaser to enter into this Agreement and perform its obligations hereunder, the Shareholders have agreed to make the representations, warranties, covenants and agreements of the Shareholders (including the indemnification and non-competition agreements) set forth herein.

NOW, THEREFORE, in consideration of the premises and the mutual covenants and agreements hereinafter set forth, and intending to be legally bound, the parties hereto hereby agree as follows:

SECTION I.

Purchase and Sale of the Assets

A. *Purchase and Sale of the Assets.* Subject to the terms and conditions of this Agreement and on the basis of the representations, warranties, covenants and agreements herein contained, at the Closing (as hereinafter defined):

  (i)   The Companies agree to sell, assign and convey to the Purchaser or its designee and the Purchaser (or its designee) agrees to purchase, acquire and accept from the Companies, the Assets.

  (ii) The Companies agree to assign to the Purchaser (or its designee) and the Purchaser (or its designee) agrees to accept and assume from the Companies, the Assumed Liabilities. The Purchaser (and the designee, if any) shall not assume and shall have no responsibility with respect to, and shall be indemnified as set forth in Section X hereof by the Companies and the Shareholders, jointly and severally, from and against, any and all liabilities or obligations of the Companies other than the Assumed Liabilities.

B. *Purchase Price and Non-Competition Price.* The purchase price (the "Purchase Price") for the Assets is $__*__, in cash. The consideration (the "Non-Competition Price") for the covenants not to compete made by the Shareholders in Section XI hereof is $__*__, in cash. The Purchase Price shall be paid by the delivery to the Companies at the Closing of certified or official bank checks in the following amounts: $__*__ to AS; $__*__ to APT; and $__*__ to J-R. The Non-Competition Price shall be paid by the delivery to each Shareholder at the Closing of a certified or official bank check payable to the order of such Shareholder in the amount of $\_\_*\_\_$.

C.   *Assets; Assumed Liabilities.*

   (i)   The Assets shall consist of the assets listed in Schedule I-(A) hereto, but excluding the assets listed in Schedule I-(B) hereto.

   (ii) The Assumed Liabilities shall consist of and shall be limited solely to the obligations and liabilities of the Companies listed in Schedule II hereto.

D.   *Allocation.* The Purchase Price for the Assets (including the Assumed Liabilities assumed by the Purchaser (or its designee)) shall be allocated as set forth in Schedule III hereto. The parties hereto agree that the allocation of the Purchase Price is intended to comply with the allocation method required by Section 1060 of the Internal Revenue Code of 1986, as amended (the "Code"). The parties shall cooperate to comply with all substantive and procedural requirements of Section 1060 of the Code and any regulations thereunder, and the allocation shall be adjusted if, and to the extent, necessary to comply with the requirements of Section 1060 of the Code. Neither the Purchaser nor any of the Companies will take, or permit any affiliated person to take, for federal, state or local income tax purposes, any position inconsistent with the allocation set forth in Schedule III hereto, or, if applicable, such adjusted allocation. Each of the Companies and the Purchaser hereby agrees that it shall attach to its tax returns for the tax year in which the Closing shall occur an information statement on Form 8594, which shall be completed in accordance with allocations set forth in Schedule III hereto.

E.   *Assignment.* The parties hereto acknowledge and agree that the Purchaser may designate a direct or indirect wholly owned subsidiary of the Purchaser to acquire the Assets and assume the Assumed Liabilities; provided, however, that all of the Purchaser's obligations hereunder shall not be affected by such designation by the Purchaser.

SECTION II.

Representations, Warranties, Covenants and Agreements of the Companies and the Shareholders

The Companies and the Shareholders, jointly and severally, hereby represent and warrant to, and covenant and agree with, the Purchaser, as of the date hereof and as of the date of the Closing, that:

A.   *Organization and Qualification.*

   (i)   AS is duly organized, validly existing and subsisting under the laws of the Commonwealth of Pennsylvania and has full corporate power and authority to own its properties and to conduct the businesses in which it is now engaged. AS is in good standing in each other jurisdiction wherein the failure so to qualify would have a material adverse effect on its businesses or properties. AS has no subsidiaries, owns no capital stock or other proprietary interest, directly or indirectly, in any other corporation, association, trust, partnership, joint venture or other entity and has no agreement with any person, firm or corporation to acquire any such capital stock or other proprietary interest. AS has full power, authority and legal right and, to the best of the knowledge of each of the Companies and each of the Shareholders, all necessary approvals, permits, licenses and authorizations to own its properties and to conduct the AS Business. AS has full power, authority and legal right to enter into and consummate the transactions contemplated under this Agreement. The copies of the articles of incorporation and by-laws of AS which have been delivered to the Purchaser are complete and correct.

(ii)   APT is duly organized, validly existing and subsisting under the laws of the Commonwealth of Pennsylvania and has full corporate power and authority to own its properties and to conduct the businesses in which it is now engaged. APT is in good standing in each other jurisdiction where it is presently conducting business wherein the failure so to qualify would have a material adverse effect on its businesses or properties. APT has no subsidiaries, owns no capital stock or other proprietary interest, directly or indirectly, in any other corporation, association, trust, partnership, joint venture or other entity and has no agreement with any person, firm or corporation to acquire any such capital stock or other proprietary interest. APT has full power, authority and legal right and, to the best of the knowledge of each of the Companies and each of the Shareholders, all necessary approvals, permits, licenses and authorizations to own its properties and to conduct the APT Business. APT has full power, authority and legal right to enter into and consummate the transactions contemplated under this Agreement. The copies of the articles of incorporation and by-laws of APT which have been delivered to the Purchaser are complete and correct.

(iii) J-R is duly organized and validly existing under the laws of the Commonwealth of Pennsylvania and has full partnership power and authority to own its properties and to conduct the businesses in which it is now engaged. J-R does not do business in any jurisdiction other than the Commonwealth of Pennsylvania. J-R has no subsidiaries, owns no capital stock or other proprietary interest, directly or indirectly, in any other corporation, association, trust, partnership, joint venture or other entity and has no agreement with any person, firm or corporation to acquire any such capital stock or other proprietary interest. J-R has full power, authority and legal right and, to the best of the knowledge of each of the Companies and each of the Shareholders, all necessary approvals, permits, licenses and authorizations to own its properties and to conduct the J-R Business. J-R has full power, authority and legal right to enter into and consummate the transactions contemplated under this Agreement. The copy of the partnership agreement which has been delivered to the Purchaser is complete and correct.

B. *Authority.* The execution and delivery of this Agreement by each of the Companies, the performance by each of the Companies of their covenants and agreements hereunder and the consummation by the Companies of the transactions contemplated hereby have been duly authorized by all necessary corporate or partnership action. This Agreement constitutes valid and legally binding obligations of each of the Companies, enforceable against each of the Companies in accordance with its terms, except as such enforceability may be limited by bankruptcy, insolvency, moratorium or other similar laws affecting creditors' rights generally and general principles of equity relating to the availability of equitable remedies.

C. *No Legal Bar; Conflicts.* Neither the execution and delivery of this Agreement, nor the consummation of the transactions contemplated hereby, violates any provision of the articles of incorporation or by-laws of either AS or APT or the agreement or certificate of partnership of J-R or any statute, ordinance, regulation, order, judgment or decree of any court or governmental agency or board, or conflicts with or will result in any breach of any of the terms of or constitute a default under or result in the termination of or the creation of any lien pursuant to the terms of any contract or agreement to which any of the Companies is a party or by which any of the Companies or any of the Assets is bound. No consents, approvals or authorizations of, or filings with, any governmental authority or any other person or entity are required in connection with the execution and delivery of this Agreement and the consummation of the transactions contemplated hereby, except for required consents to assignment of the contracts as set forth or cross-referenced on Exhibit C which, with the Purchaser's consent, the Companies are not obtaining.

D. *Financial Statements; No Undisclosed Liabilities.* The Companies and the Shareholders have delivered to the Purchaser schedules of revenues and expenses included in the tax returns for each of Companies for the years ended December 31, 1993, 1992 and 1991, which tax returns (hereinafter referred to as the "Financial Statements") have been prepared by Countz & Associates, the Companies' independent accountants. The Financial Statements are true and correct in all material respects and have been prepared using the income tax basis of accounting. The Financial Statements fully and fairly present the financial condition of each of the Companies as at the dates thereof and the results of the operations of each of the Companies for the periods indicated. None of the Companies and none of the Shareholders is aware of any material omissions in the Financial Statements. A true and correct copy of the Financial Statements is attached hereto as Exhibit D.

E. *Absence of Certain Changes.* Except as set forth in Exhibit E, subsequent to December 31, 1993, there has not been any (i) adverse or prospective adverse change in the condition of the Business, financial or otherwise, or in the results of the operations of any of the Companies or the Business; (ii) damage or de-

struction (whether or not insured) affecting the properties or business operations of any of the Companies; (iii) labor dispute or threatened labor dispute
involving the key employees of any of the Companies or any resignations or
threatened resignations of physical or occupational therapists, or notice that
any employees of any of the Companies intend to take leaves of absence, with
or without pay; (iv) actual or threatened disputes pertaining to the Business
with any major accounts or referral sources of any of the Companies, or actual
or threatened loss of business from any of the major accounts or referral
sources of any of the Companies; or (v) changes in the methods or procedures
for billing or collection of customer accounts or recording of customer accounts receivable or reserves for doubtful accounts with respect to any of the
Companies.

F.   *Real Property Owned or Leased.* A list and description of all real property owned by
     or leased to or by each of the Companies or in which each of the Companies has
     any interest is set forth in Exhibit F. All such leased real property is held subject
     to written leases or other agreements which are valid and effective in accor-
     dance with their respective terms, and there are no existing defaults or events of
     default, or events which with notice or lapse of time or both would constitute de-
     faults, thereunder on the part of the Companies. None of the Companies and
     none of the Shareholders has any knowledge of any default or claimed or pur-
     ported or alleged default or state of facts which with notice or lapse of time or
     both would constitute a default on the part of any other party in the perform-
     ance of any obligation to be performed or paid by such other party under any
     lease referred to in Exhibit F. None of the Companies and none of the Share-
     holders has received any written or oral notice to the effect that any lease will
     not be renewed at the termination of the term thereof or that any such lease will
     be renewed only at a substantially higher rent.

G.   *Title to Assets; Condition of Property.* Each of the Companies has good and valid title
     to the Assets it is transferring hereunder. Each of the Companies has the right,
     power and authority to sell and transfer the Assets it is transferring hereunder to
     the Purchaser (or its designee) and upon such transfer, the Purchaser (or its de-
     signee) will acquire good and valid title to the Assets, free and clear of all liens,
     charges, encumbrances, security interests or valid claims whatsoever. The Assets
     include substantially all properties and assets necessary for the operations of the
     Business consistent with its current operations, other than insurance, the tele-
     phone system, employees, permits and licenses, cash in excess of $25,000, the
     charts and records of Dr. Richard Sawbones and the Sawbones Receivables (as
     hereinafter defined), oral agreements with AssureCare and U.S. CareGuard and
     the Companies' names and logos. All such properties and assets are in good con-
     dition and repair, reasonable wear and tear excepted, consistent with their re-
     spective ages, and have been maintained and serviced in accordance with the
     normal practices of each of the Companies and as necessary in the normal
     course of business. None of the Assets is subject to any liens, charges, encum-
     brances or security interests. None of the Assets (or uses to which they are put)
     fails to conform with any applicable agreement, law, ordinance or regulation in a
     manner which is likely to be material to the operations of the Business.

H. *Taxes.* Each of the Companies has filed or caused to be filed on a timely basis all federal, state, local and other tax returns, reports and declarations required to be filed by it and has paid or adequately reserved for all taxes, including, but not limited to, income, excise, franchise, gross receipts, sales, use, property, unemployment, withholding, social security and workers' compensation taxes and estimated income and franchise tax payments, and penalties and fines, due and payable with respect to the periods covered by such returns (whether or not reflected on such returns), reports or declarations and all subsequent periods or pursuant to any assessment received by it in connection with such returns, reports or declarations so as to prevent any lien or charge from attaching to the Assets. All returns, reports and declarations filed by or on behalf of each of the Companies are true, complete and correct in all material respects. No deficiency in payment of any taxes for any period has been asserted by any taxing authority which remains unsettled at the date hereof, no written inquiries have been received by any of the Companies from any taxing authority with respect to possible claims for taxes or assessments and, to the knowledge of each of the Companies and each of the Shareholders, there is no basis for any additional claims or assessments for taxes. Since December 31, 1993, none of the Companies has incurred any tax liability other than in the ordinary course of business. For the prior three years, no tax return of any of the Companies has ever been audited and no written inquiries have been received by any of the Companies from a taxing authority with respect to a possible claim for taxes or assessments. None of the Companies has agreed to the extension of the statute of limitations with respect to any tax return. There are no assessments relating to the tax returns of the Companies pending or threatened. Each of the Companies has delivered to the Purchaser copies of the federal and state income (or franchise) tax returns filed by each of the Companies for the past three years.

I. *Permits; Compliance with Applicable Law.*

   (i)   *General.* Except as set forth on Exhibit I(i), none of the Companies, to its knowledge, is in default under any, and each has, to its knowledge, complied with all, statutes, ordinances, regulations, orders, judgments and decrees of any court or governmental entity or agency, relating to the Business or the Assets as to which a default or failure to comply might result in a material adverse effect on the Business. None of the Companies and none of the Shareholders has any knowledge of any basis for assertion of any violation of the foregoing or for any claim for compensation or damages or otherwise arising out of any violation of the foregoing. None of the Companies and none of the Shareholders has received any notification of any asserted present or past failure to comply with any of the foregoing which has not been satisfactorily responded to in the time period required thereunder.

   (ii) *Permits.* Set forth in Exhibit I(ii) is a complete and accurate list of all permits, licenses, approvals, franchises, notices and authorizations issued by governmental entities or other regulatory authorities, federal, state or local (collectively the "Permits"), held by each of the Companies in connection with the Business. To the best of the knowledge of each of the Companies and each of the Shareholders, the Permits set forth in Exhibit I(ii) are all the Permits required for the conduct of the Business. All the Permits set forth in Exhibit I(ii) are in full force and effect, and, to the best of the knowledge of each of the Companies and each of the Shareholders, none of the Companies has engaged in any activity which would cause or permit revocation or suspension of any such Permit, and no action or proceeding looking to or contemplating the revocation or suspension of any such Permit is pending or threatened. There are no existing defaults or events of default or event or state of facts which with notice or lapse of time or both would constitute a default by any of the Companies under any such Permit. None of the Companies and none of the Shareholders has any knowledge of any default or claimed or purported or alleged default or state of facts which with notice or lapse of time or both would constitute a default on the part of any party in the performance of any obligation to be performed or paid by any party under any Permit set forth in Exhibit I(ii). The consummation of the transactions contemplated hereby will in no way affect the continuation, validity or effectiveness of the Permits set forth in Exhibit I(ii) or require the consent of any person. Except as set forth on Exhibit I(ii), the Companies are not required to be licensed by, nor are they subject to the regulation of, any governmental or regulatory body by reason of the conduct of the Business.

(iii)   *Environmental.*

    (a)   To the knowledge of each of the Companies and each of the Shareholders, each of the Companies has duly complied with and the real estate owned by each of the Companies and the improvements thereon, and the real estate subject to the leases listed on Exhibit F and improvements thereon, and all other real estate leased by each of the Companies, and the improvements thereon (all such owned or leased real estate hereinafter referred to collectively as the "Premises"), are, to the knowledge of each of the Companies and each of the Shareholders, in compliance with the provisions of all federal, state and local environmental, health and safety laws, codes and ordinances and all rules and regulations promulgated thereunder.

    (b)   To the knowledge of each of the Companies and each of the Shareholders, each of the Companies has been issued, and will maintain until the date of the Closing, all required federal, state and local permits, licenses, certificates and approvals relating to (i) air emissions, (ii) discharges to surface water or ground water, (iii) noise emissions, (iv) solid or liquid waste disposal, (v) the use, generation, storage, transportation or disposal of toxic or hazardous substances or wastes (intended hereby and hereafter to include any and all such materials listed in any federal, state or local law, code or ordinance and all rules and regulations promulgated thereunder, as hazardous or potentially hazardous), or (vi) other environmental, health and safety matters.

(c) None of the Companies has received any notice of, and neither any of the Companies nor any of the Shareholders knows of any facts which might constitute, violations of any federal, state or local environmental, health or safety laws, codes or ordinances, and any rules or regulations promulgated thereunder, which relate to the use, ownership or occupancy of any of the Premises or of any premises formerly owned, leased or occupied by the Companies. The Companies are not in violation of any rights-of-way or restrictions affecting any of the Premises or any rights appurtenant thereto.

(iv) *Medicare and Medicaid.* Except as set forth in Exhibit I(iv), each of the Companies has complied with all laws, rules and regulations of the Medicare, Medicaid and other governmental health-care programs, and has filed all claims, invoices, returns, cost reports and other forms, the use of which is required or permitted by such programs, in the manner prescribed. Except as set forth in Exhibit I(iv), all claims, returns, invoices, cost reports and other forms made by the Companies to Medicare, Medicaid or any other governmental health or welfare related entity or any other third party payor since the inception of the Business are in all respects true, complete, correct and accurate. Except as set forth in Exhibit I(iv), no deficiency in any such claims, returns, cost reports and other filings, including claims for over-payments or deficiencies for late filings, has been asserted or threatened by any federal or state agency or instrumentality or other provider or reimbursement entities relating to Medicare or Medicaid claims or any other third- party payor, and there is no basis for any claims or requests for reimbursement, except for claims for disallowances in the ordinary course. None of the Companies has been subject to any audit relating to fraudulent Medicare or Medicaid procedures or practices. Except as set forth in Exhibit I(iv), there is no basis for any claim or request for recoupment or reimbursement from any of the Companies by, or for reimbursement by any of the Companies of, any federal, district or state agency or instrumentality or other provider reimbursement entities relating to Medicare or Medicaid claims. Net revenues from the Medicare program represented approximately 50% of the net revenues of the APT Business and approximately 10% of the AS Business during calendar years 1991, 1992, 1993 and during the first five months of 1994, in each case with a plus or minus five percent variance. During 1991, 1992, 1993 and the first five months of 1994, the Companies had no revenues from the Medicaid program.

J. *Licenses.* None of the Companies produces or distributes any product, or performs any service under a license granted by another entity and has not licensed its rights in any current or planned products, designs or services to any other entities.

K. *Accounts Receivable; Inventories.* The accounts receivable of each of the Companies which are part of the Assets are in their entirety valid accounts receivable, arising in the ordinary course of business. On or before 180 days from the date of the Closing, the Purchaser shall collect at least $160,000 of such accounts receivable. The inventories and equipment of the Companies are on the whole merchantable (other than for obsolete or damaged inventory which on the whole is not material) and fully usable in the ordinary course of business consistent with the prior practice of the Business. The Companies shall have available to the Purchaser, and the Assets shall include, unrestricted cash and cash equivalents of at least $25,000.

L. *Contractual and Other Obligations.* Set forth in Exhibit L is a list and brief description of all contracts, agreements, licenses, leases, arrangements (written or oral) and other documents to which each of the Companies is a party or by which each of the Companies or any of the Assets is bound (including, in the case of loan agreements, a description of the amounts of any outstanding borrowings thereunder and the collateral, if any, for such borrowings); all of the foregoing being hereinafter referred to as the "Contracts." There are no material contingent obligations and liabilities of each of the Companies other than for lawsuits set forth on Exhibit AA. Neither the Companies nor, to the best of the knowledge of each of the Companies and each of the Shareholders, any other party is in default in the performance of any covenant or condition under any Contract and no claim of such a default has been made and no event has occurred which with the giving of notice or the lapse of time would constitute a default under any covenant or condition under any Contract. None of the Companies is a party to any Contract which would terminate or be materially adversely affected by consummation of the transactions contemplated by this Agreement. Except as set forth in Exhibit L, none of the Companies is a party to any Contract expected to be performed at a loss. Originals or true, correct and complete copies of all written Contracts have been provided to the Purchaser.

M. *Compensation.* Set forth in Exhibit M attached hereto is a list of all agreements between each of the Companies and each person employed by or independently contracting with such Company with regard to compensation, whether individually or collectively, and set forth in Exhibit M is a list of all employees of each of the Companies who are employed in the Business (except for Dr. Sawbones and Donald Lachman) entitled to receive annual compensation in excess of $20,000 and their respective salaries. The transactions contemplated by this Agreement will not result in any liability for severance pay to any employee or independent contractor of any of the Companies. None of the Companies has informed any employee or independent contractor providing services to any of the Companies that such person will receive any increase in compensation or benefits or any ownership interest in any of the Companies or the Business other than increases in the ordinary course.

N. *Employee Benefit Plans.* Except as set forth in Exhibit N attached hereto, the Companies do not maintain or sponsor, nor are they required to make contributions to, any pension, profit-sharing, savings, bonus, incentive or deferred compensation, severance pay, medical, life insurance, welfare or other employee benefit plan. All pension, profit-sharing, savings, bonus, incentive or deferred compensation, severance pay, medical, life insurance, welfare or other employee benefit plans within the meaning of Section 3(3) of the Employee Retirement Income Security Act of 1974, as amended (hereinafter referred to as "ERISA"), in which the employees of the Business participate (such plans and related trusts, insurance and annuity contracts, funding media and related agreements and arrangements, other than any "Multiemployer plan" (within the meaning of Section 3(37) of ERISA), being hereinafter referred to as the "Benefit Plans" and any such Multiemployer plans being hereinafter referred to as the "Multiemployer Plans") comply in all material respects with all requirements of the Department of Labor and the Internal Revenue Service, and with all other applicable law, and the Companies have not taken or failed to take any action with respect to either the Benefit Plans or the Multiemployer Plans which might create any liability on the part of the Companies or the Purchaser. Each "fiduciary" (within the meaning of Section 3(21)(A) of ERISA) as to each Benefit Plan and as to each Multiemployer Plan has complied in all material respects with the requirements of ERISA and all other applicable laws in respect of each such Plan. Each of the Companies has furnished to the Purchaser copies of all Benefit Plans and Multiemployer Plans. All financial statements, actuarial reports and annual reports and returns filed with the Internal Revenue Service with respect to such Benefit Plans and Multiemployer Plans are true and correct in all material respects, and none of the actuarial assumptions underlying such documents have changed since the respective dates thereof. In addition:

(i)   Each Benefit Plan has received a favorable determination letter from the Internal Revenue Service as to its qualification under Section 401(a) of the Code;

(ii)   No Benefit Plan which is a "defined benefit plan" (within the meaning of Section 3(35) of ERISA) (hereinafter referred to as the "Defined Benefit Plans") or Multiemployer Plan has incurred an "accumulated funding deficiency" (within the meaning of Section 412(a) of the Code), whether or not waived;

(iii)   No "reportable event" (within the meaning of Section 4043 of ERISA) has occurred with respect to any Defined Benefit Plan or any Multiemployer Plan;

(iv)   The Companies have not withdrawn as a contributing sponsor (partially or totally within the meaning of ERISA) from any Benefit Plan or any Multiemployer Plan; and neither the execution and delivery of this Agreement nor the consummation of the transactions contemplated herein will result in the withdrawal (partially or totally within the meaning of ERISA) from any Benefit Plan or Multiemployer Plan, or in any withdrawal or other liability of any nature to the Companies or the Purchaser under any Benefit Plan or Multiemployer Plan;

(v)   No "prohibited transaction" (within the meaning of Section 406 of ERISA or Section 4975(c) of the Code) has occurred with respect to any Benefit Plan or Multiemployer Plan;

(vi)   The excess of the aggregate present value of accrued benefits over the aggregate value of the assets of any Defined Benefit Plan (computed both on a termination basis and on an ongoing basis) is not more than $-0-, and the aggregate withdrawal liability of any of the Companies with respect to any Multiemployer Plan, assuming the withdrawal of any of the Companies from said Multiemployer Plan, is not more than $-0-;

(vii)   No provision of any Benefit Plan or of any agreement, and no act or omission of any of the Companies, in any way limits, impairs, modifies or otherwise affects the right of the Companies or the Purchaser unilaterally to amend or terminate any Benefit Plan after the Closing, subject to the requirements of applicable law;

(viii) Except for a contribution of not in excess of $50,000 for the recently completed plan year, there are no contributions which are or hereafter will be required to be made to trusts for the prior fiscal year in connection with any Benefit Plan that would constitute a "defined contribution plan" (within the meaning of Section 3(34) of ERISA) with respect to services rendered by employees of the Companies prior to the date of Closing;

(ix)   Other than claims in the ordinary course for benefits with respect to the Benefit Plans or the Multiemployer Plans, there are no actions, suits or claims (including claims for income taxes, interest, penalties, fines or excise taxes with respect thereto) pending with respect to any Benefit Plan or any Multiemployer Plan, or any circumstances which might give rise to any such action, suit or claim (including claims for income taxes, interest, penalties, fines or excise taxes with respect thereto);

(x)   All reports, returns and similar documents with respect to the Benefit Plans required to be filed with any governmental agency have been so filed;

(xi)   None of the Companies has incurred any liability to the Pension Benefit Guaranty Corporation (except for required premium payments). No notice of termination has been filed by the plan administrator (pursuant to Section 4041 of ERISA) or issued by the Pension Benefit Guaranty Corporation (pursuant to Section 4042 of ERISA) with respect to any Benefit Plan subject to ERISA. There has been no termination of any Defined Benefit Plan or any related trust by any of the Companies;

(xii)   No Benefit Plan which is a Defined Benefit Plan subject to Title IV of ERISA has applied for or received a waiver of the minimum funding standards imposed by Section 412 of the Code; and

(xiii) None of the Companies has any obligation to provide health or other welfare benefits to former, retired or terminated employees, except as specifically required under Section 4980B of the Code. Each of the Companies has substantially complied with the notice and continuation requirements of Section 4980B of the Code and the regulations thereunder.

In connection with the transactions contemplated hereby, as soon as practicable in accordance with applicable laws and the plan documents, following the date of the Closing, the Shareholders shall cause the trustees of the Albertson Medical Specialists, P.C. 401(k) Profit Sharing Plan (the "Profit Sharing Plan") to offer to distribute the account balances in the Profit Sharing Plan of the Employees (as hereinafter defined) who are participants in the Profit Sharing Plan in accordance with the terms of the plan documents and any and all applicable laws, rules or regulations. AS shall have fully vested all Employees of any of the Companies in their account balances in the Profit Sharing Plan.

AS agrees that any contributions now due or that may become due to the Profit Sharing Plan shall be the sole responsibility of AS and shall be immediately paid, when due, by AS.

O. *Labor Relations.* To the knowledge of each of the Companies and each of the Shareholders, there have been no violations of any federal, state or local statutes, laws, ordinances, rules, regulations, orders or directives with respect to the employment of individuals by, or the employment practices or work conditions of, any of the Companies, or the terms and conditions of employment, wages and hours. To the knowledge of each of the Companies and each of the Shareholders, none of the Companies is engaged in any unfair labor practice or other unlawful employment practice and there are no charges of unfair labor practices or other employee-related complaints pending or, to the knowledge of each of the Companies and each of the Shareholders, threatened against any of the Companies before the National Labor Relations Board, the Equal Employment Opportunity Commission, the Occupational Safety and Health Review Commission, the Department of Labor or any other federal, state, local or other governmental authority. There is no strike, picketing, slowdown or work stoppage or organizational attempt pending, threatened against or involving the Business. No issue with respect to union representation is pending or threatened with respect to the employees of any of the Companies. No union or collective bargaining unit or other labor organization has ever been certified or recognized by any of the Companies as the representative of any of the employees of any of the Companies.

P. *Increases in Compensation or Benefits.* Except as set forth in Exhibit P, subsequent to December 31, 1993, there have been no increases in the compensation payable or to become payable to any of the Employees and there have been no payments or provisions for any awards, bonuses, loans, profit sharing, pension, retirement or welfare plans or similar or other disbursements or arrangements for or on behalf of such employees (or related parties thereof), in each case, other than pursuant to currently existing plans or arrangements, if any, set forth in Exhibit N. Except as set forth in Exhibit P, all bonuses heretofore granted to employees of any of the Companies have been paid in full to such employees. The vacation policy and the amount of accrued and unused vacation time for each Employee of each of the Companies is set forth in Exhibit P. Except as set forth in Exhibit P, no employee of any of the Companies who is employed in the Business is entitled to vacation time in excess of three weeks during the current calendar year and no employee of any of the Companies who is employed in the Business has any accrued vacation or sick time with respect to any prior period.

Q. *Insurance.* Each of the Companies maintains insurance policies covering the Assets and the various occurrences which may arise in connection with the operation of the Business. Such policies are in full force and effect and all premiums due thereon prior to or on the date of the Closing have been paid. Each of the Companies has complied in all respects with the provisions of such policies. A list and brief description of the insurance policies maintained by each of the Companies is set forth in Exhibit Q. There are no notices of any pending or threatened termination or premium increases with respect to any of such policies. The Companies have not had any casualty loss or occurrence which may give rise to any claim of any kind not covered by insurance (other than for the deductible) and none of the Companies nor any of the Shareholders is aware of any occurrence which may give rise to any claim of any kind not covered by insurance. Except as set forth in Exhibit Q, no third party has filed any claim against the Companies or the Business for personal injury or property damage of a kind for which liability insurance is generally available which is not fully insured, subject only to the standard deductible. All known claims against any of the Companies or the Business covered by insurance have been reported to the insurance carrier on a timely basis.

R. *Conduct of Business.* None of the Companies is restricted from conducting the Business in any location by agreement or court decree.

S. *Allowances.* Except as set forth in Exhibit S, none of the Companies has any obligation outside of the ordinary course of business to make allowances to any customers with respect to the Business.

T. *Patents, Trademarks, etc.* No patents, registered and common law trademarks, service marks, tradenames or copyrights constitute part of the Assets.

U. *Use of Names.* All names under which each of the Companies currently conducts the Business are listed in Exhibit U attached hereto. To the knowledge of each of the Companies and each of the Shareholders, there are no other persons or businesses conducting businesses similar to those of the Companies in the Commonwealth of Pennsylvania having the right to use or using the names set forth in Exhibit U or any variants of such names; and no other person or business has ever attempted to restrain any of the Companies or any of the Shareholders from using such names or any variants thereof.

V. *Power of Attorney.* None of the Companies has granted any power of attorney (revocable or irrevocable) to any person, firm or corporation for any purpose whatsoever.

W. *Accounts Payable, Indebtedness, Etc.* The accounts and notes payable and accrued expenses which are part of the Assumed Liabilities are in all respects valid claims that arose in the ordinary course of business. Since December 31, 1993, the accounts and notes payable and accrued expenses of each of the Companies have been paid in a manner consistent with past practices. The aggregate unpaid accounts payable and accrued expenses (excluding expenses constituting part of the Assumed Liabilities with respect to the Employees) of the Companies on the date of the Closing relating to Assumed Liabilities shall not exceed $5,000.

X. *No Foreign Person.* None of the Shareholders is a foreign person within the meaning of Section 1445(b)(2) of the Code.

Y. *Licensure, etc.* To the best of the knowledge of each of the Companies and each of the Shareholders, each individual employed or contracted with by each of the Companies to provide therapy services is duly licensed to provide such therapy services and is otherwise in compliance with all federal, district and state laws, rules and regulations relating to such professional licensure and otherwise meets the qualifications to provide such therapy services. To the best of the knowledge of each of the Companies and each of the Shareholders, each individual now or formerly employed or contracted by each of the Companies to provide professional services was duly licensed to provide such services during all periods prior to the Closing when such employee or independent contractor provided such services on behalf of any of the Companies. Each of the Companies, to the best of its knowledge, is in compliance with all relevant state laws and precedents relating to the corporate practice of licensed professions, and there are no material claims, disputes, actions, suits, proceedings or investigations currently pending, filed or commenced, or, to the best of its knowledge, threatened against or affecting the Assets or the Business relating to such laws and precedents, and no such material claim, dispute, action, suit, proceeding or investigation has been filed or commenced during the two-year period preceding the date of this Agreement relating to such laws and precedents, and none of the Companies is aware of any basis for such a valid claim.

Z. *Books and Records.* The books and records of each of the Companies are in all material respects complete and correct, have been maintained in accordance with good business practices and accurately reflect the basis for the financial position and results of operations of each of the Companies set forth in the Financial Statements. All of such books and records have been made available for inspection by the Purchaser and its representatives.

AA. *Litigation; Disputes.* Except as set forth in Exhibit AA, there are no claims, disputes, actions, suits, investigations or proceedings pending or threatened against or affecting any of the Companies, the Business or any of the Assets, no such claim, dispute, action, suit, proceeding or investigation has been pending or, to the best knowledge of each of the Companies and each of the Shareholders, threatened during the two-year period preceding the date of this Agreement and, to the best of the knowledge of each of the Companies and each of the Shareholders, there is no basis for any such claim, dispute, action, suit, investigation or proceeding. None of the Companies nor any of the Shareholders has any knowledge of any default under any such action, suit or proceeding. None of the Companies is in default in respect of any judgment, order, writ, injunction or decree of any court or of any federal, state, municipal or other government department, commission, bureau, agency or instrumentality or any arbitrator.

BB. *Location of Business and Assets.* Set forth in Exhibit BB is each location (specifying state, county and city) where each of the Companies (i) has a place of business, (ii) owns or leases real property and (iii) owns or leases any other property, including inventory, equipment and furniture.

CC. *Disclosure.* No representation or warranty made under any Section hereof and none of the information set forth herein, in the exhibits hereto or in any document delivered by any of the Companies or any of the Shareholders to the Purchaser, or any authorized representative of the Purchaser, pursuant to the express terms of this Agreement contains any untrue statement of a material fact by the Companies or the Shareholders or omits to state a material fact by the Companies or the Shareholders necessary to make the statements herein or therein not misleading.

SECTION III.

Representations, Warranties, Covenants and Agreements of the Shareholders

Each of the Shareholders, jointly and severally, hereby represents and warrants to, and covenants and agrees with, the Purchaser, as of the date hereof and as of the date of the Closing, that:

A.   *Authority.* Such Shareholder is fully able to execute and deliver this Agreement and to perform his covenants and agreements hereunder, and this Agreement constitutes a valid and legally binding obligation of such Shareholder, enforceable against him in accordance with its terms, except as such enforceability may be limited by bankruptcy, insolvency, moratorium or other similar laws affecting creditors' rights generally and general principles of equity relating to the availability of equitable remedies.

B.   *No Legal Bar; Conflicts.* Neither the execution and delivery of this Agreement, nor the consummation of the transactions contemplated hereby, violates any statute, ordinance, regulation, order, judgment or decree of any court or governmental agency, or conflicts with or will result in any breach of any of the terms of or constitute a default under or result in the termination of or the creation of any lien pursuant to the terms of any contract or agreement to which any such Shareholder is a party or by which any such Shareholder or any of his assets is bound.

SECTION IV.

Representations, Warranties, Covenants and Agreements of the Purchaser

The Purchaser hereby represents and warrants to, and covenants and agrees with, the Companies and each of the Shareholders, as of the date hereof and as of the Selling date of the Closing, that:

A. *Organization.* The Purchaser is a corporation duly organized, validly existing and in good standing under the laws of the State of Delaware and has full corporate power and authority to purchase the Assets, to conduct the business in which it is now engaged and to enter into this Agreement and consummate the transactions contemplated by this Agreement. The Purchaser is qualified as a foreign corporation in the Commonwealth of Pennsylvania.

B. *Authority.* The execution and delivery of this Agreement by the Purchaser, the performance by the Purchaser of its covenants and agreements hereunder and the consummation by the Purchaser of the transactions contemplated hereby have been duly authorized by all necessary corporate action, and this Agreement constitutes a valid and legally binding obligation of the Purchaser, enforceable against the Purchaser in accordance with its terms.

C. *No Legal Bar; Conflicts.* Neither the execution and delivery of this Agreement, nor the consummation of the transactions contemplated hereby, violates any provision of the certificate of incorporation or by-laws of the Purchaser or any statute, ordinance, regulation, order, judgment or decree of any court or governmental agency, or conflicts with or will result in any breach of any of the terms of or constitute a default under or result in the termination of or the creation of any lien pursuant to the terms of any contract or agreement to which the Purchaser is a party or by which the Purchaser or any of its assets is bound. No consents, approvals or authorizations of, or filings with, any governmental authority or any other person or entity are required in connection with the execution and delivery of this Agreement and the consummation of the transactions contemplated hereby, except post-Closing filings with respect to Medicare and Medicaid reimbursement and consent of the landlord of the premises at 2 Green Boulevard.

SECTION V.

[Intentionally Left Blank].

SECTION VI.

Additional Covenants of the Companies, the Shareholders and the Purchaser

A. *Company Acquisition Proposal.* The Companies and each of the Shareholders covenant and agree that, from and after the date of this Agreement and until the Closing, none of them shall directly or indirectly (i) take any action to solicit, initiate or encourage any Company Acquisition Proposal (as hereinafter defined) or (ii) engage in negotiations with, or disclose any nonpublic information relating to any of the Companies or afford access to the properties, books or records of any of the Companies to, any person or entity that may be considering making, or has made, a Company Acquisition Proposal. The Companies and each of the Shareholders shall promptly notify the Purchaser after receipt of any Company Acquisition Proposal or any indication that any person or entity is considering making a Company Acquisition Proposal or any request for non-public information relating to any of the Companies or for access to the properties, books or records of the Companies by any person or entity that may be considering making, or has made, a Company Acquisition Proposal. For purposes of this Agreement, "Company Acquisition Proposal" means any offer or proposal for, or any indication of interest in, a merger or other business combination involving any of the Companies or the acquisition of any equity interest in any of the Companies or any portion of the Assets, other than the transactions contemplated by this Agreement.

B.   *Goodwill; Publicity.* Each of the Companies and each of the Shareholders covenants and agrees that it or he, either before or after the Closing, will not make any untrue statement, written, oral or other, adverse to the interests of any of the Companies or the business reputation or good name of any of the Companies and that any and all publicity (whether written or oral) and, for a period of one hundred and twenty days after Closing, notices to third parties (other than employees of any of the Companies) concerning the sale of the Assets and other transactions contemplated by this Agreement, other than as required by law or disclosure to its lender for the real property located at 4204 Maryland Road, Willow Grove, Pennsylvania and to its insurer and accountants, shall be subject to the prior written approval of the Purchaser, which approval may be withheld in the sole discretion of the Purchaser. Notwithstanding the foregoing, the Companies and the Shareholders may disclose the transaction to senior executives of Community Hospital. The Purchaser agrees that any press release concerning the Closing hereunder shall be subject to the prior approval of the Shareholders, which such approval will not be unreasonably withheld.

The Purchaser agrees that, unless and until the Closing has been consummated, the Purchaser and its officers, directors, employees, agents and representatives will hold in strict confidence, and will not use any confidential or proprietary data or information obtained from any of the Companies or the Shareholders with respect to the Business or its financial condition, operation, contracts or other assets, except for the purposes of consummating the transaction contemplated by this Agreement.

The Purchaser agrees that, from and after the date of the Closing, the Purchaser and its officers, directors, employees, agents and representatives will hold in strict confidence and will not disclose to any person or entity the consideration paid to the Companies or the Shareholders or the financial terms of the leases contemplated hereby, except to its accountants, its insurers, any institutional lender from whom the Purchaser or any of its affiliates has, or may, borrow money and as may be required by law.

C.   *Further Assurances.* Subject to the terms and conditions of this Agreement, each of the Companies and each of the Shareholders will use its or his reasonable best efforts to take, or cause to be taken, all actions and to do, or cause to be done, all things necessary or desirable under applicable laws and regulations to consummate the transactions contemplated by this Agreement; provided, however, that subsequent to the Closing, such efforts or actions shall be at no additional cost to the Companies or the Shareholders unless otherwise agreed to in writing by the Companies or the Shareholders.

D. *Correspondence, etc.* Each of the Companies and each of the Shareholders covenants and agrees that, subsequent to the Closing each of them will deliver to the Purchaser, promptly after the receipt thereof, all inquiries, correspondence and other materials received by any of them from any person or entity relating to the Business or the Assets.

E. *Books and Records.* Each of the Companies and each of the Shareholders covenants and agrees that, subsequent to the Closing, each of them shall give the Purchaser, upon reasonable prior notice and during normal business hours, access to the historical financial books and records of each of the Companies, to the extent such books and records are not included in the Assets, for a period of five years from the date of the Closing. Each of the Companies shall retain all such books and records in substantially their condition at the time of the Closing. Prior to the expiration of five years from the Closing, none of such books and records shall be destroyed without the prior written approval of the Purchaser or without first offering such books and records to the Purchaser.

F. *Discharge of Obligations.* Each of the Companies and each of the Shareholders covenants and agrees, subsequent to the Closing, to pay promptly and to otherwise fulfill and discharge all valid obligations and liabilities of each of the Companies which are not Assumed Liabilities hereunder when due and payable and otherwise prior to the time at which any of such obligations or liabilities could in any way result in or give rise to a claim against the Assets, the Business or the Purchaser, result in the imposition of any lien, charge or encumbrance on any of the Assets, or adversely affect the Purchaser's title to or use of any of the Assets.

G. *Delivery of Funds.* Subsequent to the Closing, the Companies and the Shareholders shall deliver on a daily basis any funds and any checks, notes, drafts and other instruments for the payment of money, duly endorsed to the Purchaser, received by any of them (i) comprising payment of any of the accounts receivable of the Companies constituting a part of the Assets and (ii) comprising payment of any amounts due from customers of the Companies or others for services rendered by the Companies, including pursuant to any provider agreements constituting part of the Assets.

H. *Tax Clearance.* APT will obtain the required bulk sales tax clearance certificates ("Tax Certificates") as mandated by §1403 of the Pennsylvania Fiscal Code (72 P.S. §1403).

I. *Employees.* As of the Closing, the Purchaser shall offer employment to all those persons employed by each of the Companies in the Business, each of whom is listed on Exhibit M hereto (all such employees, the "Employees"). As of the Closing, each of the Companies shall terminate the employment of all of the Employees. Nothing herein shall be deemed either to affect or to limit in any way the management prerogatives of the Purchaser with respect to the Employees who accept such offer of employment (including without limitation the right of the Purchaser to modify compensation or the right of the Purchaser to terminate the employment of any Employee), or to create or to grant to such Employees any third-party beneficiary rights or claims or causes of action of any kind or nature against the Purchaser or its affiliates. To the extent not inconsistent with applicable law, the Employees who accept such offer of employment shall be afforded employment at substantially the same compensation, seniority and benefit levels as such Employees currently enjoy; provided, however, that in all cases with respect to benefits such terms and conditions shall be, on the whole, consistent with the terms and conditions applicable to all other employees of the Purchaser, it being understood that the Employees shall be required to make the same contributions and payments in order to receive any such benefits as may be required of similarly situated employees of the Purchaser. Nothing herein shall prevent the Purchaser from terminating the employment of any such Employee at any time for any reason as determined by the Purchaser in its sole discretion; provided, however, that if the Purchaser should terminate the employment of any Employee within six months of the Closing, the Purchaser shall provide prior written notice of such termination to AS ten days before such termination. The Purchaser agrees to credit to each Employee hired by the Purchaser an amount of vacation time and sick, personal and disability days to the extent specifically set forth opposite such Employee's name in Exhibit M hereto. The Purchaser agrees that it will pay all premiums for COBRA benefits for any Employee who is denied coverage under the Purchaser's health insurance plan due to a "pre-existing" condition.

J.   *Sawbones Receivables.* The Purchaser, for a period of six months from and after the Closing (the "Collection Period"), agrees to collect the accounts receivable generated by the business of Dr. Sawbones (the "Sawbones Receivables") and to pay the amounts so collected to AS on a monthly basis and deliver along therewith a statement reflecting the patient (and third party) which paid such accounts receivable and the amounts. The Purchaser agrees to use the same collection methods to collect the Sawbones Receivables as it employs to collect its receivables.Payments of accounts receivable shall be credited against the oldest receivable unless the patient or payor has directed otherwise. At the end of the Collection Period, the Purchaser agrees to return to AS all documentation in its possession with respect to the Sawbones Receivables and cease its collection efforts. Purchaser shall promptly give AS and its representatives, upon request, access to all of its books and records relating to the Sawbones Receivables. Purchaser shall have no right of set-off against any payments owed it under this Section VI(J).

K.   *Support Services.* For a period of six months from the date of the Closing, the Purchaser agrees to provide to Dr. Sawbones support services consistent with those currently provided to Dr. Sawbones by AS including but not limited to billing, typing services and telephone services (including without limitation message taking and appointment making).

L. *Landlord Consent.* Each of the Shareholders and each of the Companies covenants and agrees to use his or its reasonable efforts to obtain any required consent of the landlord of the premises at 2 Green Boulevard to permit the Purchaser to occupy such premises in accordance with the terms of the sublease agreement attached hereto as Exhibit L-III.

M. *Medical Insurance Coverage.* Purchaser shall provide to Meg Flynn and Marsha Berger Grant, so long as each is an employee of Purchaser or an Affiliate thereof, at no cost, medical coverage for each person's husband or shall increase each person's compensation a sufficient amount to pay for such medical coverage and the additional taxes on the increased compensation.

N. *Phones.* The Companies and the Shareholders may use the phone system at the Green Boulevard Location consistent with their prior practice and the Purchaser shall pay for such telephone bills.

SECTION VII.

Closing

A. *Time and Place of Closing.* The closing of the purchase and sale of the Assets, as set forth herein (the "Closing") shall be held at the offices of Blank Rome Comisky & McCauley, Four Penn Center Plaza, Philadelphia, Pennsylvania, at 10:00 A.M., local time, on June 30, 1994. The parties agree that the collected revenues and expenses (other than the Assumed Liabilities) of the Business up to and including June 30, 1994 shall belong to the Companies.

B. *Delivery of Assets.* Delivery of the Assets shall be made by the Companies to the Purchaser (or its designee) at the Closing by delivering such bills of sale, assignments and other instruments of conveyance and transfer, and such powers of attorney, as shall be effective to vest in the Purchaser (or its designee) title to or other interest in, and the right to full custody and control of, the Assets, free and clear of all liens, charges, encumbrances and security interests whatsoever.

C. *Assumption of Assumed Liabilities.* At the Closing, the Purchaser (or its designee) shall deliver to the Companies such instruments as shall be sufficient to effect the assumption by the Purchaser (or its designee) of the Assumed Liabilities.

D. *Contracts and Books.* At the Closing, each of the Companies and each of the Shareholders shall make available to the Purchaser the Contracts and the books and records of each of the Companies constituting a part of the Assets.

E. *Additional Steps.* At the Closing, each of the Companies and each of the Shareholders shall take all steps required to put the Purchaser in actual possession and control of the Assets.

F. *Sales or Use Taxes.* Any and all sales or use taxes assessed in connection with this transaction shall be paid as specified by applicable law.

G. *Delivery of Funds.* The Companies agree to deliver to the Purchaser at the Clos-
    ing a check in the amount of $25,000 representing the cash portion of the As-
    sets.

SECTION VIII.

Conditions to the Companies' Obligation to Close

The obligations of the Companies to sell the Assets and otherwise consummate
the transactions contemplated by this Agreement at the Closing are subject to the
following conditions precedent, any or all of which may be waived by the Companies
in their sole discretion, and each of which the Purchaser hereby agrees to use its best
efforts to satisfy at or prior to the Closing:

A. *No Litigation.* No action, suit or proceeding against the Companies, the Share-
    holders or the Purchaser relating to the consummation of any of the transac-
    tions contemplated by this Agreement or any governmental action seeking to
    delay or enjoin any such transactions shall be pending or threatened.

B. *Representations and Warranties.* The representations and warranties made by the
    Purchaser herein shall be correct as of the date of the Closing in all material re-
    spects with the same force and effect as though such representations and war-
    ranties had been made as of the date of the Closing, and on the date of the
    Closing, the Purchaser shall deliver to the Companies a certificate dated the
    date of the Closing to such effect. All the terms, covenants and conditions of this
    Agreement to be complied with and performed by the Purchaser on or before
    the date of the Closing shall have been duly complied with and performed in all
    material respects, and on the date of the Closing, the Purchaser shall deliver to
    the Companies a certificate dated the date of the Closing to such effect.

C. *Opinion of Counsel.* The Companies shall have received an opinion of Smith &
    Rogers, counsel for the Purchaser, delivered to the Companies pursuant to the
    instructions of the Purchaser, dated the date of the Closing, in form and sub-
    stance satisfactory to the Companies and their counsel, Blank Rome Comisky &
    McCauley.

D. *Leases.* The Purchaser's designee and J-R shall have entered into leases for the
    premises located at 200 Main Street, Anywhere, Pennsylvania (the "Main Street
    Location") and 1776 Independence Road, Philadelphia, Pennsylvania (the "In-
    dependence Location"), respectively, substantially in the form of Exhibits L-I
    and L-II. Furthermore, the Purchaser's designee shall have entered into a sub-
    lease agreement for the premises located at 2 Green Boulevard, Suite 22,
    Philadelphia, Pennsylvania (the "Green Boulevard Location"), substantially in
    the form of Exhibit L-III.

E. *Other Certificates.* The Companies shall have received such additional certificates,
    instruments and other documents, in form and substance satisfactory to them
    and their counsel, as it shall have reasonably requested in connection with the
    transactions contemplated hereby.

SECTION IX.

Conditions to the Purchaser's Obligation to Close

The obligation of the Purchaser to purchase the Assets and otherwise consummate the transactions contemplated by this Agreement at the Closing is subject to the following conditions precedent, any or all of which may be waived by the Purchaser in its sole discretion, and each of which each of the Companies and each of the Shareholders hereby agrees to use their best efforts to satisfy at or prior to the Closing:

A. *Opinion of Counsel.* The Purchaser shall have received an opinion of Blank Rome Comisky & McCauley, counsel for the Companies and the Shareholders, delivered to the Purchaser pursuant to the instructions of the Companies and the Shareholders, dated the date of the Closing, in form and substance satisfactory to the Purchaser and its counsel, Messrs. Smith & Rogers.

B. *No Litigation.* No action, suit or proceeding against the Companies, any of the Shareholders or the Purchaser relating to the consummation of any of the transactions contemplated by this Agreement nor any governmental action seeking to delay or enjoin any such transactions shall be pending or threatened.

C. *Representations and Warranties.* The representations and warranties made by each of the Companies and each of the Shareholders herein shall be correct as of the date of the Closing in all material respects with the same force and effect as though such representations and warranties had been made as of the date of the Closing, and on the date of the Closing, each of the Companies and each of the Shareholders shall deliver to the Purchaser a certificate dated the date of the Closing to such effect. All the terms, covenants and conditions of this Agreement to be complied with and performed by each of the Companies and each of the Shareholders on or before the date of the Closing shall have been duly complied with and performed in all material respects, and on the date of the Closing, the Companies and the Shareholders shall deliver to the Purchaser a certificate dated the date of the Closing to such effect.

D. *Other Certificates.* The Purchaser shall have received such other certificates, instruments and other documents, in form and substance satisfactory to it and its counsel, as it shall have reasonably requested in connection with the transactions contemplated hereby.

E. *Sale of All the Assets.* All the Assets shall be sold to the Purchaser (or its designee) at the Closing.

F. *Lease Terminations.* J-R and each of AS and APT, as applicable, shall deliver to the Purchaser terminations of lease agreements for all those Assets listed in Schedule I-(A) that are leased to AS or APT by J-R and which Assets are being acquired by Purchaser.

G. *Leases.* The Purchaser's designee and J-R shall have entered into leases for the premises located at the Main Street Location and the Independence Location, respectively, substantially in the form of Exhibits L-I and L-II. Furthermore, the

Purchaser's designee shall have entered into a sublease agreement for the premises located at 2 Green Boulevard, Suite 22, Philadelphia, Pennsylvania substantially in the form of Exhibit L-III.

SECTION X.

Indemnification

A. *Indemnification by the Companies and the Shareholders.* From and after the date of the Closing and subject to this Section X, each of the Companies and each of the Shareholders, jointly and severally, shall indemnify and hold harmless the Purchaser from and against all losses, claims, assessments, demands, damages, liabilities, obligations, costs and/or expenses, including, without limitation, reasonable fees and disbursements of counsel (hereinafter referred to collectively as "Damages") sustained or incurred by the Purchaser (or its designee) (i) by reason of the breach of any of the obligations, covenants or provisions of, or the inaccuracy of any of the representations or warranties made by, any of the Companies or any of the Shareholders herein, or (ii) arising out of or relating to any liabilities or obligations of each of the Companies not assumed by the Purchaser (or its designee) hereunder, or (iii) any tax obligations or other liabilities resulting from the failure of any of the Companies to obtain Tax Certificates, or (iv) arising out of or relating to liabilities or obligations imposed upon the Purchaser by a third party due to any violations by the Companies of any federal, state or local statute, laws, ordinances, rules, regulations, orders, or directives with respect to the employment practices or work conditions of the Companies, or violation by the Companies of the terms and conditions of employment, wages and hours, or (v) arising out of or relating to the Profit Sharing Plan. Notwithstanding anything to the contrary, no indemnification shall be due pursuant to clause (i) of this Section X(A) unless and to the extent that the aggregate Damages exceed $25,000 or with respect to any claim for Damages which is made or asserted by the Purchaser after the date on which the representation or warranty on which such claim for Damages is based expires as provided in Section XIII(B), and provided further, that in no event shall the Companies and the Shareholders be obligated to indemnify the Purchaser pursuant to clause (i) of this Section X(A) for an aggregate amount of Damages in excess of $1,800,000.

Notwithstanding anything to the contrary contained in this Agreement, neither the Companies nor the Shareholders shall be liable under the indemnification provisions of this Section X or otherwise have any liability for any misrepresentation or breach of warranty or covenant under this Agreement or otherwise have any liability in connection with the transactions contemplated by this Agreement to the extent that the existence of such liability, the breach of warranty or covenant or the falsity of the representation upon which such liability would be based is fully disclosed in this Agreement or in the Schedules attached hereto or is discovered by the Purchaser before the Closing; provided, however, that any such misrepresentation or breach of warranty or covenant so disclosed to the Purchaser by the Shareholders after the execution and delivery of this Agreement and prior to the Closing or otherwise discovered by the Purchaser shall not affect the right of the Purchaser to elect not to close the transactions contemplated by this Agreement as provided herein (it being understood and agreed that if, despite such right of the Purchaser to elect not to close by reason of the misrepresentation or breach so disclosed, the Purchaser nevertheless elects to close, thereby waiving such misrepresentation or breach, the Purchaser shall thereafter have no claim against the Companies or any of the Shareholders by reason of any such disclosed or discovered misrepresentation or breach of warranty or covenant).

B. *Indemnification by the Purchaser.* The Purchaser shall indemnify and hold harmless the Companies and each of the Shareholders from and against any and all Damages sustained or incurred by the Companies or any of the Shareholders (i) by reason of the breach of any of the obligations, covenants or provisions of, or the inaccuracy of any of the representations or warranties made by, the Purchaser herein, (ii) arising out of the Assumed Liabilities and/or (iii) arising from the Purchaser's conduct of the Business subsequent to the Closing.

C. *Procedure for Indemnification.* In the event that any party hereto shall incur any Damages in respect of which indemnity may be sought by such party pursuant to this Section X, the party from whom such indemnity may be sought (the "Indemnifying Party") shall be given written notice thereof by the party seeking such indemnity (the "Indemnified Party"), which notice shall specify the amount and nature of such Damages and include the request of the Indemnified Party for indemnification of such amount. The Indemnifying Party shall within 30 days pay to the Indemnified Party the amount of the Damages so specified.

D. *Recision, Punitive Damages.* It is specifically understood and agreed that in the event a misrepresentation or breach of warranty or covenant is discovered by the Purchaser after the Closing, the Purchaser shall not be entitled to a recision of this Agreement. In addition, the Purchaser shall not be entitled to recover consequential or punitive damages from the Companies or the Shareholders.

E. *Tax Benefits.* In the event that, notwithstanding the limitations contained in this Section X or elsewhere in this Agreement, the Companies or any Shareholder nevertheless becomes liable to the Purchaser under the provisions of this Agreement or otherwise, the Companies (and the Shareholders) shall be entitled to a credit or offset against any such liability of the value of any net tax benefit realized (by reason of a tax deduction, basis reduction, shifting of income, credits and/or deductions or otherwise) by the Purchaser in connection with the loss or damage suffered by the Purchaser which forms the basis of the Companies' or the Shareholders' liability hereunder. In addition, if any of the Companies or any of the Shareholders becomes obligated to indemnify Purchaser, the party so indemnifying, upon payment in full, shall be subrogated to all rights of the Indemnified Party with respect to all claims to which such indemnification relates.

F.   *Exclusions.* Notwithstanding anything to the contrary contained in this Agreement or in the Bill of Sale executed pursuant hereto, there shall be excluded from the sale, transfer, conveyance and assignment hereunder, and the Assets shall not include, any debt, liability or obligation of, or claim against, any past or present shareholder, director or officer of the Companies, except as explicitly included in the Assets.

G.   *Equitable Remedies.* With the exception of equitable remedies and except with respect to claims based on fraud, the indemnification provisions set forth in this Section X shall be the sole and exclusive remedy of the Purchaser with respect to any actions resulting or arising from the matters referred to in this Section X and, to the extent permitted by law, the Purchaser waives all other remedies available at law with respect thereto.

H.   *Consents.* The Purchaser hereby waives its right to any claims it may have against the Companies and/or the Shareholders for their failure to obtain consents to assignment of any contracts (written or oral) which constitute part of the Assets.

I.   *Accounts Receivable.*If the Companies and/or the Shareholders pay the Purchaser for uncollected accounts receivable as contemplated by the second sentence of Section II(K), then the Purchaser on a nonrecourse basis shall assign such uncollected accounts receivable to the Companies simultaneous to receiving the payment referred to in this Section X from the Companies and/or the Shareholders.

SECTION XI.

Non-Competition Agreement

Following the consummation of the transactions contemplated hereby, and in consideration thereof, none of the Companies and none of the Shareholders shall, subsequent to the date of the Closing and until seven years after the date of the Closing, directly or indirectly, (i) engage, whether as principal, agent, distributor, representative, investor, stockholder (except for passive investments of not more than 5% of the outstanding shares of any company listed on a national exchange or NASDAQ with shareholder equity exceeding $75,000,000), or employee of, or otherwise benefit from, any activity or business venture, anywhere within a fifty (50) mile radius of any location or facility where any of the Companies conduct the Business as of the date of the Closing, providing physical or occupational therapy, (ii) solicit or entice or endeavor to solicit or entice away from any member of the Purchaser Group (as hereinafter defined) any Employee, either on any of the Companies' or any of the Shareholders' own account or for any person, firm, corporation or other organization, whether or not such person would commit any breach of such person's contract of employment by reason of leaving the service of such member of the Purchaser Group, (iii) solicit or entice or endeavor to solicit or entice away any of the clients or customers of any member of the Purchaser Group, either on any of the Companies' or any of the Shareholders' own account or for any other person, firm, corporation or organization for the purpose of providing physical or occupational therapy services, or (iv) employ any person who was an Employee, or (v) at any time during such seven-year period, make any untrue statement, written, oral or other, adverse to the interests of any member of the Purchaser Group or the business reputation or good name of any member of the Purchaser Group. Following the consummation of the transactions contemplated hereby, and in consideration thereof, none of the Companies and none of the Shareholders shall, subsequent to the date of the Closing and for the term (either seven years if the tenant thereunder buys out the lease as contemplated thereunder or otherwise ten years) of the lease for the Main Street Location, lease any space at the premises at the Main Street Location to any person or entity, other than a member of the Purchaser Group, who is engaged in the practice of physical or occupational therapy; provided, however, that the Shareholders and the Companies shall not be bound by this provision in the event that the Purchaser or its designee, as applicable, exercises its option to terminate the lease for the Main Street Location pursuant to the terms of Paragraph 48 of such lease. Because the remedy at law for any breach of the foregoing provisions of this Section XI would be inadequate, each of the Companies and each of the Shareholders hereby consents, in case of any such breach, to the granting by any court of competent jurisdiction of specific enforcement, including, but not limited to, pre- judgment injunctive relief of such provisions, as provided for in Section XIII hereof.

Notwithstanding the foregoing, it shall not be a breach of this Section XI for the Shareholders to engage in the practice of orthopedic medicine and the practice of psychiatry in connection with such medical practice.

In addition, notwithstanding the foregoing, the Companies and the Shareholders shall be permitted to provide consulting or medical services to inpatient rehabilitation facilities for compensation directly related to such services so long as none of the Shareholders expends more than twenty-five percent of his working time (the "Time Limit") providing consulting or medical services to inpatient rehabilitation facilities and the Companies or the Shareholders notify Purchaser in writing before providing such services. If any of the Shareholders does expend more than twenty-five percent of his working time providing consulting or medical services to inpatient rehabilitation facilities, then prior to exceeding the Time Limit in each instance he will first obtain written consent from Purchaser, such consent not to be unreasonably withheld by the Purchaser. Purchaser has been advised in writing that the Shareholders provide services to inpatient rehabilitation facilities at Community Hospital and at two nursing homes.

The parties hereto agree that if, in any proceeding, the court or other authority shall refuse to enforce the covenants herein set forth because such covenants cover too extensive a geographic area or too long a period of time, any such covenant shall be deemed appropriately amended and modified in keeping with the intention of the parties to the maximum extent permitted by law.

For purposes hereof, "Purchaser Group" shall mean, collectively, the Purchaser and its subsidiaries, affiliates and parent entities operating in the same lines of business.

SECTION XII.

Brokers and Finders

A. *The Shareholders' Obligations.* The Purchaser shall not have any obligation to pay any fee or other compensation to any person, firm or corporation dealt with by each of the Companies or any of the Shareholders in connection with this Agreement and the transactions contemplated hereby, and the Companies and each of the Shareholders, jointly and severally, hereby agree to indemnify and save the Purchaser harmless from any liability, damage, cost or expense arising from any claim for any such fee or other compensation.

B. *The Purchaser's Obligation.* Neither the Companies nor any of the Shareholders shall have any obligation to pay any fee or other compensation to any person, firm or corporation dealt with by the Purchaser in connection with this Agreement and the transactions contemplated hereby, and the Purchaser hereby agrees to indemnify and save the Companies and each of the Shareholders harmless from any liability, damage, cost or expense arising from any claim for any such fee or other compensation.

SECTION XIII.

Miscellaneous

A. *Notices.* All notices, requests or instructions hereunder shall be in writing and delivered personally, sent by telecopy or sent by registered or certified mail, postage prepaid, as follows:

1) If to the Companies or the Shareholders:
    Albertson Medical Specialists, P.C.
    1776 Independence Road,
    Philadelphia, Pennsylvania

    with a Copy to:

    Blank Rome LLP
    One Logan Square
    Philadelphia, Pennsylvania 19103

(2) If to the Purchaser:

    Clincare Corporation
    1018 West Ninth Avenue
    New York, New York

    with a Copy to:

    Smith & Rogers
    237 Main Street
    New York, New York

Any of the above addresses may be changed at any time by notice given as provided above; provided, however, that any such notice of change of address shall be effective only upon receipt. All notices, requests or instructions given in accordance herewith shall be deemed received on the date of delivery, if hand delivered or telecopied, and two business days after the date of mailing, if mailed.

B. *Survival of Representations.* Each representation, warranty, covenant and agreement of the parties hereto herein contained shall survive the Closing, notwithstanding any investigation at any time made by or on behalf of any party hereto, for a period of two (2) years, except (a) for covenants and agreements contained in this Agreement which by their terms extend for more than two (2) years and (b) that nothing in the foregoing shall be deemed to diminish any Indemnitor's indemnification obligations to an Indemnitee respecting (x) any claim for Damages under Section X hereof for which notice to the Indemnitor has been given prior to the end of such two (2) year period, (y) the representations and warranties contained in Sections II(G), (H), (I)(iv) and (AA) and claims for common law fraud, each of which shall survive for the duration of the applicable statutes of limitations governing third-party claims made with respect thereto.

C. *Entire Agreement.* This Agreement and the documents referred to herein contain the entire agreement among the parties hereto with respect to the transactions contemplated hereby, and no modification hereof shall be effective unless in writing and signed by the party against which it is sought to be enforced.

D. *Further Assurances.* Each of the parties hereto shall use such party's reasonable best efforts to take such actions as may be necessary or reasonably requested by the other parties hereto to carry out and consummate the transactions contemplated by this Agreement; provided, however, that subsequent to the Closing, such efforts or actions shall be at no additional cost to the Companies or the Shareholders, unless otherwise agreed to in writing by the Companies or the Shareholders.

E. *Expenses.* Each of the parties hereto shall bear such party's own expenses in connection with this Agreement and the transactions contemplated hereby.

F. *Injunctive Relief.* Notwithstanding the provisions of Section XIII(G) hereof, in the event of a breach or threatened breach by any of the Companies or any of the Shareholders of the provisions of Section XI of this Agreement, each of the Companies and each of the Shareholders hereby consents and agrees that the Purchaser shall be entitled to an injunction or similar equitable relief restraining the Companies or the Shareholders, as the case may be, from committing or continuing any such breach or threatened breach or granting specific performance of any act required to be performed by the Companies or any of the Shareholders, as the case may be, under any such provision, without the necessity of showing any actual damage or that money damages would not afford an adequate remedy and without the necessity of posting any bond or other security. The parties hereto hereby consent to the jurisdiction of the Federal courts for the Eastern District of Pennsylvania and the Pennsylvania state courts located in such District for any proceedings under this Section XIII(F). The parties hereto agree that the availability of arbitration in Section XIII(G) hereof shall not be used by any party as grounds for the dismissal of any injunctive actions instituted by the Purchaser pursuant to this Section XIII(F). Nothing herein shall be construed as prohibiting the Purchaser from pursuing any other remedies at law or in equity which it may have.

G.   *Arbitration.* Any controversy or claim arising out of or relating to this Agreement, or any breach hereof, shall, except as provided in Section XIII(F) hereof, be settled by arbitration in accordance with the rules of the American Arbitration Association then in effect and judgment upon the award rendered by the arbitrator may be entered in any court having jurisdiction thereof. The arbitration shall be held in the Philadelphia, Pennsylvania area.

H.   *Invalidity.* Should any provision of this Agreement be held by a court or arbitration panel of competent jurisdiction to be enforceable only if modified, such holding shall not affect the validity of the remainder of this Agreement, the balance of which shall continue to be binding upon the parties hereto with any such modification to become a part hereof and treated as though originally set forth in this Agreement. The parties further agree that any such court or arbitration panel is expressly authorized to modify any such unenforceable provision of this Agreement in lieu of severing such unenforceable provision from this Agreement in its entirety, whether by rewriting the offending provision, deleting any or all of the offending provision, adding additional language to this Agreement, or by making such other modifications as it deems warranted to carry out the intent and agreement of the parties as embodied herein to the maximum extent permitted by law. The parties expressly agree that this Agreement as modified by the court or the arbitration panel shall be binding upon and enforceable against each of them. In any event, should one or more of the provisions of this Agreement be held to be invalid, illegal or unenforceable in any respect, such invalidity, illegality or unenforceability shall not affect any other provisions hereof, and if such provision or provisions are not modified as provided above, this Agreement shall be construed as if such invalid, illegal or unenforceable provisions had never been set forth herein.

I.   *Knowledge.* Whenever used in this Agreement, the words "to the best of the knowledge of the Companies," or similar words, shall mean the knowledge or awareness which the Shareholders and Mr. Donald Lachman would obtain in the exercise of reasonable diligence or after due inquiry, it being understood and agreed that such knowledge or awareness of any or all of such persons, for purposes hereof, shall be attributed to the Company.

J.   *Successors and Assigns.* This Agreement shall be binding upon and inure to the benefit of the successors and assigns of each of the Companies and the Purchaser, respectively, and the legal representatives and heirs of each of the Shareholders.

K.   *Governing Law.* The validity of this Agreement and of any of its terms or provisions, as well as the rights and duties of the parties under this Agreement, shall be construed pursuant to and in accordance with the laws of the Commonwealth of Pennsylvania.

L. *Counterparts.* This Agreement may be executed in counterparts, each of which
    shall be deemed an original, but all of which taken together shall constitute one
    and the same instrument.

    IN WITNESS WHEREOF, this Agreement has been duly executed by the parties
hereto as of the date first above written.

Albertson Medical Specialists, P.C.

By: _____

     Name:

     Title:

Albertson Physical Therapy, P.C.

By: _____

     Name:

     Title:

Jenkins-Michael Associates

By: _____

     Name:

     Title:

Sara Ann Rubin, M.D.

Michael Daniel Rubin, M.D.

Kimberly Lageman, M.D.

Andrew Mortenson, M.D.

Clincare Corporation

By: _____

(Schedules and Exhibits Omitted)

APPENDIX 8

SAMPLE AGREEMENT AND PLAN OF MERGER

AGREEMENT AND PLAN OF MERGER

THIS AGREEMENT AND PLAN OF MERGER (this "Agreement"), dated as of April 20, 2004 is entered into by and between Omega Financial Corporation ("Omega" or the "Surviving Corporation" as the context may require), a corporation organized and existing under the laws of Pennsylvania, which is registered as a bank holding company and whose principal offices are located at 366 Walker Drive, State College, Pennsylvania 16804, and Sun Bancorp, Inc. ("Sun"), a corporation organized and existing under the laws of the Commonwealth of Pennsylvania, which is registered as a financial holding company and whose principal offices are located at 155 North 15th Street, Lewisburg, Pennsylvania, 17837.

Omega and Sun are sometimes referred to herein as the "Parties."

RECITALS

A.   The Board of Directors of Sun deems it desirable and in the best interests of Sun and its shareholders that Sun be merged with and into Omega (which would survive the merger as the Surviving Corporation) on the terms and subject to the conditions set forth in this Agreement and in the manner provided in this Agreement.

B.   The Board of Directors of Omega deems it desirable and in the best interests of Omega and its shareholders that Sun be merged with and into Omega on the terms and subject to the conditions set forth in this Agreement and in the manner provided in this Agreement.

C.   Pursuant to this Agreement, each share of Sun Common Stock outstanding at the Effective Time will be converted into either (i) cash in the amount of $23.25, or (ii) 0.664 shares of Omega Common Stock.Holders of Sun Common Stock will be entitled to elect their preference with respect to each share of Sun Common Stock held by them, subject to pro rata allocation, such that 20% of Sun Common Stock shall be paid in cash, and 80% of Sun Common Stock will be in the form of Omega Common Stock, including the effect of cash paid in lieu of fractional shares of Omega Common Stock, if any.

D.   As an inducement and condition to Omega entering into this Agreement, each director and executive officer of Sun is agreeing to vote all shares of Sun Common Stock owned by them in favor of the transactions contemplated by this Agreement at the meeting of Sun Shareholders at which this Agreement is considered pursuant to a voting agreement in the form attached hereto as Exhibit A ("Voting Agreement").

E.   The Parties desire to make certain representations, warranties and agreements in connection with the Merger and also to prescribe certain conditions to the Merger, all as set forth herein.

DEFINITIONS

Except as otherwise provided herein, as used in this Agreement, the following terms shall have the indicated meanings (which shall be applicable to both the singular and plural forms of the terms defined).

"Acquisition Proposal" means a proposed tender offer, written agreement, understanding or other proposal of any nature pursuant to which any Person or group, other than Omega or any Omega Subsidiary, would directly or indirectly (i) acquire or participate in a merger, share exchange, consolidation or any other business combination involving Sun or any Sun Subsidiary; (ii) acquire the right to vote 10% or more of the outstanding voting securities of Sun or any Sun Subsidiary; (iii) acquire 25% or more of the assets or earning power of Sun or of any Sun Subsidiary; or (iv) acquire in excess of 10% of any class of capital stock of Sun or any Sun Subsidiary.

"Acquisition Transaction" means any of the following events:

(i)   the acquisition by any Person, other than Omega or any Omega Subsidiary, alone or together with such Person's Affiliates or any group, of beneficial ownership of 10% or more of the outstanding shares of Sun Common Stock or the right to vote 10% or more of the outstanding voting securities of Sun or any Sun Subsidiary (for purposes of this Subsection (i), the terms "group" and "beneficial ownership" shall be as defined in Section 13(d) of the Exchange Act and regulations promulgated thereunder and as interpreted thereunder);

(ii)   a merger, consolidation, share exchange, business combination or any other similar transaction involving Sun or any Sun Subsidiary; or

(iii) any sale, lease, exchange, mortgage, pledge, transfer or other disposition of 25% or more of the assets or earning power of the Sun or any Sun Subsidiary, in a single transaction or series of transactions.

"Affiliate" means, with respect to any Person, any other Person that, directly or indirectly, through one or more intermediaries, controls, is controlled by, or is under common control with, such Person.For the purposes of this definition, "control" means, when used with respect to any Person, the possession, directly or indirectly, of the power to direct or cause the direction of the management and policies of such Person, whether through the ownership of voting securities, by contract, or otherwise, and the terms "controlling" and "controlled" have correlative meanings.

"Aggregate Consideration" shall mean the amount that is equal to the sum of (i) the number of Cash Election Shares multiplied by the Cash Merger Consideration, plus (ii) the number of Stock Election Shares multiplied by the dollar amount of the Stock Merger Consideration, determined based upon the Determination Price.The Aggregate Consideration shall be determined after all adjustments and pro rations required to be made under this Agreement.

"Aggregate Shares" shall mean the number of shares of Sun Common Stock issued and outstanding on the Closing Date, excluding shares for which no consideration is payable as described in Section 2.2(a).

"Applicable Law" means any statute, law, code, rule, or regulation, or any judgment, order, ordinance, writ, injunction, or decree of, any Governmental Authority to which a specified Person or its property or activities is subject.

"Balance Sheet Date" means December 31, 2003.

"Banking Approvals" means (a) the approval of the application filed with the FDIC under the Bank Merger Act and (b) any other approvals and/or Consents required to be obtained from or made to or with the Banking Department, the FDIC, the FRB or the OCC.

"Banking Department" means the Pennsylvania Department of Banking.

"Cash Election" means the election by a Sun Shareholder to receive the Cash Merger Consideration for such Shareholder's shares of Sun Common Stock.

"Cash Election Shares" means shares of Sun Common Stock as to which a Cash Election has been made.

"Cash Merger Consideration" means $23.25.

"Charter Documents" means, with respect to a particular Person that is not an individual, such Person's articles or certificate of incorporation or formation, organization certificate, bylaws and any other similar governing documents, all as may be amended or amended and restated from time to time.

"Closing" means consummation of the Merger.

"Closing Date" means the date of the Closing, which shall be on the eighth business day after the last condition precedent pursuant to this Agreement has been fulfilled or waived (including the expiration of any applicable waiting period) or such other date upon which the Parties may mutually agree.

"Code" means the Internal Revenue Code of 1986, as amended.

"Consent" means any consent, non-objection after notice to, approval or authorization of, notice to, or designation, registration, declaration or filing with, any Person.

"Determination Date" means the day which is eight business days before the Closing Date.

"Determination Price" means the mean average market price of Omega Common Stock for the twenty trading days immediately preceding the Determination Date.In calculating the average market price of Omega Common Stock, the market price on any trading day for which there are trades reported on the NASDAQ National Market shall be the last quoted trading price on that day, and the market price on any trading day for which no trades have been reported on the NASDAQ National Market shall be the average of the high bid and low asked prices on that day as reported by NASDAQ.

"Effective Time" shall be the close of business on the date on which the Merger is consummated by the filing of Articles of Merger with the Secretary of State of the Commonwealth of Pennsylvania.

"Election Form" shall mean the form mutually prepared by Omega and Sun which shall be distributed to the Sun Shareholders and by which the Sun Shareholders can indicate their election to receive the Cash Merger Consideration or the Stock Merger Consideration.

"Election Deadline" means 4:00 p.m. eastern standard time on the business day immediately preceding the date of the meeting of Sun Shareholders to approve the transactions contemplated by this Agreement, or such other date as may be mutually agreed upon by Omega and Sun.

"Environmental Laws" mean all federal, state and local laws, including statutes, regulations, ordinances, codes, rules and other governmental restrictions, standards and requirements relating to the discharge of air pollutants, water pollutants or process waste water or substances, as now or at any time hereafter in effect, including, but not limited to, the Federal Solid Waste Disposal Act, the Federal Hazardous Materials Transportation Act, the Federal Clean Air Act, the Federal Clean Water Act, the Federal Resource Conservation and Recovery Act of 1976, the Federal Comprehensive Environmental Responsibility Cleanup and Liability Act of 1980, as amended ("CERCLA"), regulations of the Environmental Protection Agency, regulations of the Nuclear Regulatory Agency, regulations of the Occupational Safety and Health Administration, and any so-called "Superfund" or "Superlien" Laws.

"ERISA" means the Employee Retirement Income Security Act of 1974, as amended.

"Exchange Act" means the Securities Exchange Act of 1934, as amended, and the rules and regulations promulgated from time to time thereunder.

"Exchange Agent" means such bank, trust company, transfer agent or other entity selected by Omega, with the consent of Sun, not to be unreasonably withheld.

"Expenses" means all reasonable in amount and reasonably incurred out-of-pocket expenses (including all reasonable fees and reasonable expenses of counsel, accountants, investment bankers, experts and consultants to the applicable Party and its Affiliates) incurred by or on behalf of a Party to this Agreement in connection with this Agreement or the transactions contemplated by this Agreement.

"FDIC" means the Federal Deposit Insurance Corporation.

"FRB" means the Board of Governors of the Federal Reserve System.

"GAAP" means generally accepted accounting principles, as in effect at the relevant date.

"Governmental Approvals" means all Consents of Governmental Authorities that are necessary so that the consummation of the Merger and the other transactions contemplated hereby will be in compliance with Applicable Law, other than the Banking Approvals.

"Governmental Authority" shall mean any court or tribunal in any domestic jurisdiction or any federal, state, municipal or local government or other domestic governmental body, agency, authority, department, commission, board, bureau, instrumentality, arbitrator or arbitral body, including, without limitation, the Banking Department, the FDIC, the FRB and the OCC.

"Intellectual Property" means (i) trademarks, service marks, trade names, Internet domain names, designs, logos, slogans, and general intangibles of like nature, together with all goodwill, registrations and applications related to the foregoing; (ii) patents and industrial designs (including any continuations, divisionals, continuations-in-part, renewals, reissues, and applications for any of the foregoing); (iii) copyrights (including any registrations and applications for any of the foregoing); (iv) Software; and (v) technology, trade secrets and other confidential information, know-how, proprietary processes, formulae, algorithms, models, and methodologies.

"Knowledge" or "aware" or any term of similar import means, (i) with respect to Sun, the actual knowledge of each director and officer of Sun or any Sun Subsidiary after all due and reasonable inquiry, and (ii) with respect to Omega, the actual knowledge of each director and officer of Omega or any Omega Subsidiary after all due and reasonable inquiry.

"Material Adverse Effect" shall mean, with respect to a Party, an effect that is material and adverse to (a) the assets, properties, business, future prospects, financial condition or results of operations of such Party and its Subsidiaries, taken as a whole; provided, however, that, for purposes of this clause (a), a Material Adverse Effect shall not be deemed to include (i) any change in the value of the respective investment and loan portfolios of either Party resulting from a change in interest rates generally within the banking industry, (ii) any change occurring after the date of this Agreement in any Applicable Law or in GAAP, which change affects banking institutions generally, including any changes affecting the Bank Insurance Fund, (iii) changes in general economic (except in the context of determining a Material Adverse Effect for purposes of asset quality), legal, regulatory or political conditions affecting banking institutions generally, (iv) actions or omissions of a Party (or any of its Subsidiaries) taken pursuant to the terms of this Agreement with the prior written consent of the other Party in contemplation of the transactions contemplated hereby; or (b) the ability of such Party to consummate the transactions contemplated hereby .

"Merger" means the merger of Sun with and into Omega, with Omega surviving the merger.

"NASDAQ Bank Index" means the NASDAQ Bank Index as currently published by the Nasdaq Stock Market, Inc., or, if not then published, a comparable index as mutually agreed upon by Omega and Sun.

"Non-Election" means the failure of a Sun Shareholder to indicate a preference as to the form of Per Share Merger Consideration to be received for its shares of Sun Common Stock.

"Non-Electing Shares" means outstanding shares of Sun Common Stock, as to which there is a Non-Election.

"OCC" means the Office of Comptroller of the Currency, an agency of the United States Department of the Treasury.

"Omega Bank" means Omega Bank N.A.

"Omega Benefit Plans" means (i) each pension, profit sharing, stock bonus, thrift, savings, employee stock ownership or other plan, program or arrangement, which constitutes an "employee pension benefit plan" within the meaning of Section 3(2) of ERISA, which is maintained by Omega or any Omega Subsidiary or to which Omega or any Omega Subsidiary contribute, or are obligated to contribute, for the benefit of any current or former employee, officer, director, consultant or agent; and (ii) every other retirement or deferred compensation plan, bonus or incentive compensation plan or arrangement, stock option plan, stock purchase plan, severance or vacation pay arrangement, or other fringe benefit plan, program, agreement or arrangement through which Omega or any Omega Subsidiary provide benefits for or on behalf of any current or former employee, officer, director, consultant or agent, and, with respect to each such plan, the amounts contributed but not yet paid to participants or beneficiaries thereunder, and the amount of any contribution deficiencies with respect thereto.

"Omega Common Stock" means the common stock of Omega, $5.00 par value.

"Omega Financial Statements" means the audited financial statements of Omega for the years ended December 31, 2003, 2002 and 2001, together with all notes to such financial statements, as included in Omega's annual report on Form 10-K filed with the SEC for the fiscal year ended December 31, 2003.

"Omega Schedule" means the schedule of exceptions and other information prepared by Omega and delivered to Sun as described in the introductory paragraph of Article 4.

"Omega Subsidiaries" means Omega Bank and the other Subsidiaries of Omega referenced in Section 4.1(c).

"PBCL" means Pennsylvania Business Corporation Law.

"Person" means an individual, partnership (general or limited), corporation, joint venture, business trust, limited liability company, cooperative association or other form of business organization, trust, estate or any other entity.

"Per Share Merger Consideration" means either the Cash Merger Consideration or Stock Merger Consideration.

"Proceeding" means any proceeding, action, claim, suit, arbitration, mediation, investigation or inquiry by or before any Governmental Authority.

"Prospectus/Proxy" means the combined prospectus and proxy statement constituting the prospectus for the issuance of the Omega Common Stock as the Stock Merger Consideration pursuant to this Agreement and also constituting the proxy statement sent to the shareholders of Omega and Sun to solicit their votes on the approval of the Merger, as the same is included in the Registration Statement, as declared effective by the SEC, together with any supplement or amendment thereto included as part of any post-effective amendment.

"Registration Statement" means the Securities Act registration statement on Form S-4 as filed with the SEC in order to register the offering of the Omega Common Stock constituting the offering of the aggregate Stock Merger Consideration, together with all filed amendments to such registration statement.

"SEC" means the United States Securities and Exchange Commission.

"Securities Act" means the Securities Act of 1933, as amended, and the rules and regulations promulgated from time to time thereunder.

"Securities Laws" means the Securities Act and the Exchange Act.

"Sentry Plans" means the Sentry Trust Company 1997 Stock Incentive Plan, as amended, and the Sentry Trust Company 1999 Stock Incentive Plan assumed by Sun in connection with the acquisition of Sentry Trust Company pursuant to that certain Agreement and Plan of Reorganization dated as of April 23, 2003, as amended, by and among Sun, Sun Interim Trust Company (In Organization), Sentry Trust Company and Patriot Federal Credit Union.

"Shareholder Materials" means a letter of transmittal, an instruction sheet and a return mailing envelope sent or made available to Sun Shareholders who have not duly submitted the certificates for shares of Sun Common Stock by the Election Deadline.

"Shares" means the shares of Omega Common Stock issued, or to be issued, to Sun Shareholders as consideration for the Merger pursuant to this Agreement.

"Software" means computer programs, whether in source code or object code form (including any and all software implementation of algorithms, models and methodologies), databases and compilations (including any and all data and collections of data), and all documentation (including user manuals and training materials) related to the foregoing.

"Stock Election" means the election by a Sun Shareholder to receive the Stock Merger Consideration for such Shareholder's shares of Sun Common Stock.

"Stock Election Shares" means shares of Sun Common Stock as to which a Stock Election has been made.

"Stock Merger Consideration" means 0.664 shares of Omega Common Stock.

"Subsidiary" means, with respect to a Person, a corporation, partnership, limited liability company or other business entity in which such Person owns, directly or indirectly, 50% or more of any class of equity securities or a comparable percentage equity ownership interest.

"SunBank" means SunBank, a Pennsylvania state-chartered bank.

"Sun Common Stock" means the common stock of Sun, no par value.

"Sun Financial Statements" means the audited financial statements of Sun for the years ended December 31, 2003, 2002 and 2001, together with all notes to such financial statements, as included in Sun's annual report on Form 10-K filed with the SEC for the fiscal year ended December 31, 2003.

"Sun Intellectual Property" means the Intellectual Property used in or held for use in the conduct of the business of Sun or any Sun Subsidiary.

"Sun Real Property" means the real property owned, leased, rented, occupied or operated by Sun or any Sun Subsidiary.

"Sun Schedule" means the schedule of exceptions and other information prepared by Sun and delivered to Omega as described in the introductory paragraph of Article 3.

"Sun Stock Options" mean options or other rights to purchase shares of Sun Common Stock granted pursuant to (i) Sun's 1998 Stock Incentive Plan, 1998 Employee Stock Purchase Plan or 1998 Independent Directors Stock Option Plan, each as approved by shareholders of Sun on April 23, 1998 or (ii) the Sentry Plans.

"Sun Shareholder" means a record holder of one or more shares of Sun Common Stock.

"Sun Subsidiaries" means SunBank and any other Subsidiaries of Sun, including, without limitation, the Subsidiaries identified on Section 3.1(c) to the Sun Schedule.

"Superior Proposal" means an unsolicited, bona fide proposal to enter into an Acquisition Transaction that the board of directors of Sun determines in its good faith business judgment (after consultation with its financial advisors and legal counsel) (i) would result in a transaction that is more favorable to its shareholders, from a financial point of view, and its other stakeholders than the transactions contemplated by this Agreement, (ii) that the Person proposing such Acquisition Transaction is reasonably likely to have or obtain, any necessary funds or customary commitments to provide any funds necessary to consummate such Acquisition Proposal, and (iii) that any Consents required in order to consummate such Acquisition Transaction are reasonably likely to be obtained; provided, however, that, for the purposes of this definition, the term "Acquisition Transaction" shall have the meaning ascribed to it herein except that the references therein to 10% and 25% shall be deemed to be a reference to 50%.

"Tax" means any federal, state, local or foreign income, gross receipts, license, payroll, employment, excise, severance, stamp, occupation, premium, windfall profits, environmental, customs duties, capital stock, franchise, profits withholding, social security (or similar), unemployment, disability, real property, personal property, sales, use, transfer, registration, value added, alternative or add-on minimum, estimated, or other tax of any kind whatsoever, including any interest, penalty, or addition thereto, whether disputed or not.

"Tax Return" means any returns, declaration, report, claim for refund, or information return or statement relating to Taxes, including any schedule or attachment thereto, and including any amendment thereof.

NOW THEREFORE, in consideration of the foregoing premises and the mutual representations, warranties, covenants and agreements herein contained and for other good and valuable consideration, the receipt and sufficiency of which is hereby acknowledged, the Parties agree as follows:

ARTICLE I
TERMS OF THE MERGER

1.1 *The Merger.* Subject to the satisfaction (or lawful waiver) of each of the conditions to the obligations of each Party specified herein, at the Effective Time, Sun shall be merged with and into Omega, which latter corporation shall survive the Merger and is referred to herein in such capacity as the "Surviving Corporation." The Merger shall have the effects set forth here and the provisions of the PBCL relating to mergers of corporate entities.

(a) *Effects of the Merger.* At the Effective Time, the separate existence of Sun shall cease, and Omega, as the Surviving Corporation, shall thereupon and thereafter possess all of the assets, rights, privileges, appointments, powers, licenses, permits and franchises of the two merged corporations, whether of a public or a private nature, and shall be subject to all of the liabilities, restrictions, disabilities and duties of Sun. The Merger is intended to be treated by the Parties as a reorganization within the meaning of Section 368(a) of the Code.

(b) *Transfer of Assets.* At the Effective Time, all rights, assets, licenses, permits, franchises and interests of Sun in and to every type of property, whether real, personal, or mixed, whether tangible or intangible, and choses in action shall be deemed to be vested in Omega as the Surviving Corporation by virtue of the Merger becoming effective and without any deed or other instrument or act of transfer what-soever.

(c) *Assumption of Liabilities.* At the Effective Time, the Surviving Corporation shall become and be liable for all debts, liabilities, obligations and contracts of Sun whether the same shall be matured or unmatured; whether accrued, absolute, contingent or otherwise; and whether or not reflected or reserved against in the balance sheets, other financial statements, books of account or records of Sun.

1.2 *Articles of Incorporation, Bylaws, Directors, Officers and Name of the Surviving Corporation.*

(a) *Articles of Incorporation.* At and after the Effective Time, the Articles of Incorporation of Omega, as in effect immediately prior to the Effective Time, shall continue to be the Articles of Incorporation of Omega as the Surviving Corporation, unless and until amended thereafter as provided by Applicable Law and the terms of such Articles of Incorporation.

(b) *Bylaws.* At and after the Effective Time, the Bylaws of Omega, as in effect immediately prior to the Effective Time, shall continue to be the Bylaws of Omega as the Surviving Corporation, unless and until amended or repealed as provided by Applicable Law, the Articles of Incorporation of Omega and such Bylaws.

(c) *Directors and Officers.* The directors and officers of Omega in office immediately prior to the Effective Time shall continue to be directors and officers of the Surviving Corporation, to hold office as provided in the Articles of Incorporation and Bylaws of the Surviving Corporation, unless and until their successors shall have been elected or appointed and shall have qualified or until they shall have been removed in the manner provided in said Articles of Incorporation and Bylaws; provided, however, that the Board of Directors of Omega shall appoint, as of the Effective Time, three directors of Sun, as mutually agreed by Sun and Omega, as directors of Omega (each, a "Sun Director").Each Sun Director shall be appointed to one of the three classes of directors of the Omega Board of Directors and shall serve the remaining term of the class to which such Sun Director was appointed.The Omega Board of Directors shall recommend, subject to its fiduciary duties, the nomination of each Sun Director for election, by the shareholders of Omega, for one additional term of three years after such Sun Director's initial term expires.If one or more Sun Director is unable or unwilling to serve as a member of Omega's Board of Directors, such person shall be replaced by another person mutually selected by Omega and Sun who was a director of Sun immediately prior to the Effective Time.

(d) *SunBank Board of Directors; SunBank Advisory Board; Omega Bank Board of Directors.*

(i) For a period of two years following the Effective Time, Omega shall offer the current directors of SunBank either seats on the SunBank Board of Directors if SunBank has not been merged with Omega Bank or any other Omega Subsidiary or, in the event that SunBank is merged with Omega Bank or any other Omega Subsidiary, seats on a to-be-formed Advisory Board of SunBank (the "Advisory Board") which shall, in either case, address and deal with issues in the market area served by SunBank.For a period of one year following the Effective Time, the members of the SunBank Board of Directors or the Advisory Board, as applicable, will receive board fees (excluding any stock option grants) for each meeting actually attended equal to the fees for each meeting attended payable to the members of the SunBank Board of Directors immediately prior to the Effective Time.Omega shall have the right to appoint one or more representatives to seats on the SunBank Board of Directors and, if formed, the Advisory Board, and/or to send one or representatives to attend meetings thereof.After the Effective Time, the Board of Directors of SunBank and, if formed, the Advisory Board, shall give Omega at least five (5) days notice of the date, time and place of all meetings thereof.

(ii) In the event that SunBank is merged with Omega Bank or any other Omega Subsidiary within two years of the Effective Time, the Board of Directors of the entity surviving such merger ("Surviving Bank") shall appoint Robert J. McCormack (provided that he is then employed as an executive officer of either Omega or Omega Bank) and three other directors of SunBank (each, a "SunBank Director"), as mutually agreed by Omega and the directors of SunBank immediately prior to the effectiveness of such merger, to serve on the Board of Directors of Surviving Bank until the next election of directors of Surviving Bank.The Board of Directors of Surviving Bank shall recommend, subject to its fiduciary duties, the nomination of each SunBank Director for election as a director of Surviving Bank for three additional terms of one year each after such SunBank Director's initial term expires.If one or more SunBank Director is unable or unwilling to serve as a member of Surviving Bank's Board of Directors, such person shall be replaced by another person who was a director of SunBank immediately prior to the Effective Time, as mutually selected by Omega and the directors of SunBank immediately prior to the effectiveness of the merger of SunBank with Omega Bank (or any other Omega Subsidiary).All directors described in this Section 1.2(d)(ii) shall be entitled to the same fees and benefits as other directors of Surviving Bank, but no director of Surviving Bank shall be entitled to receive any directors fees while an employee of Surviving Bank.

(e) *Fees.* All directors described in Sections 1.2(c) shall be entitled to the same fees and benefits as other directors of Omega, but no director of Omega shall be entitled to receive any directors fees while an employee of Omega.

(f) *Name.* The name of the Surviving Corporation following the Merger shall be "Omega Financial Corporation."

1.3 *Availability of Information.* Promptly after the execution by the Parties of this Agreement, each Party shall provide to the other Party, its officers, employees, agents, and representatives, access, on reasonable notice and during customary business hours, to the books, records, properties and facilities of the Party and shall use its best efforts to cause its officers, employees, agents and representatives to cooperate with any of the reviewing Party's reasonable requests for information.

1.4 *Anti-dilution Provisions.* In the event Omega changes the number of shares of Omega Common Stock issued and outstanding prior to the Effective Time as a result of a stock split, stock dividend, recapitalization or any other distribution to shareholders of Omega, the Stock Merger Consideration shall be proportionately adjusted; provided, however, that no such adjustments shall be made for issuances of Omega Common Stock (a) under any benefit or compensatory plan of Omega or any Omega Subsidiary, or (b) as consideration in connection with an acquisition of a controlling interest in any Person (by merger, business combination or otherwise), or all or a portion of a Person's business or assets by Omega or any Omega Subsidiary.

ARTICLE 2
DESCRIPTION OF TRANSACTION

2.1   *Terms of the Merger.*

(a)   *Satisfaction of Conditions to Closing.* After the transactions contemplated herein have been approved by the shareholders of Omega and Sun and each other condition to the obligations of the Parties hereto, other than those conditions which are to be satisfied by delivery of documents by either Party to the other Party, has been satisfied or, if lawfully permitted, waived by the Party entitled to the benefits thereof, the Closing will be held on the date and at the time of day and place referred to in this Agreement.At the Closing, the Parties shall deliver the certificates, letters and opinions which constitute conditions to effecting the Merger and each Party will provide the other Party with such proof or indication of satisfaction of the conditions to the obligations of such other Party to consummate the Merger as such other Party may reasonably require.If all conditions to the obligations of each Party shall have been satisfied or lawfully waived by the Party entitled to the benefits thereof, the Parties shall, at the Closing, duly execute the Articles of Merger and such other documents as are required to be filed with the Secretary of State of the Commonwealth of Pennsylvania to effect the Merger, and promptly thereafter Sun and Omega shall take all steps necessary or desirable to consummate the Merger in accordance with all Applicable Laws.The Parties shall thereupon take such other and further actions as may be required by Applicable Law or this Agreement to consummate the transactions contemplated herein.

(b)   *Effective Time.* Upon the satisfaction of all conditions to Closing set forth herein, the Merger shall become effective on the date and at the time of filing of the Articles of Merger with the Secretary of State of the Commonwealth of Pennsylvania or at such later date and/or time as may be agreed upon by the Parties and set forth in the Articles of Merger so filed.

2.2   *Conversion of Stock.*

(a)   *Consideration.* At the Effective Time, each share of Sun Common Stock then issued and outstanding (other than shares held directly or indirectly by Omega, excluding shares held in a fiduciary capacity or in satisfaction of a debt previously contracted) shall, by virtue of the Merger and without any action on the part of the holder thereof, be converted into and represent the right to receive from Omega the

Cash Merger Consideration and/or Stock Merger Consideration of Omega constituting the Per Share Merger Consideration; provided, however, that any shares of
Sun Common Stock that are owned by any trust created under Sun's Defined Contribution Plan or any other benefit plan and that have not been contributed or
awarded to employees or directors at the Effective Time shall be canceled and no
payment therefor shall be made.Omega covenants and agrees to pay the Cash
Merger Consideration and the Stock Merger Consideration, as applicable, to Sun
Shareholders, subject to the satisfaction of the conditions set forth in this Agree-
ment.As of the Effective Time, each share of the Sun Common Stock held directly or
indirectly by Omega, excluding shares held in a fiduciary capacity or in satisfaction
of a debt previously contracted, shall be canceled, retired and cease to exist, and no
exchange or payment shall be made with respect thereto.

(b) *Cash or Stock Merger Consideration.* Each Sun Shareholder shall have the
right to elect to receive the Cash Merger Consideration or the Stock Merger Consideration as to each share of Sun Common Stock owned by such shareholder, subject
however to the election, allocation, adjustment and proration procedures set forth
below.

(c) *Fractional Shares.* Fractional shares of Omega Common Stock shall not
be issued and each holder of Sun Common Stock who would otherwise be entitled to
receive any such fractional shares (taking into account all share amounts to which
such holder is otherwise entitled hereunder) shall receive cash (without interest) in
lieu thereof in an amount equal to the fraction of the share of Omega Common
Stock to which such holder would otherwise be entitled multiplied by the Determination Price.No Person entitled to receive a fractional share of Omega Common
Stock will be entitled to dividends, voting rights or any other rights of a shareholder
of Omega with respect to such fractional share.

(d) *Treatment of Options.*

(i)   At the Effective Time, each holder of an option (collectively, "Sun
Options") to purchase shares of Sun Common Stock that (i) is outstanding at the Effective Time, (ii) has been granted pursuant to Sun's 1998 Stock Incentive Plan or
1998 Independent Directors Stock Option Plan or the Sentry Plans; and (iii) would
otherwise survive the Effective Time shall be entitled to receive, in substitution for
such Sun Option, an option to acquire shares of Omega Common Stock on the
terms set forth below (each Sun Option as substituted, an "Omega Option").

(ii) An Omega Option shall be a stock option to acquire shares of
Omega Common Stock with the following terms: (i) the number of shares of Omega
Common Stock which may be acquired pursuant to such Omega Option shall be
equal to the product of the number of shares of Sun Common Stock covered by the
corresponding Sun Option multiplied by 0.664, provided that any fractional share of
Omega Common Stock resulting from such multiplication shall be rounded down to
the nearest whole share; (ii) the exercise price per share of Omega Common Stock
issuable upon exercise of the Omega Option shall be equal to the exercise price of
the corresponding Sun Option immediately prior to the conversion thereof to an
Omega Option, divided by 0.664, provided that such exercise price shall be rounded
down to the nearest whole cent; (iii) the duration and other terms of such Omega

Option shall be identical to the duration and other terms of the corresponding Sun Option immediately prior to the conversion thereof to an Omega Option, except that all references to Sun shall be deemed to be references to Omega and its affiliates, where the context so requires and shall remain exercisable until the stated expiration date of the corresponding Sun Option; (iv) Omega shall assume such Sun Option, whether vested or not vested, as contemplated by the Code; and (v) to the extent Sun Options qualify as incentive stock options under Section 422 of the Code, the Omega Options exchanged therefor shall also so qualify.

(iii) On or within 15 days after the Effective Time, Omega shall take appropriate action to reserve for issuance and, if not previously registered pursuant to the Securities Act, register the number of shares of Omega Common Stock necessary to satisfy Omega's obligations with respect to the issuance of Omega Common Stock pursuant to the exercise of Omega Options.

(e) *Calculation Schedule.* The calculations of the respective amounts of cash and Omega Common Stock payable and issuable pursuant to the terms of this Agreement shall be calculated by the Exchange Agent and approved by Omega and Sun as soon as practicable and no later than the Effective Time.

2.3 *Election and Allocation Procedures.*

(a) *Election by Sun Shareholders.* Subject to and in accordance with the allocation and election procedures set forth herein, each Sun Shareholder shall, prior to the Election Deadline, specify (i) the number of whole shares of Sun Common Stock held by such Shareholder as to which such Shareholder shall desire to receive the Cash Merger Consideration, and (ii) the number of whole shares of Sun Common Stock held by such Shareholder as to which such Shareholder shall desire to receive the Stock Merger Consideration.

(b) *Allocation of Cash and Stock.* Notwithstanding anything herein to the contrary, and after taking into consideration cash paid in lieu of fractional shares, and after excluding shares for which no consideration is payable as described in Section 2.2(a), 80% of the outstanding Sun Common Stock shall be exchanged for Omega Common Stock and all remaining outstanding Sun Common Stock shall be converted into the right to receive cash.Such result shall be accomplished through the following adjustments to the elections made by Sun Shareholders, and by giving due consideration to cash payments for fractional shares:

(1) If the number of Cash Election Shares is in excess of 20% of the Aggregate Shares, then (i) Non-Electing Shares shall be deemed to be Stock Election Shares, and (ii)(A) Cash Election Shares of each Sun Shareholder who made the Cash Election shall be reduced pro rata by multiplying the number of Cash Election Shares of such Sun Shareholder by a fraction, the numerator of which is the number of shares of Sun Common Stock equal to 20% of the Aggregate Shares, and the denominator of which is the aggregate number of Cash Election Shares of all Sun Shareholders, and (B) the shares of such Sun Shareholder representing the difference between such Sun Shareholder's initial Cash Election Shares and such Sun Shareholder's reduced Cash Election Shares pursuant to clause (A) shall be converted into and be deemed to be Stock Election Shares.

(2) If the number of Stock Election Shares is in excess of 80% of the Aggregate Shares, then (i) Non-Electing Shares shall be deemed to be Cash Election Shares and (ii) (A) Stock Election Shares of each Sun Shareholder shall be reduced pro rata by multiplying the number of Stock Election Shares of such Sun Shareholder by a fraction, the numerator of which is the number of shares of Sun Common Stock equal to 80% of the Aggregate Shares and the denominator of which is the aggregate number of Stock Election Shares of all Sun Shareholders, and (B) the shares of such Sun Shareholder representing the difference between such Sun Shareholder's initial Stock Election Shares and such Sun Shareholder's reduced Stock Election Shares pursuant to clause (A) shall be converted into and be deemed to be Cash Election Shares.

(3) If the number of Cash Election Shares is less than 20% of the Aggregate Shares and the number of Stock Election Shares is less than 80% of the Aggregate Shares, then (i) there shall be no adjustment to the elections made by electing Sun Shareholders, and (ii) Non-Electing Shares of each Sun Shareholder shall be treated as Stock Elections Shares and/or as Cash Election Shares in proportion to the respective amounts by which the Cash Election Shares and the Stock Election Shares are less than the 20% and 80% limits, respectively.

(c) Receipt of Payment.After taking into account the foregoing adjustment provisions, each Cash Election Share (including those deemed to be Cash Election Shares) shall receive in the Merger the Cash Merger Consideration pursuant to Section 2.5 and each Stock Election Share (including those deemed to be Stock Election Shares) shall receive in the Merger the Stock Merger Consideration (and cash in lieu of fractional shares) pursuant to Section 2.5.

2.4 *Election Procedures.*

(a) The Election Form shall be distributed to each Sun Shareholder at such time as Sun and Omega shall determine and shall specify the Election Deadline.

(b) Elections shall be made by Sun Shareholders by mailing to the Exchange Agent a completed Election Form.To be effective, an Election Form must be properly completed, signed and submitted to the Exchange Agent accompanied by certificates representing the shares of Sun Common Stock as to which the election is being made (or by an appropriate guaranty of delivery by a commercial bank or trust company in the United States or a member of a registered national security exchange or the National Association of Securities Dealers, Inc.), or by evidence that such certificates have been lost, stolen or destroyed accompanied by such security or indemnity as shall reasonably be requested by Omega.An Election Form and accompanying share certificates must be received by the Exchange Agent by the close of business on the Election Deadline.An election may be changed or revoked but only by written notice received by the Exchange Agent prior to the Election Deadline including, in the case of a change, a properly completed revised Election Form.

(c) Omega, or the Exchange Agent if so designated by Omega, shall determine in the reasonable exercise of discretion, whether the Election Forms have been properly completed, signed and submitted or changed or revoked and may disregard immaterial defects in Election Forms.Omega or the Exchange Agent, as applicable, will notify the applicable Sun Shareholders of any defect in an Election Form by regular United States mail or such other method of notice which can reasonably be expected to be at least as prompt as notice by regular United States mail.

(d) For the purposes hereof, a Sun Shareholder who does not submit an effective Election Form to the Exchange Agent prior to the Election Deadline shall be deemed to have made a Non-Election.

(e) In the event that this Agreement is terminated pursuant to the provisions hereof and any certificates for shares have been transmitted to the Exchange Agent pursuant to the provisions hereof, Omega and Sun shall cause the Exchange Agent to return such certificates to the Person submitting the same promptly after such termination.

2.5 *Mechanics of Payment of Consideration.*

(a) *Payment of the Merger Consideration.* Omega shall deposit with the Exchange Agent sufficient certificates representing Omega Common Stock and sufficient cash to enable the Exchange Agent to distribute the Aggregate Consideration as determined pursuant to this Agreement.Within three business days after the Effective Time, the Exchange Agent shall distribute, to all Sun Shareholders who have properly submitted Election Forms together with their share certificates or proper proofs with respect to lost certificates, the Cash Merger Consideration and the Stock Merger Consideration to which each such Sun Shareholder is entitled.Within five business days after receiving properly completed Shareholder Materials, as set forth in Section 2.5(b), from any Sun Shareholder who made a Non-Election, the Exchange Agent shall likewise distribute to such Sun Shareholder the Cash Merger Consideration or Stock Merger Consideration, or a combination of both, which such Sun Shareholder is entitled to receive pursuant to this Agreement.

(b) *Submission Procedures for Non-Electing Shares.* Within five business days after the Effective Time, the Exchange Agent shall send the Shareholder Materials to each Sun Shareholder who has made a Non-Election.All Shareholder Materials shall be sent by first class United States mail to such Sun Shareholders at the addresses set forth on the official shareholder records of Sun.Omega shall also make appropriate provisions with the Exchange Agent to enable Sun Shareholders to obtain the Shareholder Materials from, and to deliver the certificates formerly representing shares of Sun Common Stock to, the Exchange Agent in person, commencing on or not later than the second business day following the Effective Time.Upon receipt of the appropriate Shareholder Materials, together with the certificates formerly evidencing and representing all of the shares of Sun Common Stock which were validly held of record by such Sun Shareholder, the Exchange Agent shall take prompt action to process such certificates formerly evidencing and representing shares of Sun Common Stock received by it (including the prompt return of any defective submissions with instructions as to those actions which may be necessary to remedy any defects) and to mail to the Sun Shareholders in exchange for the certificate(s) surrendered by them, the consideration to be issued or paid for such Sun Shareholder's shares pursuant to the terms hereof.

(c) *Rights Appurtenant to Certificates Lost Certificates.* After the Effective Time and until properly surrendered to the Exchange Agent, each outstanding certificate or certificates which formerly evidenced and represented Sun Common Stock shall be deemed for all purposes to represent and evidence only the right to receive the aggregate Cash Merger Consideration or aggregate Stock Merger Consideration into which such Sun Common Stock was converted.The aggregate Cash Merger Consideration or aggregate Stock Merger Consideration shall not be paid to the record holder of any Sun Common Stock until the certificate therefor is surrendered in the manner required.Each Sun Shareholder will be responsible for all federal, state and local taxes which may be incurred by him or her on account of his or her receipt of the consideration to be paid in the Merger.A Sun Shareholder whose certificate(s) have been lost or destroyed may nevertheless, subject to the provisions of this Article, receive the aggregate Cash Merger Consideration or aggregate Stock Merger Consideration to which such Sun Shareholder is entitled, provided that such Sun Shareholder must first deliver to Omega or to the Exchange Agent: (i) a sworn statement certifying such loss or destruction and specifying the circumstances thereof, and (ii) a lost instrument bond in form satisfactory to Omega and the Exchange Agent which has been duly executed by a corporate surety satisfactory to Omega and the Exchange Agent, indemnifying the Surviving Corporation, Omega, the Exchange Agent (and their respective successors) to their satisfaction against any loss or expense which any of them may incur as a result of such lost or destroyed certificates being presented.Any costs or expenses which may arise from such replacement procedure, including the premium on the lost instrument bond, shall be paid by the Sun Shareholder.

(d) *Stock Transfer Books.* At the Effective Time, the stock transfer books of Sun shall be closed and no transfer of shares of Sun Common Stock shall be made thereafter.

(e) *Right to Receive Dividends on Omega Common Stock.* Each Sun Shareholder who is entitled to receive the Stock Merger Consideration shall be entitled, to the same extent as other holders of Omega Common Stock, to payments of dividends, if any, on Omega Common Stock if the record date for such dividend is on or after the Closing Date; provided, however, that such dividends shall be paid, without interest, only after the Sun Shareholder submits his or her certificate for Sun Common Stock pursuant to Sections 2.4(b) or 2.5(b) or complies with the requirements of Section 2.5(c) with respect to lost stock certificates.All dividends not paid on the dividend payment date pursuant to this Section shall be paid by Omega to the Exchange Agent, which shall remit them to the applicable shareholder upon satisfaction of the conditions set forth in this Section 2.5(e).

2.6 *Time and Place of Closing.* Unless this Agreement shall have been terminated and the transactions herein contemplated shall have been abandoned pursuant to Section 8.1, and subject to the satisfaction or waiver of the conditions set forth in Article 7, the Closing will take place at 10:00 a.m. on the Closing Date, at Omega's corporate offices in State College, Pennsylvania, unless another date, time or place is agreed to in writing by the parties hereto.

2.7 *Voting Agreements.* As a material inducement for Omega entering into this Agreement, simultaneously with the execution of this Agreement by the Parties, each director and executive officer of Sun shall enter into a Voting Agreement.

2.8 *Reservation of Shares.* Omega agrees that, prior to the Effective Time, it will take appropriate action to reserve a sufficient number of authorized but unissued shares of Omega Common Stock to be issued as Stock Merger Consideration in accordance with this Agreement.

2.9 *Certain Actions Relating to Rule 16b-3.* Prior to the Effective Time, Omega and Sun shall take all such steps as may be required to cause any dispositions of shares of Sun Common Stock (including derivative securities with respect to such shares) resulting from the transactions contemplated by Article 2 of this Agreement by each individual who is subject to the reporting requirements of Section 16(a) of the Exchange Act with respect to Sun to be exempt under Rule 16b-3 promulgated under the Exchange Act.

[BALANCE OF AGREEMENT AND PLAN OF MERGER OMITTED]

Index